A COUNTRY BAKING TREASURY

Also by Lisa Yockelson

THE EFFICIENT EPICURE

FRUIT DESSERTS

BROWNIES AND BLONDIES

BAKING FOR GIFT-GIVING

COBBLERS, CRISPS, AND DEEP-DISH PIES

A COUNTRY BAKING TREASURY

PIES, CAKES, COOKIES

Lisa Yockelson

ILLUSTRATIONS BY WENDY WHEELER

HarperCollins*Publishers*

HarperCollins books may be purchased for educational, business, or sales promotional use. For information please write: Special Markets Department, HarperCollins Publishers, Inc., 10 East 53rd Street, New York, NY 10022.

FIRST EDITION

LIBRARY OF CONGRESS CATALOGING-IN-PUBLICATION DATA
Yockelson, Lisa.
  A country baking treasury : pies, cakes, cookies / Lisa Yockelson.
    p.   cm.
  Includes index.
ISBN: 0-06-017296-7
  1. Baking.   2. Pies.   3. Cakes.   4. Cookies.   I. Title.
TX763.Y632   1995
641.8'15—dc20   95-22590

  95   96   97   98   99   DT/RRD   10   9   8   7   6   5   4   3   2   1

To the memory of Lilly Yockelson,
with love and admiration

Contents

———◆◆◆———

Acknowledgments 9

Preface 11

COUNTRY PIES

THE CHARM OF COUNTRY PIES 13

ABOUT BAKING COUNTRY PIES 17

SUMMER COUNTRY PIES 35

AUTUMN COUNTRY PIES 59

WINTER COUNTRY PIES 89

SPRING COUNTRY PIES 109

SWEET AND CREAMY PIE COMPANIONS 127

THE COUNTRY PIE SWAP 133

COUNTRY CAKES

OLD-FASHIONED BAKING GOODNESS 137

THE SIMPLE ART OF COUNTRY CAKES 141

THE COUNTRY CAKE KITCHEN 145

BACK PORCH CAKES 153

COFFEE CAKES 169

TRAVELING CAKES 191

TEATIME UPSIDE-DOWN CAKES 203

POUND CAKES 213

FRESH FRUIT PICNIC CAKES 235

LITTLE CAKES 249

CAKE AND ICE CREAM 263

THE COUNTRY CAKE TEA PARTY 273

COUNTRY COOKIES

THE JOY OF COUNTRY COOKIES 281

GOOD AND FRESH: NOTES FROM A COOKIE KITCHEN 285

ON COOKIE BASKETS 293

COOKIE JAR TREATS 297

BAKE SALE GEMS 317

LUNCH BOX COOKIES 343

COFFEE AND TEA SWEETS 359

''SNACKING'' COOKIES 377

REFRESHMENTS FOR A COUNTRY DAY 397

THE COUNTRY COOKIE EXCHANGE 403

Index 409

Acknowledgments

————— ❖❖❖ —————

For their talent and spirit, I extend my brightest thanks to these individuals who, in one way or another, guided the formation of *Country Pies, Country Cakes,* and *Country Cookies* with style and grace:

To Patricia Brown, editor and consultant, who recommended *Country Pies* for publication and became my editor at Harper & Row, and to Susan Friedland, my current editor at HarperCollins*Publishers,* who helped me finish up the series by taking on *Country Cookies* and championed this collection of books.

To Susan Lescher, my literary agent, for steady and expert counsel on cookbook writing in particular and publishing in general. And to Carolyn Larson, assistant to Susan Lescher at the Lescher Agency, for taking care of business so thoughtfully.

For their insights and hard work before, during, and after the compilation of these three volumes, my gratitude also reaches to the following professionals: Susan Derecskey, cookbook editor; Lisa Ekus, at the Lisa Ekus Public Relations Company; Wende Gozan, publicist at HarperCollins*Publishers;* Jennifer Griffin, associate editor at HarperCollins*Publishers;* Joseph Montebello, creative director at HarperCollins *Publishers;* and Wendy Wheeler, the illustrator for my country baking books.

Preface

———◈◈◈———

During the years I wrote my country baking books, *Country Pies, Country Cakes,* and *Country Cookies,* homestyle American sweets were only beginning to make a resolute and valid mark in the world of "fancy" baking. A pan full of moist and fudgy brownies or a gossamer sweet potato pie—made with the freshest ingredients and a sure hand—could rival any cookie or intricate multilayered cake.

It has been a remarkable experience writing these small primers. I was prompted, occasionally, to look backward—through the recipes my mother and grandmother passed on to me—and to sort through other recipes that had long been a part of my own baking tradition. The memories of all those good things, in addition to so many new bakery treats I had developed, were turned into a handsome trilogy of baking books.

The book you now have in your hands, a compilation of those exceptionally sturdy and beloved books, combines all of the recipes in one tidy volume. Consider this book, which is a significant part of my own baking dossier, now part of *your* file. In it you'll discover that terrific recipe for Double-Crust Apple Pie (so many of my readers make this one during the breezy months of autumn), the Chocolate Pan Cake with Chocolate Fudge Frosting (a never-fail cake for fans of both chocolate and fudge), or the Three Nut Bars (perfect to have on hand around Thanksgiving and the Christmas holidays).

Readers, friends, and colleagues have told me that their individual copies of my books are dog-eared and ingredient-stained. This is as fine a commendation as any baking author can earn. As I've said before, the recipes within these pages clearly and characteristically reflect a very personal trip through one author's kitchen—a trip that has, undoubtedly, appealed to all of those who have tried out the formulas and methods that follow. For new bakers and practiced bakers, I hope that my recipes swiftly become yours.

Lisa Yockelson
Washington, D.C.
October 1994

THE CHARM OF COUNTRY PIES

*F*rom apple streusel to spicy sweet potato to mile-high coconut cream, country pies evoke an informal, simple goodness. They are casual, old-fashioned, and oftentimes hearty; because they are made with pure ingredients, the flavor of the pies is clear and vibrant.

Mary Ellisor Emmerling, author of *American Country: A Style and Sourcebook* (Clarkson N. Potter, Publishers, New York, 1980), describes the overall warmth and easygoing charm of country food in this way: "Country foods are simple, wholesome, and fresh. They are foods that are chosen with care, easy to prepare, and eaten with a hearty appetite. At best they are foods acquired close to their source, whether picked from your garden, fished from the sea, or bought at local roadside stands." Country pies, along with the rest of country cooking, are equally unpretentious and satisfying.

Pie making is one of the specialties of the true American kitchen. The tradition originated from cooks who had to improvise and create and feed large hungry families and make do, relying solely upon the foodstuffs their own land (or a neighbor's) gave forth. Recipes for pies resulted from a blend of ethnic traditions and personal cooking sensibilities, always making full use of what was seasonal and ripe or was stashed in the pantry.

The pies in this collection are meant to capture that sense of plain good taste and seasonal bounty. The pies are arranged seasonally, to take advantage of the freshest offerings from the market, farmstand, food cooperative, or garden.

A country pie makes an ideal dessert, whether it is a soft, quivery custard pie, a dense chocolate or sparkling lemon pie, a sweet-tart fresh fruit pie, or one of those rich mincemeat pies. A baked pie set out on a cooling rack, accompanied by a pitcher of Vanilla Pouring Custard (page 129), is irresistible.

❖❖❖

THE COUNTRY PIE LARDER

Notes on ingredients from a pie baker's journal

A country pie is made up of many delicious things: simple larder ingredients, known as "goods on hand" (flour, sugar, nuts, extracts, chocolate); dairy staples (milk, butter, eggs, cream, buttermilk); and a range of seasonal fruits and vegetables. Using what's ripe from the tree or bush, or dug up from the ground, when nature produces it makes for some of the best-tasting pies.

I love to bake all kinds of pies, so my small pantry is continually supplied with the basic ingredients for making them. But I have found that even the most casual bakers keep all the basics for pie making in their kitchen pantries.

Once the cupboard shelves are stocked, any of the pies in this book can be put together with ease. In my pantry, I have set aside a few shelves for all my baking needs. One shelf holds bleached all-purpose flour and plain granulated sugar. I keep the sugar (which is pressed free of all lumps before storing) and flour in enormous apothecary jars sealed tightly with their ground-glass lids; I use big jars that hold ten pounds each. The contents are continually replenished. Dark and light brown sugar are stored in containers with tight-fitting lids.

Every so often, I make a batch or two of flavored granulated sugar. These sugars are scented with vanilla beans or a variety of citrus peel, such as lemon, orange, or tangerine. Vanilla sugar, for example, is a delicious sweetener to use in all fresh fruit pies and in most custard pies, where the taste of vanilla could be heightened. Lemon-flavored sugar adds a special taste to all lemon-based pies, such as the Lemon Pudding Pie (page 121), Lemon Slice Pie (page 119), Lemon Meringue Pie (page 123), or Lemon-Almond Pie (page 122). I store the flavored sugars in jars next to the plain granulated sugar. Other sweeteners (such as liquid brown sugar and deep amber-colored maple syrup) and other flavorings (such as extracts) are arranged on the same shelf.

Different kinds of chocolate—bittersweet, semisweet, unsweetened, plus miniature chocolate chips—are stacked alongside tins of coconut, cans of sweetened condensed milk, tubes of vanilla beans, and small tins of nuts. Larger five-pound bags of nutmeats are squirreled away in the freezer for longer storage.

In addition to dairy products, I keep bottles of various homemade fruit syrups in the refrigerator. The syrups are made from fresh fruits simmered in a little water until softened; the resulting strained liquid is slowly cooked with sugar to make a translucent, lightly thickened syrup. I love the way just a tablespoon or so of fruit syrup enlivens a pie filling. The syrups are easy to make and look beautiful in slender glass bottles. The method for making a range of syrups is outlined in the beginning of the chapter on summer country pies (page 37). Beyond adding to pie fillings, syrups can also be added to a fruit mousse or ice cream to build up the flavor; a few tablespoons can be stirred into a tall glass of ice-cold seltzer to make a light and fizzy summer thirst quencher; or a quarter cup of syrup can be whisked into almost any liquid used for poaching fresh fruit. A bottle of syrup also makes a lovely hostess gift to bestow on any friend who likes to bake or enjoys making desserts.

ABOUT
BAKING
COUNTRY
PIES

A country pie is the perfect union of a simple filling and a light, tender pie crust. The filling may be sliced fresh fruit, sweetened, spiced, and lightly bound with cornstarch; a thin egg-and-cream-fortified mixture which bakes into a trembling custard; or a wicked coconut-walnut-chocolate-chip filling, reminiscent of a fudgy candy bar.

The pie crust is plain and buttery—nothing more than butter cut into the flour until reduced to small, crumbly flakes. A blend of egg yolk and ice-cold water binds it into a pliable dough. The pie dough is rolled out with a sturdy rolling pin and fitted into a standard sloping 9- or 10-inch pie tin. The top of a double-crust or deep-dish pie can be festooned with cutouts of pastry dough pressed onto the lid in a whimsical pattern.

The rolling pin I use is a straight 3-inch-thick dowel of smoothly polished oak, without ball-bearing handles. The pin is the same thickness throughout. I collect old-fashioned antique pie tins, the kind with a brand name imprinted on the bottom, such as "Mrs. Smith's Mellow Rich Pie," "Holmes," "Crusty Pie," or "Mrs. Wagner's Pies." A long time ago, when you bought a pie in its baking tin, a ten- or fifteen-cent deposit was added to the cost of the pie. Now the tins are among the important collectibles of American bakeware. Some of my tins have bottoms with several small holes; the holes let the heat of the oven penetrate the pie shell directly, for an extra-crispy crust.

Pie pans made out of tin help to turn the crust golden brown and flaky; tin also retains the heat so the pie crusts hold their shape. Fluted edges and pastry cutouts applied to the top of a pie baked in a tin pie pan retain their shape, too.

Country pies are usually baked in standard 9- or 10-inch pie tins that are between 1½ and 1¾ inches deep. If a recipe calls for a deep 9-inch pie pan, select one between 2 and 2¼ inches deep. Some old pie tins were made 2 to 2½ inches deep; look for them at flea markets, tag sales, and antique shows. A plain 10-inch pie pan can be substituted for a deep 9-inch tin, with excellent results.

Most of the pie fillings, with the exception of those cooked in a saucepan on the stovetop, can be put together in a large mixing bowl. I like to combine ingredients for a pie filling in a classic "batter" bowl. My batter bowl has the traditional pouring spout and easy-to-grab handle, holds about 10 cups, and is made of glazed pottery. If I am filling a pie shell with a liquid mixture, I just tip my batter bowl over the pastry shell and pour; fruit mixtures get spooned out from the bowl and any juices that linger get poured over the filling.

Once a double-crust or deep-dish pie is assembled, the top crust can be decorated with cutouts of pastry dough. Or you can design a cover of cutouts to apply over the filling of a double-crust pie instead of a solid cover. To make a pattern of cutouts, use a cookie cutter to stamp out shapes from a sheet of pie dough. Cookware and hardware stores (and even some supermarkets) offer a large selection of shapes—animals of all kinds, scalloped rounds, hearts, flowers, leaves, stars, and so on. Nests of cutters, such as graduated heart-shaped cookie cutters, are good to have on hand and are fun to work with, as are the tiny cutters designed to stamp out aspic.

———————❖❖❖———————

FLAKY PIE CRUSTS

A flaky pie crust is what good pie baking is all about, and whoever said that a pie crust should be made with a warm heart and a cold hand was a very wise person.

Years ago, I perfected two recipes for pie dough, one for a single-crust pie shell and another for a double-crust pie shell. Each dough is lightly sweetened and flaky and bakes to a handsome golden brown color. A single-crust pie shell made out of Flaky Pie Crust (recipe follows) is strong enough to hold any kind of filling. The Flaky Pie Crust for a Double-Crust Pie (page 30) bakes up tender but sturdy and is perfect for enclosing all kinds of fruit fillings. With these two recipes in hand, you'll be able to make all the pies in this book.

Pie crusts are simple and rewarding to assemble, whether made by hand or in a food processor. Both procedures have been outlined in each of the pie crust recipes. When making pie dough, remember all liquids and fats should be used cold so your pie crust will bake up tender and flaky. When working with pie dough, your hands should be cool; if they are warm, rinse them in cold water before handling the dough.

❖❖❖❖❖❖❖❖❖❖❖❖❖❖❖

Flaky Pie Crust

1½ cups all-purpose flour
(stir gently to aerate
the flour; measure by
scooping down into
the flour with a dry
measure and level the
top with a straight edge
of a knife)

¼ teaspoon salt

8 tablespoons (¼ pound
or 1 stick) cold
unsalted butter, cut
into tablespoon-size
chunks

1 tablespoon granulated
sugar

1 extra-large egg yolk,
cold

2 tablespoons ice-cold
water, or more as
needed

1 extra-large egg white,
for waterproofing,
optional (page 24)

---

*Makes enough pie dough for
one 9- or 10-inch single-crust
pie or one pastry cover for a
9- or 10-inch deep-dish pie*

This buttery pie dough is the one I've been using for many pie-baking years; it's flaky and tender, yet stands up to any kind of filling, whether fruit-based, custard- or pudding-like, or the thin and rich filling for a translucent pie, such as pecan. The dough is especially easy to patch, holds up beautifully in humid weather, and takes well to pinching and crimping into a fluted edge.

The flaky pie crust can be rolled out and fitted into the pie pan, popped into a self-sealing plastic bag, and refrigerated for up to 2 days before baking. Unbaked pie crusts freeze well, too (see "To freeze a pie shell," page 25).

To make the dough by hand, stir the flour and salt together in a large mixing bowl. Add butter and, using two round-bladed knives, cut into the flour until reduced to small bits. Using the tips of your fingers, further blend the fat into the flour by dipping down into the mixture and crumbling it between your fingertips as you are lifting it to the surface. The mixture should look like coarse cornmeal. Sprinkle with sugar and stir in with a few brief strokes. Blend together the egg yolk and water in a small mixing bowl. Pour over the flour mixture. Quickly combine to make a firm but pliable dough, using a fork or the fingertips of one hand. (Keep the other hand clean for answering the telephone, which always seems to ring when you are trying to make a pie dough.) Add additional droplets of ice-cold water if the dough seems too dry or crumbly. Turn out the dough onto a large sheet of waxed paper, shape into a rough, flat cake, and wrap with the paper. Refrigerate for 15 to 20 minutes.

To make the dough in a food processor, place the flour and salt in the work bowl of a food processor fitted with the steel knife. Add the butter and process, using quick on-off pulses, until the butter is reduced to small flakes. Sprinkle with the sugar and process for 1 to 2 seconds to blend. Beat the egg yolk and water in a small mixing bowl and pour over the flour-butter mixture. Process, using short, on-off pulses, until the dough begins to mass together. Add extra droplets of water if the dough seems crumbly or dry. Turn out the dough onto a large sheet of waxed paper, shape into a flat cake, and wrap with the paper. Refrigerate the dough for 15 to 20 minutes.

To roll out the pie dough, tear off two long sheets of waxed paper at least 17 to 18 inches long. Place the dough in the center of one sheet of waxed paper and top with the remaining sheet. Gently press the top sheet. Using short, quick, rolling motions, roll the dough to a scant ¼-inch thickness (approximately 13 inches in diameter). Transfer to a cookie sheet and chill for 20 minutes.

To line a rimmed pie pan, peel off the top layer of waxed paper from the sheet of pie crust. Cut strips of dough about ⅓ inch thick from the outside of the circle of dough, keeping the shape intact as you cut away strips of dough. Lightly brush the rim of the pie pan with cold water, press the strips onto the rim, and lightly brush with cold water. Invert the circle of dough onto the bottom of the pan and peel off the waxed paper. Press the dough lightly on the bottom first, then up and against the sides. Press the overhang of dough onto the rim and cut off the overhang using a sharp paring knife. Make long ¹⁄₁₆-inch-deep scoring marks on the outside edges of the dough to "rough up" the rim and give it some texture and thickness. Flute or crimp the edges decoratively, using the sampler of finished edges on pages 27–29 as a guide.

Prick the bottom of the pie shell with the tines of a fork. Refrigerate, loosely covered, for about 30 minutes. For longer storage, wrap in a sheet of plastic, slide into a large plastic bag, and seal, and refrigerate or freeze. Save the dough scraps, bag separately, and refrigerate; use to patch tears in a pie shell.

To cover a deep-dish pie with a round of pie dough, peel off the top layer of waxed paper from the sheet of pie crust. Cut strips of dough about ¹⁄₃ inch thick from the outside of the circle of dough. Lightly brush the rim of an ovenproof oval or round deep-dish pie pan with cold water; press on the strips of dough. Spoon the filling into the pie dish, mounding it slightly. Brush the top of the pastry-lined rim with cold water. Lay the pie crust over the filling by inverting the circle of dough over the filled pie pan. Peel away the waxed paper. Press the dough firmly around the rim. Cut away any overhang of dough using a sharp paring knife. Make long ¹⁄₁₆-inch-deep scoring marks on the outside edges of the dough to "rough up" the rim and give it some texture and thickness. Flute or crimp the edges decoratively, using the sampler of finished edges on pages 27–29 as a guide.

If you are using pastry cutouts, place on the top crust by brushing each with cold water and affixing to the crust. Refrigerate for 10 minutes, then glaze and cut several steam vents in the top crust.

To completely prebake a pie shell, line the well-chilled pie shell with a single length of aluminum foil. Fill with raw rice or dried beans. Preheat the oven to 425 degrees with a cookie sheet on the lower-third-level rack. Bake the pie on the cookie sheet for 10 minutes, remove the foil and rice, reduce the oven temperature to 375 degrees, and continue baking for 10 to 12 minutes longer, or until baked through and a medium-amber color. Prebaked pie shells are used throughout this book when single-crust pie shells are called for; prebaking the crust guards against soggy or underbaked pie crusts and vastly improves the taste and texture of the finished pie.

To waterproof the pie shell, remove the shell from the oven a few minutes before it finishes baking. Lightly beat an egg white until frothy. Brush the inside of the pie shell up to the decorative rim with the beaten white, using a soft pastry brush. Return to the oven for 1 to 2 minutes longer to finish baking and to dry the egg wash. The pie shell is now ready to be filled.

I like to waterproof the inside of a single-crust pie to keep the pastry shell from becoming soggy and damp after it is filled.

I always waterproof pie shells when I am making custard pies [Vanilla Custard Pie (page 92) and Coconut Custard Pie (page 93)], streusel pies [Apple Streusel Pie (page 104), Peach Streusel Pie (page 38), and Cinnamon-Pear Pie with Walnut Streusel (page 69)], lemon pies [Lemon Pudding Pie (page 121) and Lemon-Almond Pie (page 122)], all the vegetable custard pies [Pumpkin Custard Pie (page 76), Pumpkin Crunch Pie (page 78), Orange–Butternut Squash Pie (page 82), Apricot-Yam Pie (page 81), Brandied Golden Acorn Squash Pie (page 84), and Fresh Sugar Pumpkin Pie (page 80)], and for Brown Sugar Pie (page 87), Lime Cream Pie (page 126), and Buttermilk Pie (page 106).

To freeze a pie shell, wrap in several sheets of plastic wrap, slide into a self-locking plastic bag, and freeze. The pie shell should be used within 2 months; bake directly from the freezer without defrosting.

For a frozen single-crust pie shell, increase baking time at 375 degrees by 5 to 6 minutes, or until the shell is a golden brown color.

VARIATIONS

To vary the basic recipe for Flaky Pie Crust dough, use the following additions or substitutions:

Substitute *¼ cup cold solid shortening* for half of the butter, for a pie crust with a more fragile, melting crumb.

Substitute *½ cup of cold pure rendered lard* for the entire amount of butter, for a tender crust to use for apple or pear pies and for pies that combine fruit and nuts or fruit and mincemeat.

Blend *½ teaspoon ground cinnamon, ¼ teaspoon freshly grated nutmeg, and ¼ teaspoon ground ginger* into the flour with the salt, for a spicy pie crust that tastes right with all kinds of fruit pies, sweet vegetable custard pies (such as pumpkin, acorn squash, and butternut squash), and fruited mincemeat pies.

Add *¼ teaspoon pure vanilla extract* to the egg yolk and ice-cold water mixture to lightly flavor the crust; this crust is appealing with any kind of fruit, nut, or custard pie.

A SAMPLER OF PIE FINISHES

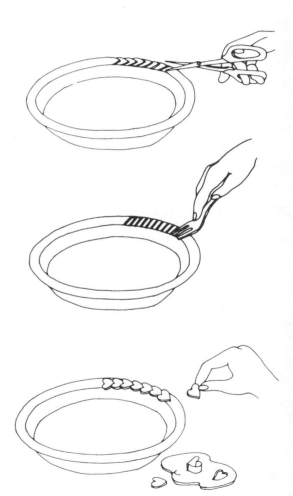

FEATHERY EDGE

With the open tip of a pair of scissors, cut slanting Vs around the edge of the pie crust, spacing each cut ½ inch apart.

SIMPLE FORK-FLUTED EDGE

Press the back of the tines of a fork firmly into rim of pie crust, using a quick rocking motion. Repeat around pie crust edge.

HEART-SHAPED EDGE

With a small heart-shaped cutter, stamp out hearts from sheet of pastry dough. Lightly brush rim of crust with cold water; place hearts around rim, overlapping slightly, pressing down gently to adhere.

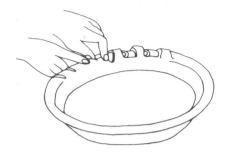

CHECKERBOARD EDGE

Omit long scoring marks designed to give depth to edge of pie crust (page 23). Cut pie crust edge at ½-inch intervals, making each cut ½ inch long, creating square tabs. Roll or fold down every other section.

RUFFLED EDGE

Press left thumb on rim of pie crust. Draw the back of a knife (blunt edge) in toward the center of the pie about ½ inch. Repeat at even intervals around rim of crust, creating deep ruffled scallops.

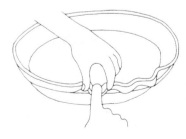

PINCHED SCALLOPED EDGE

Put forefinger of right hand on edge of pie crust. Pinch dough into a deep scallop with forefinger and thumb of left hand by drawing in the dough about ¼ inch. Repeat at even intervals around rim of crust.

LEAFY EDGE

With a sharp paring knife or leaf-shaped cutter, cut small oval-shaped leaves from a sheet of pastry dough. With the back of a knife, mark veins on the leaves. Lightly brush rim of crust with cold water; place leaves touching each other, zigzag fashion, around rim of crust, pressing down gently to adhere.

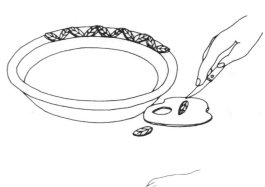

SQUEEZED ROPE EDGE

Press thumb of right hand on edge of pie crust at a slight angle. Squeeze pie dough edge at even ½-inch intervals between thumb and knuckle of forefinger to create a rope effect.

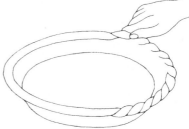

HIGH PEAKED EDGE

Using thumb and forefinger of both hands, pinch together ½-inch sections of pie crust edge, creating a rim that stands up. Repeat at even intervals around edge of crust.

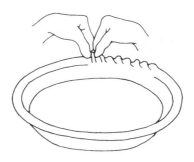

❖❖❖❖❖❖❖❖❖❖❖❖❖❖❖

Flaky Pie Crust for a Double-Crust Pie

2 cups all-purpose flour
(stir gently before
measuring to aerate
the flour; measure by
scooping down into
the flour with a dry
measure and level the
top with the straight
edge of a knife)

¼ teaspoon salt

10⅔ tablespoons (¼
pound or 1 stick plus
2⅔ tablespoons) cold
unsalted butter, cut
into tablespoon-size
chunks

1 tablespoon plus 1
teaspoon granulated
sugar

1 extra-large egg yolk,
cold

3 tablespoons ice-cold
water, or more as
needed

This is an ideal pastry dough to use for double-crust pie; it bakes up golden and flaky, and holds its shape.

To make the dough by hand, stir the flour and salt together in a large mixing bowl. Add butter and, using two round-bladed knives, cut into the flour until reduced to small bits. Using the tips of your fingers, further blend the fat into the flour by dipping down into the mixture and crumbling it between your fingertips as you are lifting it to the surface. The mixture should look like coarse cornmeal. Sprinkle with sugar and stir in with a few swift strokes. Blend together the egg yolk and water in a small mixing bowl. Pour over the flour mixture. Quickly combine to make a firm but pliable dough, using a fork or the fingertips of one hand. Add additional droplets of ice-cold water if the dough seems too dry or crumbly. Divide the dough in half and press each half into a flat cake on separate sheets of waxed paper. Wrap dough and refrigerate for 15 to 20 minutes.

To make the dough in a food processor, place the flour and salt in the work bowl of a food processor fitted with the steel knife. Add butter and process, using quick on-off pulses, until the butter is reduced to small flakes. Sprinkle with the sugar and process for 1 to 2 seconds to blend. Beat the egg yolk and water in a small mixing bowl and pour over the flour-butter mixture. Process, using short on-off pulses, until the dough begins to mass together. Add extra droplets of water if the dough seems crumbly or dry. Divide the dough in half and press each half into a large, flat cake on separate sheets of waxed paper. Wrap the dough and refrigerate for 15 to 20 minutes.

1 extra-large egg white,
   beaten until frothy, for
   waterproofing the
   unbaked pie shell,
   optional

*Makes enough pie dough for
one 9- or 10-inch double-crust
pie or one 9- or 10-inch cover
for a deep-dish pie with dough
left over to make pastry cutout
decorations for the top of the
pie*

To roll out the pie dough, tear off four long sheets of waxed paper at least 17 to 18 inches long. Place each cake of dough in the center of one sheet of waxed paper and cover with another sheet, gently pressing each top sheet. Using short, quick, rolling motions, roll out the dough to a thickness of a scant ¼ inch; each round of dough will be about 10 to 11 inches in diameter. Transfer each to a cookie sheet and chill for 20 minutes.

To freeze pie crust dough, wrap the rolled-out dough, on its waxed paper sheets, in several layers of plastic wrap, carefully slide into a self-locking plastic bag, and freeze for up to 2 months.

To use frozen dough in making a double-crust pie, lift two sheets of dough from the freezer to the refrigerator for about half an hour, or until pliable. Remove dough from the refrigerator, peel off the waxed paper, and assemble the pie according to the instructions below.

To line a rimmed pie pan for a double-crust pie, remove one sheet of pastry dough from the refrigerator. Peel off the top layer of waxed paper. Cut strips of dough about ⅓ inch thick from the outside of the circle of dough, keeping the shape intact as you cut away strips of dough. Lightly brush the rim of the pie pan with cold water, press the strips onto the rim, and lightly brush with cold water. Invert the circle of dough onto the bottom of the pan and peel off the waxed paper. Press the dough lightly on the bottom first, then up and against the sides. Press the dough onto the rim and cut off the overhang using a sharp paring knife. If you are making the shell in advance, wrap it in a self-sealing bag and refrigerate. About 15 minutes before filling the shell, beat the egg white until frothy and brush it on the inside of the pastry shell to waterproof it; this is an optional step, but I recommend it highly to keep the bottom crust crisp. Refrigerate for 15 minutes.

Fill the pastry-lined and waterproofed shell with the filling, mounding it slightly toward the center. Lightly brush the pastry rim with cold water. Peel off the top layer of waxed paper from the second circle of dough. Invert the circle of dough over the pie filling. Peel away the sheet of waxed paper. Press the dough firmly onto the moistened rim. Cut away any overhang of dough using a sharp knife. Make long $\frac{1}{16}$-inch-deep scoring marks on the outside edges of the dough to give some texture and thickness to the rim. Flute or crimp the edges decoratively, using the sampler of finished edges on pages 27–29 as a guide.

If you are using pastry cutouts, place on the top crust by brushing each with cold water and affixing to the crust in an attractive pattern. Refrigerate for 10 minutes, then glaze and cut several steam vents in the top crust.

To fashion a pie cover of pastry cutouts, select a cookie cutter for stamping out cutouts. Diamonds, hearts, scalloped rounds, triangles, rectangles, animals, or fruits are all distinctive shapes. Stamp cutouts from the second sheet of dough and chill on a cookie sheet. After the filling has been piled into the pie shell, cover the top with the cutouts, overlapping one over the next to form a top crust. Since some small patches of filling will show through, cutting steam vents in the top crust is not necessary. Chill the pie for 10 minutes, then glaze the cutouts and bake as directed. A cutout pastry top is a whimsical and unusual touch to finish off a double-crust or deep-dish pie. It works best for deep-dish fruit pies, some pear pies [Pear Mincemeat Pie (page 68) and Spiced Pear-Currant Pie (page 71)], the Apple-Ginger Mincemeat Pie (page 63), Apple-Pear Pie with Apple Cider Syrup (page 66), and the Cranberry-Walnut Mincemeat Pie (page 72).

To make a lattice cover for a double-crust pie, cut long, narrow 1-inch-wide strips, wide 1½- to 2-inch-wide strips, or extra-wide 2- to 3-inch strips from one round of pie dough using a fluted pastry wheel or a sharp knife and a ruler. Place the strips on a waxed paper–lined cookie sheet and refrigerate for 20 minutes. Line the pie tin with the second round of pie dough according to the directions on page 31 ("To line a rimmed pie pan for a double-crust pie"), to the point of fluting the edges. The edges are left unfluted so that lattice strips can be pressed on later.

Pile the filling into the pie crust. Weave the strips of dough over the filling, securing them by pressing firmly where the rim and lattice strip come together. Trim off any overhanging edges. Flute or crimp the edges decoratively and chill for 10 minutes before baking.

To add extra pastry cutouts to the top of a deep-dish or double-crust pie, you'll need to make one recipe of Flaky Pie Crust (page 21) in addition to one recipe of Flaky Pie Crust for a Double-Crust Pie (page 30). From the extra round of pastry dough, cut out shapes using a cookie cutter or a stencil and a sharp paring knife. A cutout of a cornucopia, for example, would be nice to apply to the top of a double-crust pie served on Thanksgiving; fruit cutouts are a nice touch to add to a double-crust fruit pie. Always cut out shapes from a well-chilled sheet of dough. Brush one side with cold water and press on the top crust. Glaze the pie and bake as directed.

VARIATIONS

To vary the basic recipe for Flaky Pie Crust for a Double-Crust Pie, use the following additions or substitutions:

Substitute *5⅔ tablespoons of cold solid shortening* for part of the butter (thus using a mixture of 5 tablespoons butter and 5⅔ tablespoons solid shortening); use with any double-crust apple, pear, or fruited mincemeat pies, or the double-crust Lemon Slice Pie (page 119).

Substitute *10⅔ tablespoons cold pure rendered lard* for the entire amount of butter; use with any double-crust fresh fruit pies or any double-crust pies with a mincemeat filling.

Blend *½ teaspoon ground cinnamon, ½ teaspoon freshly grated nutmeg, and ½ teaspoon ground cloves* into the flour with the salt, for a spicy pie crust that tastes right with any of the double-crust fresh fruit pies.

Add *½ teaspoon pure vanilla extract* to the egg yolk and ice-cold water mixture; use this lightly flavored dough with any fresh fruit double-crust pies in the summer section.

SUMMER COUNTRY PIES

SUMMER COUNTRY PIES

———————◆◆◆———————

Peach Streusel Pie   38
Deep-Dish Gingered Peach Pie   40
Double-Crust Blueberry-Peach Pie   42
Deep-Dish Blueberry Pie   44
Spiced Red Plum Pie   45
Prune Plum Pie   46
Deep-Dish Walnut-Rum-Plum Pie   46
Double-Crust Nectarine Spice Pie   48
Sour Cherry Pie   50
Glazed Yellow Cherry Pie   51
Deep-Dish Blackberry Pie   52
Apple-Raspberry Pie   53
Red Raspberry Pie   54
Fresh Apricot Pie   55
Late-Season Green Tomato Pie   56

*P*ies made in the summertime, loaded with sliced fresh fruit or perfect berries, are a delight. Make several rounds of pie crust dough and stack in the freezer. When you come from the farm market with an armload of ripe fruit, remove a round of dough from the freezer to make a quick-from-scratch pie.

I always buy more fruit than I need for any one pie (or other dessert) and turn the extra into fresh fruit syrups, which I love to use in summer pie fillings. Fruit syrups are made from chunked or sliced ripe fruit, water, and granulated sugar. The syrups are clear and lightly thickened—like having the essence of summer in a bottle. I almost always have six—or more—syrups on hand. I find them appealing to use in making fruit compotes, for swirling into ice cream, in mousse mixtures, and as syrup solutions for poaching fruit.

I make fruit syrups from peaches, red plums, blue plums, apricots, blueberries, red raspberries, black raspberries, sweet Bing cherries, sour "pie" cherries, yellow cherries, and nectarines. Whole fruits are sliced or cut into large cubes, with their skins and pits still attached for color and flavor. Cherries are only lightly crushed.

Fresh Fruit Syrups

To make the syrup, place 8 cups of the prepared fruit in a large nonreactive casserole. Such a casserole should be made out of stainless steel, enameled cast iron, or release-surface-coated aluminum; those substances will not taint the contents with a metallic taste. Add 1½ cups of water, cover, and simmer until the fruit is tender and falling apart, about 20 minutes. Remove from the heat and let stand, covered, for 5 minutes. By cupfuls, drain the fruit in a large stainless steel sieve set over a big bowl. Press on the solids once or twice to extract the juice, being careful not to mash the pulp through the sieve. Measure the pressed juice.

Pour the juice into a clean casserole and, for every cup of juice, add 1 cup granulated sugar. Cover and cook slowly until the sugar has dissolved. Uncover and simmer the syrup until lightly thickened, about 10 minutes, depending on the density of the fruit used. Cool to room temperature, funnel into clean, dry bottles, cap tightly, and refrigerate.

Two tablespoons of fruit syrup can be added to any filling for a deep-dish pie, and 1 to 2 tablespoons can be spooned over the fruit filling in a double-crust pie.

❖❖❖❖❖❖❖❖❖❖❖❖❖❖❖❖❖❖❖❖

Peach Streusel Pie

¼ cup plus 2 teaspoons all-purpose flour

½ cup granulated sugar

¼ cup firmly packed light brown sugar

¼ teaspoon ground cinnamon

This homestyle pie has two dimensions: an aromatic layer of peaches thickened with flour and seasoned with sugar, cinnamon, and lemon juice and a crunchy pile of nutty crumbs covering the peaches. The nut-sugar-flour streusel topping makes a perfect covering for almost any kind of juicy summer fruit—it's a lightly crunchy cloak that seals in the fruit as it bakes. The filling for this pie is baked in a fully baked pie shell, which I recommend to keep the pastry dough crisp. Baking the filling in an unbaked shell of dough would produce a partially cooked crust and a quite soggy one at best.

5 cups peeled, pitted, and
sliced peaches (about 7
large peaches), tossed
in 1 tablespoon freshly
squeezed lemon juice

1 fully baked 9-inch pie
shell, made from 1
recipe Flaky Pie Crust
(page 21)

FOR THE SUGAR AND SPICE
STREUSEL:

¾ cup all-purpose flour

½ teaspoon ground
cinnamon

¼ teaspoon freshly grated
nutmeg

¼ cup granulated sugar

¼ cup firmly packed light
brown sugar

½ cup chopped walnuts

5 tablespoons cold
unsalted butter, cut
into small chunks

One 9-inch pie

White peaches, if you can get them, make a succulent pie, as do the end-of-summer freestones, with their deep pink blush and sweet flesh.

Serve big slices of this pie with Double Vanilla Ice Cream (page 130) or Vanilla Pouring Custard (page 129). The ice cream will melt into the juice of the pie filling for a delicious mingling of flavors.

———❖❖❖———

Blend together the flour, granulated sugar, light brown sugar, and cinnamon in a large mixing bowl. Add the peach slices and toss well. Pile the filling into the baked pie shell.

For the streusel, combine the flour, cinnamon, nutmeg, granulated sugar, and brown sugar in a small mixing bowl. Stir in the walnuts. Add the butter and, using two round-bladed knives, cut into the nut mixture until reduced to small flakes.

Cover the top of the pie evenly but completely with the streusel, pressing it down lightly over the fruit.

Bake in a preheated 375 degree oven for about 1 hour, until the peaches are tender and the filling bubbles in spots through the streusel, looking like cooked jam.

Transfer to a cooling rack. Serve barely warm or at room temperature.

Deep-Dish Gingered Peach Pie

3 tablespoons cornstarch

¾ cup granulated sugar

3 tablespoons firmly packed light brown sugar

1 teaspoon ground ginger

¼ teaspoon ground mace

2 tablespoons chopped crystallized ginger

2 tablespoons golden raisins, plumped in ¼ cup boiling water for 1 minute, drained, and dried

6 cups peeled, pitted, and sliced peaches (about 7 to 8 large peaches), tossed in 1 tablespoon freshly squeezed lemon juice

For this pie, crystallized and ground ginger, raisins, sugar, and cornstarch are folded into ripe peach slices to make a fragrant deep-dish filling. When baked, peaches turn into a lightly thickened compote.

One of summer's pleasures is making and eating this pie— breaking through a flaky top crust, spooning out warm, spiced peaches, and devouring it with clouds of whipped cream.

———❖❖❖———

Blend together the cornstarch, granulated sugar, light brown sugar, ground ginger, and mace. Add the chopped ginger, raisins, and peaches, along with any accumulated juice.

Pile the filling in a deep 9-inch pie pan or any other deep-dish round or oval ovenproof cooking vessel. Dot with butter.

Cover the filling with the round of pie dough, seal, and crimp the edges decoratively, as explained on page 23. Refrigerate for 10 minutes.

For the glaze, brush the top of the pie with milk and sprinkle with sugar. Cut several steam vents, using a sharp paring knife.

Bake in a preheated 425 degree oven for 25 minutes, reduce the oven temperature to 350 degrees, and continue baking for 20 to 25 minutes longer, or until the crust is golden and the

1½ tablespoons unsalted
butter, cut into bits

1 recipe Flaky Pie Crust,
prepared for a
deep-dish pie cover
(page 21)

**MILK AND GINGER-SUGAR
GLAZE:**

2 tablespoons cold milk

1 tablespoon granulated
sugar blended with
¼ teaspoon ground
ginger

One 9-inch pie

fruit is tender. (Test by inserting a toothpick in the vent to
feel the consistency of the fruit.)

Transfer to a cooling rack. Serve warm or at room temperature.

Double-Crust Blueberry-Peach Pie

1 recipe Flaky Pie Crust
    for a Double-Crust Pie
    (page 30), well chilled

¼ cup plus 2 teaspoons
    all-purpose flour

1 cup granulated sugar

¼ teaspoon ground
    cinnamon

¼ teaspoon freshly grated
    nutmeg

3 cups peeled, pitted, and
    sliced peaches (about 4
    peaches)

1¾ cups blueberries,
    picked over

2 tablespoons unsalted
    butter, cut into bits

1 teaspoon freshly
    squeezed lemon juice,
    strained

During the summer, I always have several kinds of ripe fruit on hand to make an assortment of syrups, glazes, jellies, and preserves to use in cooking and baking throughout the year. One afternoon, I turned an overflow of blueberries and peaches into a double-crust pie, with delicious results. This pie has become a family favorite.

Other than adding a bit of cinnamon and nutmeg to the sugar and flour mixture, I have kept the filling plain to let the taste of each fruit come through.

The blueberry-peach filling can be covered with a lattice top, letting patches of fruit show through, or it can be covered with a plain round of pie dough.

Line a 9-inch pie pan with half of the chilled pie dough following the directions on page 31; refrigerate.

Thoroughly combine the flour, sugar, cinnamon, and nutmeg in a large mixing bowl. Add the peach slices and blueberries. Toss.

Pile the filling in the chilled pie shell, mounding it slightly toward the center. Dot with butter and drizzle with lemon juice. Cover with remaining dough (or weave a latticework top over the filling using the second sheet of dough), seal, and flute the edges decoratively, as explained on page 31. Refrigerate for 10 minutes.

CRACKLE SUGAR GLAZE:

2 tablespoons ice-cold
    water
1 tablespoon granulated
    sugar

One 9-inch pie

Brush the top of the pie with water, sprinkle with sugar, and cut several steam vents, using a sharp paring knife.

Bake in a preheated 425 degree oven for 25 minutes, reduce the oven temperature to 350 degrees, and continue baking for about 30 minutes longer, or until the pastry is golden.

Transfer to a cooling rack. Serve barely warm or at room temperature, with Vanilla Pouring Custard, if you like (page 129).

Baking Note: Pastry cutouts, forming an overlapping cover atop the fruit, may replace the full pie dough cover (see page 32).

Deep-Dish Blueberry Pie

¼ cup all-purpose flour

1 cup granulated sugar

¼ teaspoon freshly grated nutmeg

5 cups blueberries, picked over

2 teaspoons finely grated lemon rind

2 tablespoons unsalted butter, cut into bits

1 recipe Flaky Pie Crust, prepared for a deep-dish pie cover (page 21)

MILK AND SUGAR GLAZE:

2 tablespoons cold milk

1 tablespoon granulated sugar

One 9-inch pie

Plump blueberries, with a silvery sheen, are one of the easiest summer fruits to turn into a pie. Just pick over the berries for leaves, dump them into a bowl, and toss well in sugar, flour, and nutmeg.

When blueberries are baked in a pie, some of the juices invariably trickle through the steam vents in the top crust. Blueberry pie would not be blueberry pie without them.

Serve large spoonfuls of the filling with some crust attached, partnered with scoops of Double Vanilla Ice Cream (page 130). I serve this pie in deep plates. I bake it in a deep oval pie dish made of ovenproof porcelain that I bought in England many years ago. The dish and plates are decorated with clusters of fruit and look beautiful on the table.

Blend together the flour, sugar, and nutmeg in a large mixing bowl. Add the blueberries and lemon rind. Fold the berries through the sugar mixture.

Pile into a deep 9-inch pie pan or any other deep-dish round or oval ovenproof cooking vessel. Dot with butter.

Cover the filling with the round of pie dough, seal, and crimp the edges decoratively, as explained on page 23. Refrigerate for 10 minutes.

For the glaze, brush the top of the pie with the cold milk and sprinkle with sugar. Cut several steam vents in the top crust with a sharp knife.

Bake in a preheated 425 degree oven for 20 minutes, reduce the oven temperature to 350 degrees, and continue baking for about 35 minutes longer, or until the top crust is golden. Transfer to a cooling rack. Serve warm or at room temperature.

Spiced Red Plum Pie

1 recipe Flaky Pie Crust for a Double-Crust Pie (page 30), well chilled

5 tablespoons all-purpose flour

1 cup granulated sugar blended with ½ teaspoon ground cinnamon, ½ teaspoon freshly grated nutmeg, ¼ teaspoon ground ginger, and ¼ teaspoon ground allspice

5 cups pitted and sliced ripe red plums (about 11 to 12 plums)

1 tablespoon fresh plum syrup (see Fresh Fruit Syrups, page 37), optional

1 teaspoon freshly squeezed lemon juice

Two sheaths of flaky pie crust hold a solid plum filling flavored with nutmeg, cinnamon, ginger, and cloves. It is a pie to remember when perfect midsummer plums abound. Choose plump, sweet-scented, firm plums. To bring out the fruit's vivid flavor, I like to top the pie filling with a tablespoon of fresh plum syrup.

This pie is equally delicious when made with the Italian prune plums available late summer and early fall. These small, slightly elongated blue plums need only to be halved and pitted before tossed with the sugar and spices. The recipe for Prune Plum Pie, a variation of Spiced Red Plum Pie, is outlined below.

For a real treat, serve slices of Spiced Red Plum Pie on deep dessert plates and pour a big puddle of Vanilla Pouring Custard (page 129) to one side of each slice.

Line a 9-inch pie pan with half of the chilled pie dough following the directions on page 31; refrigerate.

Combine the flour and sugar-spice blend in a large mixing bowl. Add the sliced plums and toss.

Pile the filling in the chilled pie shell, mounding it slightly toward the center. Drizzle with plum syrup, if desired, and lemon juice. Cover with remaining dough, seal, and crimp the edges decoratively, as explained on page 31. Refrigerate for 10 minutes.

(continued)

CRACKLE SUGAR GLAZE:

2 tablespoons ice-cold
water

1 tablespoon granulated
sugar

One 9-inch pie

For the glaze, brush the top of the pie with water and sprinkle with sugar. Cut several steam vents, using a sharp paring knife.

Bake in a preheated 425 degree oven for 25 minutes, reduce the oven temperature to 350 degrees, and continue baking for about 30 minutes longer, or until the pastry is golden.

Transfer to a cooling rack. Serve barely warm or at room temperature.

PRUNE PLUM PIE

To make Prune Plum Pie, substitute 5 cups (about 28 to 36) halved and pitted Italian blue prune plums for the red. Very large plums should be pitted and quartered.

Baking Note: A top cover made out of pastry dough cutouts (page 32) may replace the top cover for the pie.

❖·❖·❖·❖·❖·❖·❖·❖·❖·❖·❖·❖·❖

Deep-Dish Walnut-Rum-Plum Pie

3 tablespoons cornstarch

1 cup granulated sugar

¼ teaspoon ground
cinnamon

This unusual pie uses a concentrated rum syrup, a number of spices, and chopped walnuts to enrich the sliced plum filling.

Deep-Dish Walnut-Rum-Plum Pie is a splendid dessert to take to a covered dish supper along with a container of Vanilla Pouring Custard (page 129). When the custard is poured over each serving, it mixes with the pie juices, making a delicious combination of fruit and cream.

$^{1}/_{4}$ teaspoon freshly grated nutmeg

$^{1}/_{4}$ teaspoon ground allspice

$^{1}/_{4}$ teaspoon ground ginger

$^{1}/_{2}$ cup chopped lightly toasted walnuts

6 cups pitted and sliced red plums (about 14 to 15 plums)

1 teaspoon freshly squeezed lemon juice

2 tablespoons Rum Syrup (see recipe below)

2 tablespoons unsalted butter, cut into bits

1 recipe Flaky Pie Crust, prepared for a deep-dish pie cover (page 21)

MILK AND SUGAR GLAZE:

2 tablespoons cold milk

1 tablespoon granulated sugar

One 9-inch pie

Blend together the cornstarch, sugar, cinnamon, nutmeg, allspice, and ginger. Add the walnuts, plums, and lemon juice. Stir.

Pile the filling in a deep 9-inch pie pan or any other deep-dish round or oval ovenproof cooking vessel. Drizzle with Rum Syrup and dot with butter.

Cover the filling with the round of dough, seal, and crimp the edges decoratively, as explained on page 23. Refrigerate for 10 minutes.

For the glaze, brush the top of the pie with milk and sprinkle with sugar. Cut several steam vents in the top crust with a sharp paring knife.

Bake in a preheated 425 degree oven for 20 minutes, reduce the oven temperature to 350 degrees, and continue baking for 30 to 35 minutes, or until the pastry top is golden.

Transfer to a cooling rack. Serve warm or at room temperature.

RUM SYRUP

To make Rum Syrup, combine $^{1}/_{4}$ cup dark rum, 1 tablespoon granulated sugar, and $^{1}/_{4}$ cup water in a small saucepan. Cover and cook over low heat for 3 to 4 minutes until the sugar has dissolved. Uncover, bring to a boil over moderately high heat, boil 1 minute, and cool. Use as directed.

Double-Crust Nectarine Spice Pie

1 recipe Flaky Pie Crust for a Double-Crust Pie (page 30), well chilled

¼ cup plus 2 teaspoons all-purpose flour

⅞ cup granulated sugar

¼ teaspoon ground cinnamon

¼ teaspoon freshly grated nutmeg

¼ teaspoon ground allspice

5½ cups peeled, pitted, and sliced nectarines (about 7 to 8 nectarines)

2 tablespoons nectarine syrup (see Fresh Fruit Syrups, page 37), optional

2 teaspoons freshly squeezed lemon juice, strained

2 tablespoons unsalted butter, cut into bits

The nectarine, often overlooked in favor of its cousin the peach, makes a delicious pie filling. The fruit is sweet smelling and firm, and the peel is easy to remove by dipping the fruit briefly in boiling water.

The pie crust holds nectarines tossed in a mixture of flour, sugar, cinnamon, nutmeg, allspice, and lemon juice. A tablespoon or two of fresh nectarine syrup, if you have it, would heighten the flavor of the fruit.

Serve a slice of pie along with a tall glass of minted iced tea on a hazy summer afternoon, or bring it along to a fried chicken or dinner-on-the-grill supper as your contribution.

Line a 9-inch pie pan with half of the chilled pie dough following the directions on page 31; refrigerate.

Combine the flour, granulated sugar, cinnamon, nutmeg, and allspice in a large mixing bowl. Add the sliced nectarines; toss.

Pile the filling in the chilled pie shell, mounding it slightly toward the center. Drizzle with syrup, if desired, and with lemon juice. Dot with butter. Cover with remaining dough, seal, and crimp the edges decoratively, as explained on page 31. Refrigerate for 10 minutes.

For the glaze, brush the top of the pie with the ice-cold water and sprinkle with sugar. Cut several steam vents, using a sharp paring knife.

Bake in a preheated 425 degree oven for 25 minutes, reduce

CRACKLE SUGAR GLAZE:

2 tablespoons ice-cold
water

1 tablespoon granulated
sugar

One 9-inch pie

the oven temperature to 350 degrees, and continue baking for 25 to 30 minutes longer, or until the pastry top is golden.

Transfer to a cooling rack. Serve barely warm or at room temperature.

Baking Note: A cover of pastry cutouts (page 32) can replace the cover of dough.

Sour Cherry Pie

1 recipe Flaky Pie Crust
for a Double-Crust Pie
(page 30), well chilled

¼ cup plus 2 teaspoons
all-purpose flour

1¼ cups granulated sugar

¼ teaspoon ground
cinnamon

¼ teaspoon ground mace

5 cups sour cherries,
pitted

2 tablespoons sour cherry
syrup (see Fresh Fruit
Syrups, page 37)

2 tablespoons unsalted
butter, cut into bits

MILK AND SUGAR GLAZE:

2 tablespoons cold milk

1 tablespoon granulated
sugar

One 9-inch pie

Sour cherries make your mouth pucker up when eaten
straight, but when they are pitted, tossed with sugar, and
baked in a pie shell, their tartness is gentled considerably. The
sour cherries I find at a local farm market are a pinkish-red
color with a tawny gold cast. They make as good a pie as they
do a jelly, glaze, marmalade, or jam.

Sour cherry syrup is called for in this recipe; a few spoonfuls
drizzled over the pie filling intensifies the flavor of the cherries
as they bake. (If you boil down enough to make a glaze, it
becomes a lustrous topping for fresh fruit tarts.)

Line a 9-inch pie pan with half of the chilled pie dough following the directions on page 31; refrigerate.

Combine the flour, sugar, cinnamon, and mace in a large
mixing bowl. Add the cherries; toss.

Pile the filling into the chilled pie shell. Drizzle with sour
cherry syrup and dot with butter.

Cover with the remaining dough, seal, and crimp the edges
decoratively, as explained on page 31. Refrigerate for 10 minutes.

For the glaze, brush the top of the pie with milk and sprinkle with sugar. Cut several steam vents, using a sharp paring
knife.

Bake in a preheated 425 degree oven for 25 minutes, reduce
the oven temperature to 350 degrees, and continue baking for
25 to 30 minutes longer, or until the top is golden.

Transfer to a cooling rack. Serve barely warm or at room
temperature, with scoops of Double Vanilla Ice Cream, if you
like (page 130).

Glazed Yellow Cherry Pie

3 tablespoons cornstarch

1 cup granulated sugar

¼ teaspoon ground cinnamon

⅛ teaspoon each ground allspice and ground cloves

5 cups yellow cherries, pitted

2 teaspoons freshly squeezed lemon juice, strained

1 fully baked 9-inch pie shell, made from Flaky Pie Crust (page 21)

2 tablespoons unsalted butter, cut into bits

APPLE JELLY GLAZE:

½ cup apple jelly

2 tablespoons apple juice or water

2 tablespoons toasted slivered almonds

One 9-inch pie

Plump and sweet yellow cherries are baked in a pie shell topped only with butter; after the filling has thickened, a clear apple jelly glaze is spooned over the top and sprinkled with slivered, lightly toasted almonds, adding a textural edge and a nutty taste.

Yellow cherries make a pretty pie. I often reserve a large handful of cherries with their stems attached to garnish a baked and glazed pie.

Red Bing cherries may be substituted for the yellow cherries, with delicious results.

————❖❖❖————

Blend together the cornstarch, sugar, cinnamon, allspice, and cloves in a large mixing bowl. Add the yellow cherries and toss. Sprinkle with lemon juice.

Spoon the pie filling into the baked pie shell. Scatter the butter evenly over the top.

Bake in a preheated 375 degree oven for 40 minutes, or until the filling is bubbly and the cherries are tender.

Transfer to a cooling rack.

To make the glaze: Combine the apple jelly and juice (or water) in a small saucepan. Bring to a simmer over moderate heat. Remove from the heat and spoon the hot glaze over the cherries. Cool completely.

Just before serving, sprinkle the lightly toasted slivered almonds over the top of the pie.

Deep-Dish Blackberry Pie

5 tablespoons all-purpose flour

1 cup granulated sugar

6 cups blackberries

2 tablespoons unsalted butter, cut into bits

1 recipe Flaky Pie Crust, prepared for a deep-dish pie (page 21)

CRACKLE SUGAR GLAZE:

2 tablespoons ice-cold water

1 tablespoon granulated sugar

One 9-inch pie

Sweet and plump blackberries may be turned into jam, marmalade, and jelly, or used in tarts, cobblers, puddings, and this deep-dish pie.

This is one of the simplest and best-tasting pies I can think of, laden with sweetened berries and nothing more. The blackberries are covered with pastry dough, but you could cut out hearts or diamonds and lay those, overlapping, over the berries.

Deep-Dish Blackberry Pie is scrumptious when served just-out-of-the-oven warm, with scoops of Double Vanilla Ice Cream (page 130).

Blend together the flour and sugar in a large mixing bowl. Add the berries and toss them well in the sugar mixture.

Pile into a deep 9-inch pie pan or any other deep-dish round or oval ovenproof cooking vessel, mounding the berries toward the center. Dot with butter.

Cover the filling with the round of pie dough, seal, and crimp the edges decoratively, as explained on page 23. Refrigerate for 10 minutes.

For the glaze, brush the top of the pie with water and sprinkle with sugar. Cut several steam vents, using a sharp paring knife.

Bake in a preheated 425 degree oven for 20 minutes, reduce the oven temperature to 350 degrees, and continue baking for 30 to 35 minutes longer, or until the pastry is golden.

Transfer to a cooling rack. Serve warm.

Apple-Raspberry Pie

1 recipe Flaky Pie Crust
for a Double-Crust Pie
(page 30), well chilled

¼ cup all-purpose flour

1 cup granulated sugar

¼ teaspoon freshly grated
nutmeg

¼ teaspoon ground
cinnamon

2 cups red raspberries

2⅔ cups peeled, cored,
and sliced tart cooking
apples

2 tablespoons red
raspberry syrup (see
Fresh Fruit Syrups,
page 37)

2 tablespoons unsalted
butter, cut into bits

CREAM AND SUGAR GLAZE:

2 tablespoons cold light
cream

1 tablespoon granulated
sugar

One 9-inch pie

For this pie, luscious red raspberries are combined with tart cooking apples, flour, sugar, and a hint of nutmeg and cinnamon. This flavorsome combination of fruit is enhanced with some red raspberry syrup drizzled over the filling.

Serve a cold pitcher of minted iced tea with ample slices of pie and spoonfuls of whipped cream, lightly sweetened with the raspberry syrup.

———❖❖❖———

Line a 9-inch pie pan with half of the chilled pie dough following the directions on page 31; refrigerate.

Combine the flour, sugar, nutmeg, and cinnamon in a large mixing bowl. Pick over the raspberries for any stems. Add the berries and sliced apples to the flour mixture. Toss gently.

Pile the filling in the chilled pie shell. Drizzle with raspberry syrup and dot with butter. Cover with remaining dough, seal, and crimp the edges decoratively, as explained on page 31. Refrigerate for 10 minutes.

For the glaze, brush the top of the pie with cream and sprinkle with sugar. Cut several steam vents in the top crust with a sharp paring knife.

Bake in a preheated 425 degree oven for 25 minutes, reduce the oven temperature to 350 degrees, and continue baking for 25 to 30 minutes longer, or until the top is golden.

Transfer to a cooling rack. Serve at room temperature.

Red Raspberry Pie

1 recipe Flaky Pie Crust
  for a Double-Crust Pie
  (page 30), well chilled

¼ cup plus 2 teaspoons
  all-purpose flour

1 cup granulated sugar

5 cups red or black
  raspberries, picked
  over

2 teaspoons freshly
  squeezed lemon juice

2 tablespoons unsalted
  butter, cut into bits

MILK AND SUGAR GLAZE:

2 tablespoons cold milk

1 tablespoon granulated
  sugar

One 9-inch pie

This is a simple, fresh-tasting pie. Firm red raspberries are tossed in a mixture of sugar, flour, and lemon juice to draw out their flavor. In anticipation of the berry season, when raspberries abound for a few brief weeks, I squirrel away a pile of rolled-out pastry crusts so I can make a pie whenever I bring home pints and quarts of fruit.

From extra cartons of berries, I produce a vibrant raspberry syrup (see Fresh Fruit Syrups, page 37); occasionally, I'll spoon a few tablespoons of the syrup over the pie filling. Black raspberries may be substituted for red raspberries, with excellent results.

Line a 9-inch pie pan with half of the chilled pie dough following the directions on page 31; refrigerate.

Blend together the flour and sugar in a large mixing bowl. Add the raspberries and combine gently.

Pile the filling into the chilled pie shell. Drizzle with lemon juice and dot with butter. Cover with the remaining dough, seal, and crimp the edges decoratively, as explained on page 31. Refrigerate for 10 minutes.

For the glaze, brush the top of the pie with milk and sprinkle sugar evenly over the top. Cut several steam vents, using a sharp paring knife.

Bake in a preheated 425 degree oven for 25 minutes, reduce the oven temperature to 350 degrees, and continue baking for about 25 to 30 minutes longer, or until the top is golden.

Transfer to a cooling rack. Serve at room temperature, with Vanilla Pouring Custard, if you like (page 129).

Fresh Apricot Pie

1 recipe Flaky Pie Crust
  for a Double-Crust Pie
  (page 30), well chilled

¼ cup all-purpose flour

¾ cup granulated sugar

2 tablespoons firmly
  packed light brown
  sugar

½ teaspoon freshly grated
  nutmeg

½ teaspoon ground
  cinnamon

4¾ cups pitted and
  quartered ripe apricots
  (about 20 medium to
  large apricots)

2 tablespoons fresh
  apricot syrup (see
  Fresh Fruit Syrups,
  page 37), optional

2 tablespoons unsalted
  butter, cut into bits

Fresh, fragrant apricots are one of summer's best offerings, and I know of no better way to use them than in this pie—and in fruit syrup, chutney, jelly, and marmalade.

For the pie, the apricots are halved, pitted, and thickly sliced, then tossed with flour, sugar, nutmeg, and cinnamon. Fresh apricot or apricot-plum syrup is a marvelous addition to the pie filling; spoon 2 tablespoons of the syrup over the fruit before covering with the top crust. A cutout pastry cover is a good way to enclose the fruit if you are not using the traditional top crust. I am partial to using scalloped rounds of dough as cutouts; I overlap the rounds slightly, placing them in the center of the pie first, and continue around toward the edge. Serve slices of apricot pie with Vanilla Pouring Custard (page 129), Double Vanilla Ice Cream (page 130), or Vanilla-Scented Whipped Cream (page 131).

Line a 9-inch pie pan with half of the chilled pie dough following the directions on page 31; refrigerate.

Blend together the flour, granulated sugar, light brown sugar, nutmeg, and cinnamon in a large mixing bowl. Add the apricots and toss with the sugar and spice mixture.

Spoon the filling into the chilled pie shell, mounding it slightly toward the center. Drizzle with apricot syrup, if you are using it, and dot with butter.

Cover the filling with the remaining dough, seal, and crimp the edges decoratively, as explained on page 31. Refrigerate for 10 minutes.

(continued)

CREAM AND SUGAR GLAZE:

2 tablespoons cold heavy
  cream

1 tablespoon granulated
  sugar

One 9-inch pie

For the glaze, brush the top of the pie with cream and
sprinkle with sugar. Cut several steam vents in the top crust
with a sharp paring knife.

Bake in a preheated 425 degree oven for 25 minutes, reduce
the oven temperature to 350 degrees, and continue baking for
25 to 30 minutes longer, or until the pastry crust is golden.

Transfer to a cooling rack. Serve barely warm or at room
temperature.

❖❖∶❖❖❖❖❖❖❖❖❖❖∶❖❖❖

Late-Season Green Tomato Pie

1 recipe Flaky Pie Crust
  for a Double-Crust Pie
  (page 30), well chilled

⅓ cup all-purpose flour

1 cup granulated sugar

¼ teaspoon ground
  cinnamon

¼ teaspoon freshly grated
  nutmeg

⅛ teaspoon ground
  cloves

For this pie filling, sliced green tomatoes are tossed in a lightly
spiced mixture of sugar and flour, piled into an unbaked pie
shell, and sealed with a round of dough.

When I am not using the full pastry cover, I top the filling
with an overlay of pastry cutouts (see page 32) and apply the
Crackle Sugar Glaze (recipe below). I also like to cover the
filling with a lattice top made from 2- to 3-inch-wide strips of
interwoven dough. Serve thick slices of the pie with tall glasses
of minted or herbal iced tea.

———❖❖❖———

Line a 9-inch pie pan with half of the chilled pie dough following the directions on page 31; refrigerate.

Combine the flour, granulated sugar, cinnamon, nutmeg,

4 cups green tomatoes, sliced ¼ inch thick (about 6 tomatoes)

2 tablespoons dark raisins, plumped in boiling water for 10 minutes, drained, and dried

1 teaspoon finely grated lemon rind

2 tablespoons unsalted butter, cut into bits

CRACKLE SUGAR GLAZE:

2 tablespoons ice-cold water

1 tablespoon granulated sugar

One 9-inch pie

and cloves in a large mixing bowl. Add the tomatoes, raisins, and lemon rind and fold into the flour mixture.

Spoon the filling into the chilled pie shell and dot with butter. Cover the filling with the remaining dough, seal, and flute the edges decoratively, as explained on page 31. Refrigerate for 10 minutes.

To glaze, brush the top of the pie with water and sprinkle with sugar. Cut several steam vents in the top crust with a sharp paring knife.

Bake in a preheated 425 degree oven for 15 minutes, reduce the oven temperature to 350 degrees, and continue baking the pie for about 50 minutes longer, or until the pastry is golden.

Transfer to a cooling rack. Serve at room temperature.

AUTUMN
COUNTRY
PIES

AUTUMN COUNTRY PIES

————————— ❖❖❖ —————————

Double-Crust Apple Pie   62
Apple-Ginger Mincemeat Pie   63
Apple-Pear Pie with Apple Cider Syrup   66
Pear Mincemeat Pie   68
Cinnamon-Pear Pie with Walnut Streusel   69
Spiced Pear-Currant Pie   71
Cranberry-Walnut Mincemeat Pie   72
Golden Pecan Pie   74
Bourbon Pecan Pie   75
Pumpkin Custard Pie   76
Pumpkin Crunch Pie   78
Fresh Sugar Pumpkin Pie   80
Apricot-Yam Pie   81
Orange–Butternut Squash Pie   82
Brandied Golden Acorn Squash Pie   84
Coconut-Walnut-Chocolate-Chip "Candy" Pie   86
Brown Sugar Pie   87

*J*ust about the time children go back to school, I am in the kitchen making batches of Dried Fruit and Spice Mincemeat (page 64) to use in pie fillings with pears, apples, and cranberries and quarts of Apple Cider Syrup (page 65) to splash over pie fillings whose flavor needs intensifying. Apple pies, especially, benefit from being moistened with a little cider syrup.

For sweet custard pies, a staple of the fall pie-baking kitchen, I pick out firm pumpkins, slender yams, and heavy butternut and acorn squash at the market. I steam and mash or puree chunks of the vegetables. From fresh pumpkin puree I make Pumpkin Custard Pie (page 76), Pumpkin Crunch Pie (page 78), and Fresh Sugar Pumpkin Pie (page 80). Golden acorn squash puree gets sweetened, spiced, and bound with cream and eggs to make tender custard pies. These fillings are thick, rich, and generously flavored with cinnamon, allspice, ginger, cloves, and freshly grated nutmeg.

Nuts—walnuts and pecans—are in a few fall country pies. Golden Pecan Pie (page 74) and Bourbon Pecan Pie (page 75) are semitranslucent pies made with plenty of eggs and sweetened with a combination of sugars. In the Coconut-Walnut-Chocolate-Chip ''Candy'' Pie (page 86), chopped walnuts add body and crunch to a filling made of eggs, butter, sugar, and cream.

These pies are substantial and filling; just out of the oven and warm, they are a real treat in chilly weather.

Double-Crust
Apple Pie

1 recipe Flaky Pie Crust
   for a Double-Crust Pie
   (page 30), well chilled

1 tablespoon plus 1½
   teaspoons cornstarch

⅓ cup firmly packed light
   brown sugar

⅓ cup granulated sugar

¾ teaspoon ground
   cinnamon

¼ teaspoon freshly grated
   nutmeg

4 cups peeled, cored, and
   sliced tart cooking
   apples (about 5 large
   apples), tossed in 1
   tablespoon freshly
   squeezed lemon juice

1½ tablespoons cold
   unsalted butter, cut
   into bits

MILK AND SUGAR GLAZE:

2 tablespoons cold milk

1 tablespoon granulated
   sugar

One 9-inch pie

A barely warm helping of apple pie, with a dip of ice cream to one side, is comforting. In my kitchen, making a Double-Crust Apple Pie has become an autumn ritual, along with bottling loads of apple cider syrup and simmering pots full of apple butter and applesauce.

The top of the pie may be etched in a whimsical "spider-web" pattern by using the tip of a skewer to draw the design on the pastry round before covering the pie. Or you may apply apple-shaped pastry cutouts to the top just before it is baked.

———❖❖❖———

Line a 9-inch pie pan with half of the chilled pie dough following the directions on page 31; refrigerate.

Combine the cornstarch, light brown sugar, granulated sugar, cinnamon, and nutmeg in a large mixing bowl. Blend well. Add the sliced apples and toss.

Spoon the filling into the chilled pie shell, mounding it slightly toward the center. Dot with butter. Cover with remaining dough, seal, and crimp edges decoratively, as explained on page 31. Refrigerate for 10 minutes.

For the glaze, brush the top of the pie with milk and sprinkle with sugar. Cut several steam vents in the top crust with a sharp paring knife.

Bake in a preheated 425 degree oven for 10 minutes, reduce the oven temperature to 350 degrees, and continue baking for 40 minutes longer, or until the pastry is golden.

Transfer to a cooling rack. Serve warm or at room temperature, accompanied by Vanilla Pouring Custard (page 129), Double Vanilla Ice Cream (page 130), or Vanilla-Scented Whipped Cream (page 131).

Apple-Ginger Mincemeat Pie

1 recipe Flaky Pie Crust
   for a Double-Crust Pie
   (page 30), well chilled

2 tablespoons cornstarch
   blended with 1
   tablespoon firmly
   packed light brown
   sugar

4 cups peeled, cored, and
   cubed tart cooking
   apples

1 cup Dried Fruit and
   Spice Mincemeat
   (page 64)

½ cup chopped walnuts

¼ cup ginger, preserved
   in syrup, drained, and
   chopped

1 tablespoon cold
   unsalted butter, cut
   into bits

CRACKLE SUGAR GLAZE:

2 tablespoons ice-cold
   water

1 tablespoon granulated
   sugar

One 9-inch pie

Once you've made a batch of my Dried Fruit and Spice Mince-meat—a luxurious thing to have on hand—you can make all kinds of fall and winter pies. The fruit available from September through February marries beautifully with the rich, dark mincemeat.

This homestyle pie is a mixture of mincemeat, chopped walnuts, and ginger preserved in syrup, plus a good quantity of apples. The apples are sweetened by the mincemeat's syrup and the ginger.

Triangular pieces are delicious with spoonfuls of softly whipped cream sweetened with some syrup drained from the ginger; use about 2 tablespoons of syrup to flavor 1 cup heavy cream.

Line a 9-inch pie pan with half of the chilled pie dough following the directions on page 31; refrigerate.

Place the cornstarch–brown sugar blend in a large mixing bowl. Stir in the apples, mincemeat, walnuts, and ginger. Pile the mixture into the chilled pie shell and dot with butter. Cover with remaining dough, seal, and crimp the edges decoratively, as explained on page 31. Refrigerate for 10 minutes.

To glaze, brush the top of the pie with water and sprinkle with the granulated sugar. Cut several steam vents, using a sharp paring knife.

Bake in a preheated 425 degree oven for 20 minutes, reduce the oven temperature to 350 degrees, and continue baking for about 30 to 35 minutes longer, until the pastry is golden.

Transfer to a cooling rack. Serve at room temperature.

Dried Fruit and Spice Mincemeat

1½ cups dark raisins

1½ cups golden raisins

1½ cups dried currants

1½ cups dried peaches, cut into large dice

1½ cups dried apricots, cut into large dice

1½ cups pitted dates, cut into large dice

1½ teaspoons ground cinnamon

½ teaspoon freshly grated nutmeg

¼ teaspoon ground allspice

¼ teaspoon ground ginger

⅓ cup dark corn syrup

1¼ cups dark rum

¾ cup firmly packed light brown sugar

¼ cup Apple Cider Syrup (see recipe below), optional

This is an elegant yet quick-to-prepare mincemeat that uses a full range of dried fruit. Peaches and apricots contribute tanginess, golden raisins and currants provide sweetness, and dates give a honeylike richness.

The mincemeat is especially nice to have on hand for adding a remarkable depth to fruited pie fillings. I also like to use it as a filling for crepes and sometimes I incorporate several tablespoons into a stuffing for Cornish hens or the holiday turkey. It is a blend of mincemeat that bolsters the taste of apples and cranberries, too.

This is a satisfying mincemeat to make. The procedure does not require unlimited hours stirring a bubbling kettle. It's just a matter of boiling a sweet rum and spice liquid and pouring it over the fruit. The fruit plumps in the hot solution, absorbing the spicy syrup.

Jarred, this mincemeat has a long life span—about a year—in the refrigerator, where it will continue to mellow. Dried Fruit and Spice Mincemeat makes a dandy bread-and-butter hostess gift for a friend who likes to cook. For gift giving, pack the mincemeat into pretty glass jars up to ¼ inch from the top. Cut a round of heavy brown paper to fit neatly on top of the mincemeat and moisten both sides with rum. Press the disk on top of the mincemeat and seal with the lid. The rum-charged circle will keep the mincemeat flavored throughout the year.

Combine the dark and golden raisins, currants, peaches, apricots, and dates in a large mixing bowl; set aside.

2 cups apple juice

7 tablespoons unsalted
  butter

About 11 cups

Put the cinnamon, nutmeg, allspice, and ginger in a large nonreactive saucepan. Stir in the corn syrup, rum, light brown sugar, Apple Cider Syrup (if desired), and apple juice. Add the butter. Bring the mixture to a boil over moderate heat. Boil for 3 minutes. Pour the hot liquid over the dried fruit; stir. Cool to room temperature.

When cooled completely, pour into clean glass jars, seal tightly, and refrigerate.

Apple Cider Syrup

To make a quart jug of Apple Cider Syrup, boil 1 gallon pure, unfiltered apple cider until reduced by half. Add ½ cup light corn syrup; stir well to dissolve. Continue to boil until reduced to 4 cups. Cool to room temperature. Strain through a sieve lined with a double thickness of finely meshed cheesecloth, pour into a bottle, cap tightly, and refrigerate. The syrup will keep indefinitely.

Apple Cider Syrup adds a concentrated apple flavor to the mincemeat, which I find delightful. If you have a little extra time, I think you will find it well worth making.

Apple-Pear Pie with Apple Cider Syrup

1 recipe Flaky Pie Crust for a Double-Crust Pie (page 30), well chilled

2 tablespoons plus 2 teaspoons cornstarch

⅓ cup firmly packed light brown sugar

⅓ cup granulated sugar

¼ teaspoon ground cinnamon

¼ teaspoon freshly grated nutmeg

¼ teaspoon ground allspice

2 cups peeled, cored, and sliced tart cooking apples (about 3 medium-size)

2 cups peeled, cored, and sliced just-ripe pears, preferably D'Anjou (about 3 medium-size)

2 tablespoons Apple Cider Syrup (page 65)

This fresh fruit pie uses the best of the fall market stand—tart cooking apples and ripe pears. For this pie, I like the combination of just ripe D'Anjou pears and crisp Jonathan apples. Light brown and granulated sugars sweeten the filling, giving it a soft caramel flavor.

I have found that a small amount of concentrated fruit syrup can make a simple pie filling taste extraordinary. Syrups heighten the natural fragrance of the fruit, and they are simple and rewarding to make. Here, I am fond of using a few tablespoons of Apple Cider Syrup (page 65) to intensify the flavor of the apples and pears. If you don't have any, simmer ½ teaspoon light corn syrup in 3 tablespoons apple cider or apple juice until reduced to 2 tablespoons, remove from the heat, and cool completely. When the syrup has cooled to room temperature, spoon it over the apple and pear filling.

❖❖❖

Line a 9-inch pie pan with half of the chilled pie dough following the directions on page 31; refrigerate.

Combine the cornstarch, light brown sugar, granulated sugar, cinnamon, nutmeg, and allspice in a large mixing bowl. Add the apples and pears; toss. Pile the filling in the chilled pie shell, mounding it slightly toward the center. Drizzle with Apple Cider Syrup and dot with butter. Cover the pie filling with the remaining dough, seal, and crimp the edges decoratively, as explained on page 31. Refrigerate for 10 minutes.

2 tablespoons cold
    unsalted butter, cut
    into cubes

MILK AND SUGAR GLAZE:

2 tablespoons cold milk
1 tablespoon granulated
    sugar

One 9-inch pie

For the glaze, brush the top of the pie with milk and sprinkle with sugar. Cut several steam vents, using a sharp paring knife.

Bake in a preheated 425 degree oven for 10 minutes, reduce the oven temperature to 350 degrees, and continue baking the pie for 40 minutes longer, or until the pastry top is golden.

Transfer to a cooling rack. Serve barely warm or at room temperature.

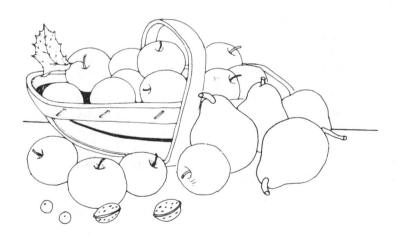

Pear Mincemeat Pie

1 recipe Flaky Pie Crust
for a Double-Crust Pie
(page 30), well chilled

3 tablespoons cornstarch

1/4 cup granulated sugar
or Vanilla-Scented
Granulated Sugar
(page 219)

1/2 teaspoon ground
cinnamon

1/4 teaspoon freshly grated
nutmeg

2/3 cup Dried Fruit and
Spice Mincemeat
(page 64)

5 cups peeled, cored, and
sliced firm but ripe
pears (about 6 pears)

1/2 cup chopped walnuts

This not-too-sweet pie is a lovely late fall dessert, perfect for when we begin to crave the flavors of ripe pears and rum-charged mincemeat. It is quick to put together, providing you've hoarded away a few jars of mincemeat.

The dried fruit mincemeat, which is swirled through the pears, is made of dark and light raisins, currants, peaches, apricots, and dates, as well as a wealth of spices. Its sweeteners (corn syrup, brown sugar, and apple juice) also complement the flavor of the sturdy fall fruit.

There are several ways to craft the top crust for the pie: You can use a solid cover, brush it with milk, and sprinkle with sugar. Or, you can weave a latticework cover (page 33) over the filling, exposing little windows of mincemeat. Finally, you can form a pastry lid from cutouts according to the directions on page 32.

———❖❖❖———

Line a 9-inch pie pan with half of the chilled pie dough following the directions on page 31; refrigerate.

Combine the cornstarch and granulated or vanilla-flavored sugar in a large mixing bowl. The mixture should look like a very fine powder. Blend in the cinnamon and nutmeg. Add the mincemeat, sliced pears, and walnuts; fold in gently.

Spoon the filling into the chilled pie shell, mounding it slightly toward the center. Cover with the remaining dough, seal, and crimp the edges decoratively, as explained on page 31. Refrigerate for 10 minutes.

2 tablespoons cold milk

1 tablespoon granulated
sugar

One 9-inch pie

For the glaze, brush the top of the pie with milk and sprinkle with the granulated sugar. Cut several steam vents, using a sharp paring knife.

Bake in a preheated 425 degree oven for 20 minutes, reduce the oven temperature to 350 degrees, and continue baking for 30 to 35 minutes longer, or until the pastry is golden.

Transfer to a cooling rack. Serve at room temperature, along with generous spoonfuls of Double Vanilla Ice Cream (page 130), if you like.

❖❖❖❖❖❖❖❖❖❖❖❖❖❖❖❖

Cinnamon-Pear Pie with Walnut Streusel

2 tablespoons plus 2
teaspoons cornstarch

¼ cup plus 1 tablespoon
firmly packed light
brown sugar

¼ cup granulated sugar

½ teaspoon ground
cinnamon

¼ teaspoon ground
allspice

The "cover" on top of the spiced pear slices is a mantle of crumbs—made of butter, walnuts, flour, and sugar. This streusel shelters the pears from the oven's heat, keeping them moist as the pie bakes.

Warm slices of this pie are good with scoops of Double Vanilla Ice Cream (page 130) or drifts of Vanilla-Scented Whipped Cream (page 131), sweetened with 1½ tablespoons liquid brown sugar or maple syrup instead of confectioners' sugar.

———❖❖❖———

Blend together the cornstarch, brown sugar, granulated sugar, cinnamon, and allspice in a large mixing bowl. Add the pears

(continued)

5 cups peeled, cored, and
   sliced firm but ripe
   pears (about 6 pears),
   tossed in 1 tablespoon
   freshly squeezed lemon
   juice
1 fully baked 9-inch pie
   shell, made from 1
   recipe Flaky Pie Crust
   (page 21)

WALNUT STREUSEL
TOPPING:

½ cup all-purpose flour

¼ cup granulated sugar

2 tablespoons firmly
   packed light brown
   sugar

¼ teaspoon ground
   cinnamon

¼ teaspoon freshly grated
   nutmeg

⅓ cup chopped walnuts

4 tablespoons (½ stick)
   cold unsalted butter,
   cut into cubes

One 9-inch pie

with any accumulated liquid. Toss gently. Pile the filling into
the pie shell, mounding it slightly toward the center.

To make the topping, blend together the flour, granulated
sugar, light brown sugar, cinnamon, nutmeg, and walnuts in a
small mixing bowl. Add the butter and, using two round-
bladed knives, cut into the flour mixture until it resembles a
very coarse meal.

Cover the pie evenly and completely with the streusel, pressing it down gently.

Bake in a preheated 375 degree oven for about 1 hour, or
until the pears are tender and the filling bubbles through the
topping in spots, looking like cooked jam.

Transfer to a cooling rack. Serve warm or at room temperature.

Spiced Pear-Currant Pie

1 recipe Flaky Pie Crust
for a Double-Crust Pie
(page 30), well chilled

¼ cup all-purpose flour

⅓ cup firmly packed light
brown sugar

⅓ cup granulated sugar

½ teaspoon ground
cinnamon

½ teaspoon freshly grated
nutmeg

¼ teaspoon ground
ginger

¼ teaspoon ground
allspice

Pinch of salt

5 cups peeled, cored,
and sliced firm but
ripe pears (about 6
pears), tossed in 1½
tablespoons freshly
squeezed lemon juice

¼ cup dried currants

2 tablespoons unsalted
butter, cut into bits

A mound of sweetened sliced and spiced pears, dotted here and there with currants, is just about as perfect a filling for a cold weather pie as you could imagine. The pears bake to a buttery tenderness underneath a tent of pastry dough.

For this double-crust pie, I like to flute the edges in a deep scallop pattern and apply five small pear-shaped pastry cutouts in a ring close to the edge of the pie. This adds a charming finishing touch and hints at what's in the filling.

———❖❖❖———

Line a 9-inch pie pan with half of the chilled pie dough following the directions on page 31; refrigerate.

Combine the flour, brown sugar, granulated sugar, cinnamon, nutmeg, ginger, allspice, and salt in a large mixing bowl. Stir well. Add the sliced pears and currants; toss gently.

Spoon the filling into the chilled pie shell, heaping it in a mound. Dot with butter. Cover with the remaining round of dough, seal, and flute the edges decoratively, as explained on page 31. Refrigerate for 10 minutes.

To glaze the pie, brush the top crust with the ice-cold water. Press on any pastry cutouts, if you are using them, and brush with water. Sprinkle with sugar. Cut several steam vents, using a sharp paring knife.

Bake in a preheated 425 degree oven for 20 minutes, reduce the oven temperature to 350 degrees, and continue baking for 35 minutes longer, or until the top is golden.

(continued)

CRACKLE SUGAR GLAZE:

2 tablespoons ice-cold
    water

1 tablespoon granulated
    sugar

_____

One 9-inch pie

Transfer to a cooling rack. Serve barely warm or at room temperature with Vanilla-Scented Whipped Cream (page 131), if you like.

Baking Note: If the dried currants are not as supple and moist as they should be, heat ½ cup apple juice in a small saucepan until hot. Remove from heat, add the currants, and steep for 5 minutes. Drain well and dry on several thicknesses of paper toweling. They are now ready to be used.

❖❖❖❖❖❖❖❖❖❖❖❖❖❖❖❖❖

Cranberry-Walnut Mincemeat Pie

1 recipe Flaky Pie Crust
    for a Double-Crust Pie
    (page 30), well chilled

2 tablespoons plus 2
    teaspoons cornstarch
    blended with 2
    tablespoons
    granulated sugar

3 cups Dried Fruit and
    Spice Mincemeat
    (page 64)

1 cup Cranberry Preserve,
    preferably homemade
    (see recipe below)

Cranberries provide just the right tart edge to mincemeat. Just about the time they flood the produce bins, we're well into fall with the season's mincemeat already made.

Line a 9-inch pie pan with half of the chilled pie dough following the directions on page 31; refrigerate.

Put the cornstarch-sugar blend in a large mixing bowl with the mincemeat; stir. Add the cranberry preserve and walnuts and fold through.

Spoon the filling into the chilled pie shell. Cover with the remaining dough, seal, and crimp the edges decoratively as explained on page 31. Refrigerate for 10 minutes.

To glaze, brush the top of the pie with cold water and sprinkle with sugar. Cut several steam vents, using a sharp paring knife.

1 cup coarsely chopped
  lightly toasted walnuts

CRACKLE SUGAR GLAZE:

2 tablespoons ice-cold
  water
1 tablespoon granulated
  sugar

One 9-inch pie

Bake in a preheated 425 degree oven for 15 minutes, reduce the oven temperature to 350 degrees, and continue baking for about 35 minutes, or until the pastry top is golden.

Transfer to a cooling rack. Serve at room temperature, with some Vanilla-Scented Whipped Cream (page 131) on the side, if you like.

Cranberry Preserve

Homemade cranberry preserve, one that's not too thick, makes the best-tasting pie. To make this condiment, combine 1¼ cups water and 1 cup granulated sugar that has been blended with ½ teaspoon ground cinnamon, ¼ teaspoon ground allspice, and ¼ teaspoon ground ginger in a large nonreactive pot. Add 2 tablespoons orange juice and 1 table-spoon finely grated orange rind. Cover and cook over low heat until the sugar dissolves. Uncover, add one 12-ounce bag fresh cranberries (washed and picked over), and bring to a boil while stirring. When the berries begin to burst rapidly, cook about 45 seconds to 1 minute longer, then remove from the heat. Cool this softly thickened preserve to room temperature, transfer to a container, cover airtight, and refrigerate. The preserve will keep for at least 6 weeks.

Golden Pecan Pie

4 extra-large eggs, at
   room temperature

1 cup granulated sugar

1/2 cup plus 1 tablespoon
   firmly packed light
   brown sugar

1/4 teaspoon salt

8 tablespoons (1/4 pound
   or 1 stick) unsalted
   butter, melted and
   cooled

1 3/4 cups coarsely
   chopped pecan pieces

1 fully baked 9-inch pie
   shell, made from 1
   recipe Flaky Pie Crust
   (page 21)

One 9-inch pie

This pie is rich in eggs and butter, and thoroughly loaded with pecans. I love to use nutmeats from freshly cracked pecans (and from walnuts, too, for that matter) because I know they will be crisp and lightly oily. As a child, I was in charge of cracking all the nuts for my mother's fruitcake, so cracking nuts is a natural part of the baking process for me.

The simple, sweet filling is easily mixed in a batter bowl; after baking it becomes partially translucent, quivery, and jellylike, interspersed with pecans.

A warm slice of Golden Pecan Pie with a hot cup of tea or coffee is a fine afternoon treat.

———❖❖❖———

Beat the eggs in a large mixing bowl. Blend in the granulated and light brown sugars. Stir in the salt, butter, and pecans.

Pour the filling into the baked pie shell. Bake in a preheated 425 degree oven for 10 minutes, reduce the oven temperature to 350 degrees, and continue baking for 25 minutes longer, or until the top is set and a knife inserted 1 to 2 inches from the center withdraws clean.

Transfer to a cooling rack. Serve barely warm or at room temperature, accompanied by Vanilla-Scented Whipped Cream (page 131).

❖❖❖❖❖❖❖❖❖❖❖❖❖❖❖❖❖❖❖❖

Bourbon Pecan Pie

4 extra-large eggs, at
   room temperature

¾ cup firmly packed dark
   brown sugar

¾ cup dark corn syrup

¼ teaspoon salt

1 tablespoon bourbon

2 teaspoons pure vanilla
   extract

6 tablespoons unsalted
   butter, melted and
   cooled

1¾ cups coarsely
   chopped pecan pieces

1 fully baked 9-inch pie
   shell, made from 1
   recipe Flaky Pie Crust
   (page 21)

One 9-inch pie

This is a dandy pie to carry along to a fall picnic or to serve as one among many desserts at a holiday meal or celebration. The little swig of bourbon does wonders for the pecans and that taste may be repeated in an accompaniment. Try blending 2 teaspoons of a good quality bourbon into the Vanilla Pouring Custard (page 129) or Vanilla-Scented Whipped Cream (page 131) just before serving.

————❖❖❖————

Beat the eggs in a large mixing bowl. Blend in the dark brown sugar and corn syrup. Stir in the salt, bourbon, vanilla, butter, and pecans.

Pour the filling into the baked pie shell. Bake in a preheated 425 degree oven for 10 minutes, reduce the oven temperature to 350 degrees, and continue baking for 25 minutes longer, or until the top is set and a knife inserted 1 to 2 inches from the center withdraws clean.

Transfer to a cooling rack. Serve warm or at room temperature.

Pumpkin Custard Pie

½ cup firmly packed light brown sugar

½ cup granulated sugar

1 tablespoon all-purpose flour

1 teaspoon ground cinnamon

¼ teaspoon freshly grated nutmeg

¼ teaspoon ground allspice

3 extra-large eggs, at room temperature

2 cups Fresh Pumpkin Puree (see recipe below) or 1-pound can solid-pack pumpkin puree (not pumpkin pie filling)

1 cup heavy cream, at room temperature

½ cup light cream, at room temperature

2 teaspoons pure vanilla extract

This pumpkin pie is one that's always requested for Thanksgiving—it's a light custard made from pumpkin puree, a few spices, eggs, and cream.

I usually make an extra batch of dough, roll it thinly, and stamp out turkey shapes using a cookie cutter. While I prebake the pie crust, I bake the pastry turkeys alongside. After the pie has been baked and cooled, I place a ring of turkeys around the perimeter for a festive look. Maple leaves cut out of dough also look pretty edging the baked pie.

Combine the light brown sugar, granulated sugar, flour, cinnamon, nutmeg, and allspice in a large mixing bowl. Add the eggs, one at a time, blending well after each addition. Beat in the pumpkin puree. Stir in the heavy cream, light cream, and vanilla.

Pour the filling into the baked pie shell. Bake in a preheated 400 degree oven for 10 minutes, reduce the oven temperature to 325 degrees, and continue baking for about 40 minutes, or until set and a knife inserted 1 to 2 inches from the center withdraws clean.

Transfer to a cooling rack. Serve tepid or at room temperature, with dollops of Vanilla-Scented Whipped Cream (page 131).

1 fully baked deep
10-inch pie shell, made
from 1 recipe Flaky Pie
Crust (page 21)

One 10-inch pie

Fresh Pumpkin Puree

Freshly cooked and pureed pumpkin makes a delightful pie filling. The puree is easy to make: Cut a pumpkin into thick wedges, scrape away the seeds, and then cut into large chunks. Steam until tender, cool, and scrape the flesh away from the skin. Discard the skin. Puree the flesh, in batches, in a food processor fitted with the steel knife or through a food mill fitted with the fine disk. Once the puree has cooled completely, it is ready to be used in a pie filling.

Pumpkin Crunch Pie

½ cup granulated sugar

1 tablespoon all-purpose flour

½ teaspoon ground cinnamon

½ teaspoon freshly grated nutmeg

¼ teaspoon ground allspice

⅛ teaspoon ground cloves

2 extra-large eggs plus 1 extra-large egg yolk, at room temperature

2 cups Fresh Pumpkin Puree (page 77) or 1-pound can solid-pack pumpkin puree (not pumpkin pie filling)

1 cup light cream, at room temperature

1 teaspoon pure vanilla extract

1 fully baked deep 9-inch pie shell, made from 1 recipe Flaky Pie Crust (page 21)

This pie's topping consists of a brittle "crunch"—a crumble of brown sugar, butter, and walnuts that crowns a simple pumpkin base. This pie is a delightful change from the more traditional pumpkin pies, and the candy-nut topping can be applied over almost any squash pie with a thick and substantial filling.

This topping is a good way to use up small odd lots of nuts. You may vary the taste of the topping by substituting chopped pecans or macadamia nuts for the walnuts.

Combine the granulated sugar, flour, cinnamon, nutmeg, allspice, and cloves in a large mixing bowl. Add the eggs, one at a time, blending well after each addition. Beat in the egg yolk. Beat in the pumpkin puree. Stir in the light cream and vanilla.

Pour the filling into the baked pie shell. Bake in a preheated 425 degree oven for 10 minutes, reduce the oven temperature to 375 degrees, and continue baking for 10 minutes longer.

CRUNCH TOPPING

While the pie is baking, make the crunch topping. Put the brown sugar in a small mixing bowl. Scatter over it the cubes of butter and chopped walnuts. Using two round-bladed knives, cut the butter into the sugar and walnuts until reduced to small flakes. Stir in the cinnamon and nutmeg.

Remove the pie from the oven, quickly sprinkle the topping in an even layer, and return to the oven. Reduce the oven

CRUNCH TOPPING:

¼ cup firmly packed light brown sugar

4 tablespoons (½ stick) cold unsalted butter, cut into cubes

¾ cup chopped walnuts

¼ teaspoon ground cinnamon

¼ teaspoon freshly grated nutmeg

One 9-inch pie

temperature to 350 degrees and continue to bake for about 30 minutes, or until set and a knife inserted 1 inch from the center withdraws clean.

Transfer to a cooling rack. Serve barely warm or at room temperature, accompanied by Vanilla-Scented Whipped Cream (page 131), if you like.

Fresh Sugar Pumpkin Pie

⅔ cup firmly packed light
   brown sugar
½ teaspoon ground
   cinnamon
½ teaspoon freshly grated
   nutmeg
¼ teaspoon ground
   cloves
1 tablespoon all-purpose
   flour
3 extra-large eggs, at
   room temperature
2 cups Fresh Sugar
   Pumpkin Puree (see
   recipe below)
1 cup light cream
   blended with ¼ cup
   heavy cream, at room
   temperature
1 tablespoon maple syrup
2 teaspoons pure vanilla
   extract
2 tablespoons unsalted
   butter, melted and
   cooled
1 fully baked deep 9-inch
   pie shell, made from 1
   recipe Flaky Pie Crust
   (page 21)

One 9-inch pie

A small, sweet baby pumpkin, affectionately known as a "sugar pumpkin," is esteemed for its thick, meaty flesh, perfect for turning into a puree and using in many pie fillings. This pie makes a handsome finish to a holiday meal.

———————❖❖❖———————

Blend together the brown sugar, cinnamon, nutmeg, cloves, and flour in a large mixing bowl. Add the eggs, one at a time, blending well after each addition. Beat in the pumpkin puree. Stir in the light and heavy cream blend, maple syrup, vanilla, and butter.

Pour the filling into the baked pie shell. Bake in a preheated 400 degree oven for 10 minutes, reduce the oven temperature to 325 degrees, and continue baking for 35 minutes longer, or until set and a knife inserted about 1 to 2 inches from the center withdraws clean.

Transfer to a cooling rack. Serve at room temperature, with Vanilla Pouring Custard (page 129) or Vanilla-Scented Whipped Cream (page 131), if you like.

Fresh Sugar Pumpkin Puree

Quarter a 2-pound sugar pumpkin, pare it, scoop out the seeds, and cut it into big chunks; the flesh gets steamed until tender (about 15 to 20 minutes), scraped away from the skin, and pureed in the bowl of a food processor fitted with the steel knife.

Apricot-Yam Pie

½ cup firmly packed light
  brown sugar

½ cup granulated sugar

1 tablespoon all-purpose
  flour

½ teaspoon ground
  cinnamon

¼ teaspoon ground
  ginger

¼ teaspoon ground
  allspice

3 extra-large eggs, at
  room temperature

2 cups fresh Yam Puree
  (see recipe below)

1 cup heavy cream, at
  room temperature

½ cup good-quality
  unfiltered apricot
  nectar

3 tablespoons unsalted
  butter, melted and
  cooled

1 fully baked 10-inch pie
  shell, made from 1
  recipe Flaky Pie Crust
  (page 21)

One 10-inch pie

This is a sweet, mellow pie made with pureed yams and en-hanced with a splash of unfiltered apricot nectar. Good-quality unfiltered nectars can be purchased at a natural foods store. The nectar contributes a fruity undertone to the pie. Peach or plum nectar can be substituted for the apricot, as can any fairly dense, concentrated fruit syrup. If you use a fruit syrup, reduce the amount of granulated sugar in this recipe to ¼ cup.

Blend together the brown sugar, granulated sugar, flour, cin-namon, ginger, and allspice in a large mixing bowl. Add the eggs, one at a time, blending well after each addition. Blend in the yam puree. Stir in the heavy cream, apricot nectar, and butter.

Pour the filling into the baked pie shell. Bake in a preheated 350 degree oven for 45 minutes, or until set and a knife in-serted 1 to 2 inches from the center withdraws clean.

Transfer to a cooling rack. Serve barely warm or at room temperature, with Vanilla-Scented Whipped Cream (page 131), if you like.

Yam Puree

To make 2 cups of yam puree, steam 3 large yams (about 1½ to 1¾ pounds) until tender. When cool enough to handle, peel away the jackets and cut the flesh into chunks. Puree in the bowl of a food processor fitted with the steel knife or pass through a food mill fitted with the fine disk. Cool completely before using.

Orange–Butternut Squash Pie

3/4 cup firmly packed light brown sugar

1 tablespoon all-purpose flour

1/2 teaspoon ground cinnamon

1/2 teaspoon ground ginger

1/4 teaspoon freshly grated nutmeg

Pinch of salt

3 extra-large eggs, at room temperature

2 cups fresh Butternut Squash Puree (see recipe below)

1 tablespoon finely grated orange rind

1 teaspoon pure orange extract

2 tablespoons good-quality orange cut marmalade

1 cup heavy cream, at room temperature

Pureed butternut squash, orange peel, and orange marmalade are combined with the usual brown sugar, spices, eggs, and cream to make a sweet vegetable custard pie.

When fall and winter squash proliferate, it's a good idea to steam several pounds at once, puree the flesh, and divide into 2-cup portions for use in pies throughout the season. Spoon the puree into heavy-duty freezer containers, press a double thickness of plastic wrap onto the surface, cover tightly, cool, and freeze.

This pie looks pretty when baked in a shell with a deeply ruffled border; make a few autumn leaves out of pastry dough, bake them, and place atop the filling when the pie emerges from the oven.

A slice of this pie is delicious when accompanied by a hot cup of orange herbal tea.

———◆◆◆———

Blend together the brown sugar, flour, cinnamon, ginger, nutmeg, and salt in a large mixing bowl. Add the eggs, one at a time, blending well after each addition. Beat in the squash puree. Stir in the orange rind, extract, marmalade, heavy cream, and light cream.

Pour the filling into the baked pie shell. Bake in a preheated 350 degree oven for 45 minutes, or until the filling has set and a knife inserted 1 to 2 inches from the center withdraws clean.

Transfer to a cooling rack. Serve at room temperature.

½ cup light cream, at
   room temperature
1 fully baked 10-inch pie
   shell, made from 1
   recipe Flaky Pie Crust
   (page 21)

One 10-inch pie

Butternut Squash Puree

To make 2 cups of butternut squash puree, halve one 2-pound
butternut squash. Scoop away the seeds, cut into large chunks,
and steam until tender, about 15 to 20 minutes. Cool slightly,
scrape the flesh from the skin, and puree in the bowl of a food
processor fitted with the steel knife or through a food mill
fitted with the fine disk. Cool completely before using.

Brandied Golden Acorn Squash Pie

½ cup firmly packed light brown sugar

2 tablespoons granulated sugar

½ teaspoon ground cinnamon

½ teaspoon freshly grated nutmeg

¼ teaspoon ground ginger

⅛ teaspoon ground mace

3 extra-large eggs, at room temperature

2 cups fresh Golden Acorn Squash Puree (see recipe below)

1 cup heavy cream, at room temperature

¼ cup light cream, at room temperature

2 tablespoons brandy

1 teaspoon pure vanilla extract

The flesh of the golden acorn squash turns tender and buttery when steamed and pureed. Brandy adds a little kick to the filling, which bakes into an exceptionally tender, lightly sweetened custard.

I have enjoyed slices of this pie on snowy evenings sitting opposite a roaring fire and on cool afternoons as a teatime sweet.

Blend together the brown sugar, granulated sugar, cinnamon, nutmeg, ginger, and mace in a large mixing bowl. Add the eggs, one at a time, blending well after each addition. Beat in the squash puree. Stir in the heavy cream, light cream, brandy, vanilla, and melted butter.

Pour the filling into the baked pie shell. Bake in a preheated 400 degree oven for 10 minutes, reduce the oven temperature to 325 degrees, and continue baking for about 35 to 40 minutes longer, or until set and a knife inserted 1 to 2 inches from the center withdraws clean.

Transfer to a cooling rack. Serve at room temperature.

2 tablespoons unsalted
  butter, melted and
  cooled
1 fully baked 10-inch pie
  shell, made from 1
  recipe Flaky Pie Crust
  (page 21)

One 10-inch pie

Golden Acorn Squash Puree

To make 2 cups of golden acorn squash puree, halve one
2-pound acorn squash. Scoop out the seeds, cut the flesh into
large chunks, and steam until tender, about 15 to 20 minutes.
Cool slightly, scrape the flesh from the skin, and puree in the
bowl of a food processor fitted with the steel knife or pass the
squash through a food mill fitted with the fine disk. Cool
completely before using.

Coconut-Walnut-Chocolate-Chip "Candy" Pie

¾ cup all-purpose flour

Pinch of salt

3 extra-large eggs, at room temperature

1 cup granulated sugar

3 tablespoons firmly packed light brown sugar

5 tablespoons unsalted butter, melted and cooled, blended with 1 tablespoon heavy cream

2 teaspoons pure vanilla extract

1 cup miniature semisweet chocolate chips

1 cup chopped walnuts

1 cup sweetened shredded coconut

1 fully baked deep 9-inch pie shell, made from 1 recipe Flaky Pie Crust (page 21)

One deep 9-inch pie

This confectionlike pie is my version of one my grandmother Lilly used to make—it's thick with shredded coconut, chopped walnuts, and miniature chocolate chips. Miniature chips were not available during Grandma's time; she chopped up bittersweet chocolate candy bars bought at her local coffee, tea, and spice shop in Georgetown. This pie is best served barely warm, with vanilla ice cream, when it tastes like a soft, faintly caramel-flavored chocolate and nut candy bar.

———❖❖❖———

Sift the flour and salt together onto a sheet of waxed paper; set aside.

Beat the eggs in a large mixing bowl. Beat in the granulated sugar, light brown sugar, butter–heavy cream blend, and vanilla. Add flour and beat in. Stir in the chocolate chips, walnuts, and coconut.

Pour the filling into the baked pie shell. Bake in a preheated 350 degree oven for 1 hour, or until it is set and a knife inserted 2 inches from the center has only a few moist particles clinging to it.

Transfer to a cooling rack. Serve warm or at room temperature, with scoops of Double Vanilla Ice Cream (page 130), if you like.

Brown Sugar Pie

1 cup firmly packed light
 brown sugar

⅓ cup all-purpose flour

Pinch of salt

1 cup heavy cream

¾ cup light cream

2 teaspoons pure vanilla
 extract

1 fully baked 9-inch pie
 shell, made from 1
 recipe Flaky Pie Crust
 (page 21)

4 tablespoons (½ stick)
 unsalted butter, cut
 into bits

¼ teaspoon freshly grated
 nutmeg

One 9-inch pie

Creamy and tasting faintly of caramel, this is a rich and satisfying version of a sugar pie. Those who remember it from their
childhood will find this homespun variation just as pleasing. I
use heavy cream and light cream as the liquid, brown sugar as
the sweetener, and flavor it lightly with nutmeg.

This pie should be enjoyed on its own, without further
adornment. I like to bake this pie in one of my antique pie
tins. In it the pie looks wholesome, fresh, and very appealing.

———❖❖❖———

Blend together the light brown sugar, flour, and salt in a small
mixing bowl. Pour the heavy cream and light cream into a
saucepan, set over moderately high heat, and warm slightly
(about 3 to 4 minutes); remove from heat and stir in vanilla.

Sprinkle the sugar-flour mixture evenly on the bottom of
the pie shell. Pour the cream-vanilla blend over the sugar
mixture.

Dot the top of the pie with the bits of butter. Sprinkle nutmeg over the top of the pie.

Bake in a preheated 350 degree oven for 50 to 55 minutes,
until golden on top.

Transfer to a cooling rack. Serve at room temperature.

WINTER COUNTRY PIES

WINTER COUNTRY PIES

———————— ❖❖❖ ————————

Vanilla Custard Pie   92

Coconut Custard Pie   93

Maple Cream Pie   94

Maple-Walnut Pie   95

Old-Fashioned Chocolate Fudge Pie   96

Mile-High Coconut Cream Pie   98

Banana Cream Pie   100

Chocolate Silk Pie   102

Spicy Sweet Potato Pie   103

Apple Streusel Pie   104

Buttermilk Pie   106

*E*very time I do my marketing in winter, I am reminded of the rich array of nuts that can be used in pies. Enormous heaps of nuts are set in large bins or burlap sacks. I buy several pounds at once and, at home, pile the nuts in an old basket or bowl. There they sit ready to be cracked, their nutmeats picked out and chopped. Winter is the time to make use of the plentiful supply of walnuts; once they are cracked, I use the chopped walnuts in Maple-Walnut Pie (page 95), an interesting variation of the translucent pecan pie. I also combine chopped walnuts with sugar, flour, butter, and spices to make a streusel covering for apple pie.

During winter, I keep cream and eggs on hand for making vanilla, coconut, maple cream, or custard pies. I keep the pantry shelf stacked with squares of unsweetened chocolate for filling an Old-Fashioned Chocolate Fudge Pie (page 96) or Chocolate Silk Pie (page 102); I have bananas ripening at room temperature for slicing into a Banana Cream Pie (page 100); and I make a special trip to a nearby dairy or natural food store to buy fresh buttermilk for my Buttermilk Pie (page 106).

Winter country pies are delicious when served with a steaming pot of tea or coffee, or little cups of espresso at the close of a meal. I also like to accompany slices of pie with large cups of mulled cider or herbal tea for a casual, afternoon tea-and-sweets break.

Vanilla Custard Pie

4 extra-large eggs, at
    room temperature

½ cup granulated sugar

1 cup heavy cream, at
    room temperature

1 cup light cream, at
    room temperature

¼ cup milk, at room
    temperature

2 teaspoons pure vanilla
    extract

1 fully baked 9-inch pie
    shell, made from 1
    recipe Flaky Pie Crust
    (page 21)

¼ teaspoon freshly grated
    nutmeg

One 9-inch pie

Custard pie is plain and delicate; it's made with fresh eggs and cream set just to the point of perfection. I usually use free-range chicken eggs; the orange-yellow yolks deeply color and enrich the custard and thicken up the filling wonderfully.

For this pie, I like to sprinkle a little nutmeg over the top before baking to enhance the flavor of the custard.

Beat the eggs in a large mixing bowl. Blend in the sugar, heavy cream, light cream, and milk. Stir in the vanilla.

Pour the filling into the baked pie shell and sprinkle the nutmeg evenly over the top. Bake in a preheated 425 degree oven for 10 minutes, reduce the oven temperature to 325 degrees, and continue baking for 35 minutes longer, or until the filling has set and a knife inserted 2 inches from the center withdraws clean.

Transfer to a cooling rack. Serve warm or at room temperature.

Coconut Custard Pie

4 extra-large eggs, at
   room temperature

½ cup granulated sugar

1 cup heavy cream, at
   room temperature

1 cup light cream, at
   room temperature

2 teaspoons pure coconut
   extract

1 teaspoon pure vanilla
   extract

1 cup sweetened
   shredded coconut

1 fully baked 9-inch pie
   shell, made from 1
   recipe Flaky Pie Crust
   (page 21)

¼ teaspoon freshly grated
   nutmeg

One 9-inch pie

Coconut Custard Pie is a toothsome variation of a silken custard pie. To make it, you stir a cupful of shredded coconut into the basic egg and cream mixture. This is a nourishing pie with body and substance, perfect to serve on a blustery winter evening with a steaming pot of coffee.

More often than not, I make this pie in an antique pie plate from my collection; the old-fashioned, worn surface produces a golden and flaky crust.

———❖❖❖———

Beat the eggs in a large mixing bowl until combined. Whisk in the sugar, heavy cream, and light cream. Blend in the coconut and vanilla extracts. Stir in the coconut.

Pour the filling into the baked pie shell and sprinkle the nutmeg evenly over the top. Bake in a preheated 425 degree oven for 10 minutes, reduce the oven temperature to 325 degrees, and continue baking for 35 minutes longer, or until the filling has set and the top is a light golden color. A knife inserted 2 inches from the center of the pie will withdraw clean.

Transfer to a cooling rack. Serve warm or at room temperature.

Maple Cream Pie

1 cup heavy cream

½ cup light cream

Pinch of salt

4 extra-large eggs plus 2 extra-large egg yolks, at room temperature

¼ cup firmly packed light brown sugar

¼ cup plus 2 tablespoons good-quality pure maple syrup

2 teaspoons pure maple extract

1 teaspoon pure vanilla extract

1 fully baked 9-inch pie shell, made from 1 recipe Flaky Pie Crust (page 21)

One 9-inch pie

This hearty pie is wonderful to make in the dead of winter when you want a satisfying and smooth-textured sweet. The filling is nothing more than a luxurious blend of maple syrup, cream, eggs, vanilla, and brown sugar, baked in a buttery pie crust.

A narrow ring of chopped, lightly toasted walnuts may be sprinkled around the edge of the baked pie, if you like, for crunch.

Put the heavy cream, light cream, and pinch of salt into a heavy, medium-size saucepan. Place over moderate heat, bring to the scalding point, remove from heat, and set aside.

Beat the eggs and egg yolks in a large mixing bowl until combined. Beat in the brown sugar and maple syrup. Blend in the maple and vanilla extracts. Stir ¼ cup of the scalded cream into the egg yolk mixture. Slowly add the remaining scalded cream to the egg yolk mixture in a thin, steady stream, whisking all the while.

Pour the filling into the baked pie shell. Bake in a preheated 400 degree oven for 10 minutes, reduce the oven temperature to 325 degrees, and continue baking for about 35 minutes longer, or until the filling has set. The filling will wiggle ever so faintly like a baked custard does and a knife inserted 2 inches from the center will withdraw clean.

Transfer to a cooling rack. Serve barely warm or at room temperature.

Maple-Walnut Pie

3 extra-large eggs, at
room temperature

⅓ cup firmly packed light
brown sugar

2 teaspoons all-purpose
flour

Pinch of salt

1 cup pure maple syrup

2 teaspoons pure vanilla
extract

¼ cup heavy cream, at
room temperature

5 tablespoons unsalted
butter, melted and
cooled

1⅓ cups coarsely
chopped fresh walnuts

1 fully baked 9-inch pie
shell, made from 1
recipe Flaky Pie Crust
(page 21)

One 9-inch pie

The earthy flavors of maple syrup and walnuts are combined in this pie filling, which joins together the best qualities of a custard and a translucent pie. Eggs, light brown sugar, maple syrup, vanilla, butter, and walnuts make a fairly rich concoction, reminiscent of the maple-walnut sauce from old-time ice cream parlors.

Warm slices of this pie are luscious when served with espresso or with freshly brewed lemon or English Breakfast tea. I like to offer wedges at a late afternoon tea or several hours after dinner, when its richness can be appreciated.

———❖❖❖———

Beat the eggs in a large mixing bowl until combined. Combine the brown sugar, flour, and salt; add to the eggs. Beat in the maple syrup, vanilla, and heavy cream. Stir in the butter and walnuts.

Pour the filling into the baked pie shell. Bake in a preheated 425 degree oven for 10 minutes, reduce the oven temperature to 325 degrees, and continue baking for about 30 minutes, or until set (the center 2 inches will quiver slightly, but the pie will still be baked through). A knife inserted about 2 to 3 inches from the edge of the pie will withdraw clean.

Transfer to a cooling rack. Serve warm or at room temperature, with spoonfuls of Vanilla-Scented Whipped Cream (page 131) or scoops of vanilla ice cream.

Old-Fashioned
Chocolate
Fudge Pie

12 tablespoons (¼ pound
plus 4 tablespoons or
1½ sticks) unsalted
butter, cut into chunks

3 squares (3 ounces)
unsweetened
chocolate, coarsely
chopped

3 extra-large eggs plus 1
extra-large egg yolk, at
room temperature

1½ cups granulated sugar

6 tablespoons all-purpose
flour

¼ teaspoon salt

2 teaspoons pure vanilla
extract

1 fully baked 9-inch pie
shell, made from 1
recipe Flaky Pie Crust
(page 21)

I've been baking this dense and rich fudge pie for as long as I can remember. The perfect balance of chocolate to butter to eggs makes this filling firm yet creamy, with an irresistible chocolate flavor.

The fudge filling may be hidden under a thick mantle of whipped cream flavored with vanilla and sweetened with confectioners' sugar. The cream topping becomes a perfect counterpoint to the dreamy filling.

———❖❖❖———

Put the butter and chocolate in a heavy saucepan set over low heat. Cook slowly until melted, stirring occasionally. Set aside to cool.

Beat the eggs and egg yolk in a large mixing bowl until combined. Blend together the sugar, flour, and salt and beat into the eggs. Whisk in the cooled chocolate and butter. Stir in the vanilla.

Pour the filling into the baked pie shell. Bake in a preheated 325 degree oven for about 40 minutes, or until the filling has just set (small bubbles may appear over the surface of the baked pie). A knife inserted 2 to 3 inches from the edge of the pie will withdraw clean.

Transfer to a cooling rack. When the pie has reached room temperature, prepare the Sweet Cream Topping.

SWEET CREAM TOPPING:

2 cups very cold heavy cream

3 tablespoons sifted confectioners' sugar

1 teaspoon pure vanilla extract

One 9-inch pie

SWEET CREAM TOPPING

To make the topping, pour the cream into a well-chilled deep bowl. Beat until soft, floppy peaks are formed. Sprinkle with confectioners' sugar, add vanilla, and continue beating until the cream forms firm peaks that hold their shape. Spoon over the chocolate filling, spread to the edge of the pie, and swirl decoratively.

Chill for at least 1 hour before serving.

Mile-High Coconut Cream Pie

¾ cup granulated sugar

¼ cup cornstarch

2 cups light cream, at room temperature

1 cup milk, at room temperature

4 extra-large egg yolks, at room temperature, lightly beaten

4 tablespoons (½ stick) unsalted butter, at room temperature

2 teaspoons pure vanilla extract

1 cup sweetened shredded coconut

1 fully baked 9-inch pie shell, made from 1 recipe Flaky Pie Crust (page 21)

A tall meringue caps off this rich coconut pie. The filling is one of those stovetop-cooked puddings made extra creamy by using light cream. The pudding is thickened with cornstarch, which I think works better than flour. The cornstarch binds the liquids and egg yolks into a soft, light-tasting semitranslucent mass.

This coconut pie has become a family favorite ever since the first one was set on the cooling rack. If you're not in the mood to make the meringue topping, serve the pie with a thick covering of sweetened whipped cream (see Sweet Cream Topping, page 97).

————— ❖❖❖ —————

Mix the granulated sugar and cornstarch in a large bowl until it resembles a fine talcum powder. Add the light cream in a thin, steady stream, whisking constantly. Beat well. Add the milk in a thin stream, blending thoroughly. Beat in the egg yolks. Pour into a heavy 2-quart saucepan (preferably made of enameled cast iron), set over moderately high heat, and bring to the boil, stirring continuously. When the mixture reaches a hard boil (the bubbles cannot be diminished by stirring), reduce the heat to low and simmer for 2 minutes, while stirring occasionally.

Pour the filling into a medium-size mixing bowl. Beat in the softened butter, a tablespoon at a time, adding the next tablespoon after the first has melted into the pudding. Beat in the vanilla and shredded coconut. Cover the surface of the pudding with a sheet of plastic wrap; let cool for about 30 minutes.

MILE-HIGH MERINGUE TOPPING:

10 extra-large egg whites, at room temperature

¾ cup plus 2 tablespoons granulated sugar

¼ teaspoon cream of tartar

1 teaspoon pure vanilla extract

One 9-inch pie

To make the meringue topping: Place the egg whites and sugar in the top of a double boiler. Pour 1½ inches of water into the bottom saucepan and bring to a simmer. Set the top pan over the simmering water and warm the whites and sugar, stirring briskly—the whites will warm in about 30 to 35 seconds. Remove saucepan from the simmering water, wipe it dry, and pour the whites into a large, deep mixing bowl. Beat the whites until foamy, add the cream of tartar, and continue beating until soft peaks form. Add the vanilla; beat until firm but moist peaks are formed. The firm peaks should hold their shape in a sharp point and be smooth and satiny.

Turn the filling into the baked pie shell and spoon the meringue over the coconut filling, spreading it to the edge of the pastry crust. Make deep, upward swirls in the meringue with the back of a spoon, spatula, or flexible palette knife.

Bake in a preheated 400 degree oven for about 10 minutes, or until the meringue has browned lightly.

Transfer to a cooling rack. Serve at room temperature.

Banana Cream Pie

¾ cup granulated sugar

¼ cup cornstarch

Pinch of salt

1 cup heavy cream, at
    room temperature

1 cup light cream, at
    room temperature

1 cup milk, at room
    temperature

4 extra-large egg yolks, at
    room temperature,
    lightly beaten

4 tablespoons (½ stick)
    unsalted butter, at
    room temperature

2 medium-size bananas,
    firm but ripe

1 fully baked 9-inch pie
    shell, made from 1
    recipe Flaky Pie Crust
    (page 21)

This pie is a real charmer, with sliced ripe bananas sitting under a vanilla cream filling; it is finished with snowy drifts of whipped cream.

For the best flavor, use bananas that are firm but ripe. Slice them on the diagonal into 1-inch pieces and have the pudding ready to pour once the last banana has been cut.

Mix the sugar, cornstarch, and salt in a large mixing bowl. Slowly whisk in the heavy cream in a thin, steady stream; whisk in the light cream, a little at a time, then blend in the milk. Whisk in the egg yolks. Pour into a heavy 2-quart saucepan (preferably made of enameled cast iron), set over moderate heat, and bring the contents of the pot to a boil, whisking slowly but constantly. When the mixture reaches a hard boil (the bubbles cannot be diminished by stirring), reduce the heat to low and simmer for 2 minutes, while stirring occasionally.

Pour the filling into a medium-size mixing bowl. Beat in the butter, a tablespoon at a time, adding the next tablespoon after the first has melted into the pudding. Press a sheet of plastic wrap directly over the surface of the pudding. Let cool to warm, about 45 minutes to 1 hour.

Slice the bananas into 1-inch pieces and scatter over the baked pie shell. Pour the filling over the bananas, spreading it evenly to conceal them. Chill for 15 minutes.

SWEET CREAM TOPPING:

1½ cups very cold heavy cream

2 tablespoons sifted confectioners' sugar

¾ teaspoon pure vanilla extract

One 9-inch pie

SWEET CREAM TOPPING

While the pie is chilling, prepare the Sweet Cream Topping: Pour the cream into a well-chilled deep bowl. Beat until soft peaks are formed. Sprinkle with confectioners' sugar, add vanilla, and continue beating until the cream forms firm peaks that hold their shape. Scoop onto the pie, spread to the edges, and, with the back of a spoon, make deep swirls in the whipped cream.

Chill for at least 1 hour before serving.

Chocolate
Silk Pie

¼ cup light cream

6 ounces bittersweet
chocolate, roughly
chopped

12 tablespoons (¼ pound
plus 4 tablespoons or
1½ sticks) unsalted
butter, at room
temperature

4 extra-large eggs, at
room temperature,
separated

2 teaspoons pure vanilla
extract

Pinch of salt

2 tablespoons granulated
sugar

½ cup very cold heavy
cream

1 fully baked 9-inch pie
shell, made from 1
recipe Flaky Pie Crust
(page 21)

One 9-inch pie

This is a thick and rich chocolate pie. I like to use a good
bittersweet chocolate—one that melts into a dense, creamy
mass—with an intense chocolate bouquet (such as Callebaut,
Lindt Excellence, or Tobler Tradition).

Vanilla-Scented Whipped Cream (page 131), served alongside wedges of the pie, is a good partner; the light cream
balances the dark flavor of the chocolate filling. A steaming
pot of freshly brewed coffee or espresso is a perfect companion to thick slices of the pie.

———❖❖❖———

Put the cream, chocolate, and butter in a heavy 1-quart saucepan, set over low heat, and cook slowly until the ingredients
have melted. Stir occasionally. Once melted, remove from
heat and pour into a large mixing bowl. Beat in the egg yolks,
one at a time, then blend in the vanilla and salt. Let the
mixture cool to room temperature, about 30 minutes.

Beat egg whites in a deep, medium-size mixing bowl until
soft peaks are formed, sprinkle with sugar, and continue beating until firm but moist peaks are formed.

Stir a large spoonful of the egg whites into the cooled chocolate mixture, until the whites disappear into the chocolate.
Fold through the remaining whites. Beat the heavy cream in a
small mixing bowl until firm peaks are formed, then fold into
the chocolate mixture.

Pour the filling into the baked pie shell and smooth the top
lightly with a rubber spatula. Refrigerate the pie for 6 hours,
or until the filling is firm.

Spicy Sweet Potato Pie

2 cups pureed steamed and peeled sweet potatoes (about 4 small sweet potatoes)

¾ cup granulated sugar blended with 1 teaspoon ground cinnamon, ½ teaspoon ground ginger, and ¼ teaspoon freshly grated nutmeg

3 extra-large eggs, at room temperature

2 tablespoons light molasses

1 cup heavy cream, at room temperature

4 tablespoons unsalted butter, melted and cooled

½ teaspoon pure vanilla extract

1 fully baked deep 9-inch pie shell, made from 1 recipe Flaky Pie Crust (page 21)

One 9-inch pie

This is a smooth sweet potato pie given body and substance by cream, eggs, and spices. A pie such as this is the essence of country itself.

If you like a chunkier pie, don't puree the sweet potatoes—press them with a potato masher to get a lumpy, slightly coarse vegetable.

Oftentimes, I'll buy many pounds of sweet potatoes, steam them, process some into a smooth puree, and coarsely mash the rest. Two-cup quantities get turned into sturdy freezer containers, transferred to the freezer, and stockpiled for pie baking throughout the fall and winter.

Spicy Sweet Potato Pie is heavenly served with whipped cream sweetened with liquid brown sugar and flavored with vanilla and a few gratings of nutmeg.

———❖❖❖———

Beat the sweet potatoes and sugar-spice mixture in a large mixing bowl. Add the eggs, one at a time, beating well after each addition. Stir in the molasses, cream, butter, and vanilla.

Pour the filling into the baked pie shell. Bake in a preheated 425 degree oven for 10 minutes, reduce the oven temperature to 325 degrees, and continue baking for about 35 minutes longer, or until the filling has set completely. A knife inserted 2 inches from the center of the pie will withdraw clean.

Transfer to a cooling rack. Serve barely warm or at room temperature.

Apple Streusel Pie

½ cup granulated sugar

¼ cup firmly packed light brown sugar

2 tablespoons plus 2 teaspoons cornstarch

½ teaspoon ground cinnamon

¼ teaspoon freshly grated nutmeg

5 cups peeled, cored, and sliced tart cooking apples (about 5 large apples)

1 fully baked 9-inch pie shell, made from 1 recipe Flaky Pie Crust (page 21)

CINNAMON-STREUSEL TOPPING:

¾ cup all-purpose flour

¼ cup granulated sugar

¼ cup firmly packed light brown sugar

5 tablespoons cold unsalted butter, cut into small chunks

The sweet scent of cinnamon, apples, nutmeg, and butter from this pie perfumes the whole house, making the wait for it seem terribly long.

Use firm, tart cooking apples, such as Granny Smith—they bake tender and succulent while holding their shape. The streusel topping, which serves as a lid, keeps the apples moist and silky as they bake. Streusel is quick to blend together and may conceal almost any sort of fruit filling, be it apple, plum, apricot, blueberry, cherry, raspberry, pear, or peach.

Thoroughly mix together the granulated sugar, light brown sugar, cornstarch, cinnamon, and nutmeg in a large mixing bowl. Add the apples, toss, and let sit for 3 minutes. Heap the apple mixture into the baked pie shell, mounding it slightly toward the center.

To make the topping, blend together the flour, granulated sugar, and light brown sugar in a small mixing bowl. Add the butter and, using two round-bladed knives, cut into the flour mixture until it resembles rough-cut oatmeal. Stir in cinnamon and nutmeg.

Cover completely with the streusel, enclosing the apples and any open spots that peek through. Press down gently without compacting it.

Bake in a preheated 375 degree oven for about 55 to 60 minutes, or until the apples are tender and the filling bubbles through the streusel, looking like cooked jam.

¼ teaspoon ground
  cinnamon
¼ teaspoon freshly grated
  nutmeg

One 9-inch pie

Transfer to a cooling rack. Serve warm or at room temperature, accompanied by scoops of Double Vanilla Ice Cream
(page 130), Vanilla-Scented Whipped Cream (page 131), or
Vanilla Pouring Custard (page 129).

Buttermilk Pie

1 cup plus 2 tablespoons
  Vanilla-Scented
  Granulated Sugar
  (page 219) or plain
  granulated sugar

3 tablespoons all-purpose
  flour

3 extra-large eggs plus 2
  extra-large egg yolks, at
  room temperature

1 cup buttermilk, at room
  temperature

2 teaspoons pure vanilla
  extract

This pie, firmly built into the American pie-making tradition, is one many cooks turned to when fruit was not available or just too expensive. Buttermilk Pie became the perfect dessert to make with "goods on hand." It uses simple dairy staples to make a satisfyingly sweet but pleasantly tart filling.

Buttermilk Pie is characteristically buttery and eggy, and is a bit richer than a plain custard pie; it is a delight when made with fresh buttermilk, the kind you can purchase from a dairy or at a natural food store. I buy buttermilk at a local Maryland dairy; it boasts big lumps of buttery curds that float through the rich liquid and makes one of the best winter pies I know.

Thoroughly stir together the granulated sugar and flour in a large mixing bowl. Add the eggs, one at a time, blending well after each addition. Beat in the egg yolks. Blend in the buttermilk, vanilla, butter, and lemon juice.

8 tablespoons (¼ pound or 1 stick) unsalted butter, melted and cooled

1 tablespoon freshly squeezed lemon juice

1 fully baked 9-inch pie shell, made from 1 recipe Flaky Pie Crust (page 21)

One 9-inch pie

Pour the filling into the baked pie shell. Bake in a preheated 400 degree oven for 10 minutes, reduce the oven temperature to 325 degrees, and continue baking for about 35 to 40 minutes, or until the filling has just set and is slightly puffy. A knife inserted 2 to 3 inches from the edge of the pie will withdraw clean.

Transfer to a cooling rack. Serve warm or at room temperature.

SPRING
COUNTRY
PIES

SPRING COUNTRY PIES

———————— ❖❖❖ ————————

Glazed Strawberry Pie   112

Deep-Dish Strawberry-Rhubarb Pie   113

Plum-Rhubarb Pie   114

Orange-Rhubarb Pie   115

Coconut "Candy" Pie   116

Shimmery Chocolate Pie   117

Mile-High Lemon Cream Pie   118

Lemon Slice Pie   119

Lemon Pudding Pie   121

Lemon-Almond Pie   122

Lemon Meringue Pie   123

Vanilla Meringue Pie   124

Lime Cream Pie   126

Several years ago, I was asked to judge a pie-baking contest at an old-fashioned country fair. Since the fair was held during late spring, most of the pies we sampled were filled with strawberry and rhubarb. To my amazement, all the judges were able to work their way through about forty different strawberry and rhubarb pies. All the fillings were crimson or deep pink in color, and the pie crusts were made from a variety of doughs. The best pies were carefully flavored with spices and citrus peel and sweetened with enough sugar to enhance the natural taste of the fruit.

I love a plain unbaked strawberry pie made of whole strawberries folded through a sweetened and thickened, crushed strawberry "jam." Hefty slices of this Glazed Strawberry Pie (page 112) are best served with heaping spoonfuls of whipped cream. I also like the combination of strawberries or plums with sliced rhubarb—sugared, spiced, and baked in a double-crust pie. When I am making a pie of sliced rhubarb and nothing more, the filling is seasoned with orange rind, orange juice, and spices.

Mostly I make these simple pies from berries I have handpicked at a nearby farm. Customers such as myself eagerly work the strawberry patches, exchanging recipes for pies, tarts, and jams while they fill their pails with berries.

Lemon pie, every bit as light and tantalizing as strawberry or rhubarb, is a refreshing sweet to serve in the springtime. The lemon pies in this chapter are sweet, tart, and sometimes creamy. The fillings vary—one is a thickened pudding flavored with lemon juice and grated lemon rind; another is a mixture of paper-thin lemon slices marinated in sugar and combined with beaten eggs; and there is a soft, puffy lemon filling that bakes into a lemon custard bottom and spongelike top. The filling for the lemon meringue and lemon-almond pies tastes vibrantly sweet and sour. Any of the lemon pies makes an ideal teatime snack with a cool fruit spritzer or pot of hot coffee or tea.

Glazed Strawberry Pie

2 cups (1 pint) whole
    strawberries, hulled

1 tablespoon freshly
    squeezed lemon juice

3 tablespoons cornstarch

1 cup granulated sugar

3 cups (1½ pints) whole
    small strawberries,
    hulled

1 fully baked 9-inch pie
    shell, made from 1
    recipe Flaky Pie Crust
    (page 21)

One 9-inch pie

A good strawberry pie is a mingling of textures and flavors: the melting crumble of the pie crust, the firm berries, and the clear, cornstarch-thickened berry "jam" that binds it. Two cups of lightly crushed whole berries are cooked with sugar, cornstarch, and lemon juice to form a "jam." The remaining whole berries are folded through that mixture (the coating thus creating a glaze) and piled into a baked pastry shell.

Blueberries and blackberries may be substituted for the strawberries when either fruit abounds.

———❖❖❖———

Dump the 2 cups strawberries into a large bowl, crush lightly with the back of a wooden spoon or a potato masher, and stir in the lemon juice; set aside.

Thoroughly blend together the cornstarch and sugar until the mixture looks like a fine baby powder. Pour in the crushed strawberries; stir. Turn into a heavy nonreactive saucepan and set over moderate heat. Cook the mixture, stirring, until it comes to a boil and thickens. Remove from the heat, pour into a bowl, and cool to tepid.

When the "jam" is tepid, fold it through the 3 cups whole berries. Pile into the baked pie shell.

Serve at room temperature, with Vanilla-Scented Whipped Cream (page 131), if you like.

Deep-Dish Strawberry-Rhubarb Pie

⅓ cup all-purpose flour

1¼ cups granulated sugar

¼ teaspoon ground cinnamon

¼ teaspoon ground allspice

¼ teaspoon ground cloves

Pinch of salt

2 cups trimmed and ½-inch-sliced rhubarb

3 cups small strawberries, hulled

2 tablespoons unsalted butter, cut into bits

1 recipe Flaky Pie Crust, prepared for a deep-dish pie cover (page 21)

CRUSHED SUGAR GLAZE:

2 tablespoons ice-cold water

12 small sugar cubes, crushed

One 9-inch pie

Nuggets of rhubarb and whole strawberries, sweetened and thickened, turn into a crimson-colored filling when baked. This pie is pleasingly sweet and tart, and very good when accompanied by scoops of Double Vanilla Ice Cream (page 130), which melt into the pie filling.

I love to use a crushed sugar glaze to give the top crust a crunchy exterior. For that, crush small sugar cubes with a rolling pin, mallet, or mortar and pestle, then brush the crust with ice-cold water and sprinkle with the shards of sugar.

Combine the flour, sugar, cinnamon, allspice, cloves, and salt in a large mixing bowl. Add the rhubarb and strawberries, toss well, and let stand for 1 minute.

Spoon the filling into a deep 9-inch pie pan or any other round or oval deep-dish ovenproof vessel, mounding the filling slightly toward the center. Dot with butter, cover with the round of dough, seal, and crimp the edges decoratively, as explained on page 27. Refrigerate for 10 minutes.

For the crushed sugar glaze, brush the top of the pie with water and sprinkle with crushed sugar. Cut several steam vents, using a sharp paring knife.

Bake in a preheated 425 degree oven for 15 minutes, reduce the oven temperature to 350 degrees, and continue baking for about 35 to 40 minutes longer, or until the pastry is golden.

Transfer to a cooling rack. Serve warm or at room temperature.

Plum-Rhubarb Pie

1 recipe Flaky Pie Crust
    for a Double-Crust Pie
    (page 30), well chilled

⅓ cup all-purpose flour

1⅓ cups granulated sugar

¼ teaspoon ground
    allspice

¼ teaspoon ground
    cinnamon

¼ teaspoon freshly grated
    nutmeg

Pinch of salt

3 cups sliced and pitted
    ripe red plums

2 cups trimmed and
    ½-inch-sliced rhubarb

1 tablespoon plum syrup
    (page 37)

2 tablespoons unsalted
    butter, cut into bits

MILK AND SUGAR GLAZE:

2 tablespoons cold milk

1 tablespoon granulated
    sugar

One 9-inch pie

The filling for this pie is a sensual mixture of sour-sweet plums and tart rhubarb, balanced by spice-seasoned granulated sugar. I like to moisten the top of the pie with a tablespoon of homemade plum syrup, which brings the flavor of the fruit into bloom. The method for making all sorts of fruit syrups may be found on page 37, at the beginning of the chapter on summer country pies.

Line a 9-inch pie pan with half of the chilled dough following the directions on page 31; refrigerate.

Combine the flour, sugar, allspice, cinnamon, nutmeg, and salt in a large mixing bowl. Add the sliced plums and rhubarb; toss well. Let stand for 2 minutes.

Spoon the filling into the chilled pie shell. Drizzle with plum syrup, dot with butter, cover with the remaining dough, seal, and crimp the edges decoratively, as explained on page 31. Refrigerate for 10 minutes.

For the glaze, brush the top of the pie with milk and sprinkle with sugar. Cut several steam vents, using a sharp paring knife.

Bake in a preheated 425 degree oven for 15 minutes, reduce the oven temperature to 350 degrees, and continue baking for 35 to 40 minutes longer, or until the top is golden.

Transfer to a cooling rack. Serve barely warm or at room temperature, accompanied by Vanilla Pouring Custard (page 129), if you like.

Orange-Rhubarb Pie

1 recipe Flaky Pie Crust
for a Double-Crust Pie
(page 30), well chilled

⅓ cup all-purpose flour

1½ cups granulated sugar

¼ teaspoon ground
cinnamon

¼ teaspoon ground
allspice

4 cups trimmed and
½-inch-sliced rhubarb
(about 6 long stalks)

1 tablespoon finely grated
orange rind

2 tablespoons freshly
squeezed orange juice

2 tablespoons unsalted
butter, cut into bits

MILK AND SUGAR GLAZE:

2 tablespoons cold milk

1 tablespoon granulated
sugar

One 9-inch pie

This is a refreshing pie that combines the tart flavor of rhubarb with the sweet tang of oranges. The ruby-colored filling is redolent of cinnamon and allspice.

Make this a double-crust pie by covering the filling with a round of pie dough or enclosing it with an overlapping pattern of pastry cutouts in the form of hearts, diamonds, stars, or triangles, as described on page 32. The fanciful cutout cover looks beautiful and does a perfect job of concealing the filling.

Slices of Orange-Rhubarb Pie are delicious when served with cups of orange herbal or English Breakfast tea.

Line a 9-inch pie pan with half of the chilled dough following the directions on page 31; refrigerate.

Combine the flour, sugar, cinnamon, and allspice in a large mixing bowl. Add the sliced rhubarb; toss well. Fold through the orange rind and lemon juice. Spoon the filling into the pie shell. Dot with butter.

If you are using the full top crust, cover with remaining dough, seal, and crimp edges decoratively, as explained on page 31; if you are using a pastry cutout top, apply cutouts as explained on page 32. Refrigerate for 10 minutes.

To glaze the crust, brush the top of the pie with milk and sprinkle with sugar. If you are using a full top crust, cut several steam vents, using a sharp paring knife.

Bake in a preheated 425 degree oven for 15 minutes, reduce the oven temperature to 350 degrees, and continue baking for 40 minutes longer, or until the pastry is golden. Transfer to a cooling rack. Serve barely warm or at room temperature.

Coconut "Candy" Pie

4 extra-large eggs plus 1
  extra-large egg yolk, at
  room temperature

1⅓ cups granulated sugar

2 teaspoons pure vanilla
  extract

Pinch of salt

8 tablespoons (¼ pound
  or 1 stick) unsalted
  butter, melted and
  cooled

½ teaspoon distilled
  white vinegar

1¼ cups sweetened
  shredded coconut

½ cup chopped pecans

1 fully baked 9-inch pie
  shell, made from 1
  recipe Flaky Pie Crust
  (page 21)

One 9-inch pie

When the fragile whisked filling for this simple pie bakes, it becomes firm and tastes like a hearty, rich candy bar.

The pie is made from ingredients usually kept on hand in the country pie larder—eggs, sugar, vanilla, butter, coconut, and pecans. It is a light coconut pie, not as rich and filling as coconut cream or any of the custard pies.

Enjoy this pie anytime. Cut in narrow triangular pieces for serving at tea, as the dessert at the close of a Sunday supper, or as a "snacking" pie to nibble on.

———❖❖❖———

Beat the whole eggs and egg yolk in a large mixing bowl. Beat in the sugar, vanilla, and salt. Blend in the melted butter. Stir in the vinegar, coconut, and pecans.

Pour the pie filling into the baked pie shell. Bake in a pre-heated 350 degree oven for about 50 minutes, or until set. A knife inserted 2 to 3 inches from the edge will withdraw clean.

Transfer to a cooling rack. Serve at room temperature.

Shimmery Chocolate Pie

1⅓ cups granulated sugar

¼ cup sifted unsweetened cocoa powder

1 tablespoon all-purpose flour

Pinch of salt

3 extra-large eggs plus 1 extra-large egg yolk, at room temperature

¼ cup light cream

2 teaspoons pure vanilla extract

8 tablespoons (¼ pound or 1 stick) unsalted butter, melted and cooled

1 fully baked 9-inch pie shell, made from 1 recipe Flaky Pie Crust (page 21)

One 9-inch pie

This translucent pie has a custardlike quiver to it; it's enriched with cocoa, eggs, and vanilla. Shimmery Chocolate Pie is ideal to serve with a steaming pot of coffee or small cups of espresso, along with a little Vanilla-Scented Whipped Cream (page 131) on the side.

Thoroughly blend together the sugar, cocoa, flour, and salt. Beat the eggs and egg yolk together, add to the sugar-cocoa mixture, and beat well. Blend in the cream, vanilla, and butter.

Pour the filling into the baked pie shell. Bake in a preheated 350 degree oven for 50 minutes, or until set. A knife inserted 1 to 2 inches from the center of the pie will emerge clean.

Transfer to a cooling rack. Serve at room temperature with spoonfuls of Vanilla-Scented Whipped Cream (page 131), if you like.

Mile-High Lemon Cream Pie

¼ cup cornstarch

¾ cup granulated sugar

Pinch of salt

2 cups light cream, at room temperature

¾ cup milk, at room temperature

4 extra-large egg yolks, at room temperature, lightly beaten

1 tablespoon finely grated lemon rind

¼ cup freshly squeezed lemon juice

3 tablespoons unsalted butter, softened to room temperature

½ teaspoon pure lemon extract

1 fully baked 9-inch pie shell, made from 1 recipe Flaky Pie Crust (page 21)

This mile-high pie has a flaky crust holding a cooked pudding. The pudding is sparked with lemon and deeply colored by egg yolks. The soft and creamy filling is the base for a dramatic meringue covering made up of 10 egg whites. The soft and thick meringue is a good counterpoint to the eggy richness of the lemon filling.

———— ❖❖❖ ————

Thoroughly blend together the cornstarch, sugar, and salt in a large mixing bowl. The mixture should look like a fine talcum powder. Slowly, while whisking, blend in the cream and milk. Whisk in the yolks. Pour into a heavy nonreactive saucepan and set over moderate heat. Stir continuously until the mixture reaches a boil. When the bubbles cannot be stirred down, reduce the heat and let the pudding simmer for 2 minutes, stirring slowly but continuously.

Remove from the heat, stir in the lemon rind and juice, beat in the butter by tablespoon-size chunks, adding the next only after the first has melted into the pudding, and blend in the lemon extract. Pour into a bowl and press a piece of plastic wrap directly over the surface. Cool the pudding for 25 to 30 minutes, then turn into the baked pie shell.

For the topping, stir together the egg whites and sugar in the top of a double boiler. Set the saucepan containing the whites over a saucepan holding about 1½ inches of barely simmering water. Let the sugar and whites warm over the water for 30 to 35 seconds, stirring constantly. Remove the saucepan, wipe dry, then transfer the whites to a large, deep

10 extra-large egg whites, at room temperature

¾ cup plus 2 tablespoons granulated sugar

½ teaspoon pure vanilla extract

¼ teaspoon cream of tartar

One 9-inch pie

mixing bowl. Beat the whites on moderately high speed until frothy, add the vanilla and cream of tartar, and continue beating on high speed until the whites have formed firm but moist peaks.

Pile the meringue on top of the pie filling, spreading it to enclose the filling completely. Peak and swirl the meringue decoratively with a narrow spatula.

Bake in a preheated 400 degree oven for about 10 minutes, or until the meringue is lightly browned.

Transfer to a cooling rack. Serve at room temperature, preferably no longer than 4 to 5 hours after baking.

❖⋅❖⋅❖⋅❖⋅❖⋅❖⋅❖⋅❖⋅❖⋅❖⋅❖⋅❖⋅❖

Lemon Slice Pie

1 recipe Flaky Pie Crust for a Double-Crust Pie (page 30), well chilled

1 lemon, cut into paper-thin slices, seeded

2 lemons, pared to remove entire outer peel and white pith, cut into paper-thin slices, seeded

This pie has an intense lemon flavor; whole lemons (both peeled and unpeeled) are thinly sliced as the basis for the filling. The lemon slices are tossed in sugar and left to macerate overnight to lessen the astringency of the lemon peel before combining with the beaten eggs.

Sometimes, if I'm in a playful mood, I'll customize the pastry cover by designing a pastry cutout overlay of whole lemons and lemon leaves. These I apply over the top and use a clear, simple glaze to show off the design. For more casual times, I make a crunchy sugar glaze flavored with lemon to finish off the pie; I rub sugar cubes over the surface of a lemon or two

(continued)

2 cups granulated sugar

4 extra-large eggs, at
room temperature

2 tablespoons unsalted
butter, cut into bits

CRUSHED LEMON-SUGAR
GLAZE:

12 small sugar cubes

1 lemon

2 tablespoons ice-cold
water

One 9-inch pie

so the essential oils permeate the cubes and turn them a light yellow color. The cubes are crushed and sprinkled over the pie.

Line a 9-inch pie tin with half of the chilled dough following the directions on page 31; refrigerate.

Combine the sliced lemons and granulated sugar in a large nonreactive mixing bowl. Toss well. Cover the mixture loosely with plastic wrap and let stand at room temperature overnight. Stir the mixture twice.

Beat the eggs in a large mixing bowl. Add the lemon-sugar mixture and stir gently. Pour the filling into the chilled pie shell. Dot with butter, cover with the remaining dough, seal, and crimp the edges decoratively, as explained on page 31. Refrigerate for 10 minutes.

For the lemon-flavored crushed sugar glaze, rub the sugar cubes over the outside of the lemon, letting the cubes absorb the oil. Crush the cubes with a rolling pin.

Brush the top of the pie with water, sprinkle with the crushed sugar, and cut several steam vents, using a sharp paring knife.

Bake in a preheated 425 degree oven for 10 minutes, reduce the oven temperature to 350 degrees, and continue baking for 30 to 35 minutes longer, or until the pastry is golden.

Transfer to a cooling rack. Serve at room temperature.

Lemon Pudding Pie

4 tablespoons (½ stick) unsalted butter, softened at room temperature

1 cup granulated sugar

3 extra-large egg yolks, at room temperature

⅓ cup freshly squeezed lemon juice, strained

2 teaspoons finely grated lemon rind

3 tablespoons plus 2 teaspoons all-purpose flour

1 cup light cream, at room temperature

2 extra-large egg whites, at room temperature

Pinch cream of tartar

1 fully baked 9-inch pie shell, made from 1 recipe Flaky Pie Crust (page 21)

One 9-inch pie

The filling for this lemon pie is a light one: butter, sugar, and egg yolks are creamed together and flavored with lemon juice and rind. A bit of flour is added to bind the mixture and cream to smooth it. The resulting batter is lightened considerably with beaten egg whites. Once the filling is poured into a pie shell and baked, something miraculous begins to happen —a soft lemon custard forms a bottom layer while a spongy, cakelike layer rises to the top.

This old-time heirloom-quality recipe is wonderful to make when all you have on hand are a few bakery staples and some juicy lemons.

———❖❖❖———

Cream the butter well in a large mixing bowl. Add ¾ cup granulated sugar in two additions, beating for 1 minute after each portion is added. Blend in the egg yolks, one at a time, beating well after each addition. Beat in the lemon juice and lemon rind; beat in the flour and cream.

Beat the egg whites on moderately high speed in a small, deep bowl until frothy. Add the cream of tartar and continue beating until soft peaks are formed; add the remaining ¼ cup sugar and beat until firm but moist peaks are formed. Stir a small spoonful of the egg whites into the lemon mixture, then fold in the remaining egg whites.

Gently pour the filling into the baked pie shell. Bake in a preheated 400 degree oven for 10 minutes, reduce the oven temperature to 350 degrees, and continue baking for about 25 minutes longer, or until the top is well risen and firm to the touch.

Transfer to a cooling rack. Cool completely, then refrigerate for 6 hours before serving.

Lemon-Almond Pie

1½ cups Lemon-Scented Granulated Sugar (at right)

1 tablespoon plus 1 teaspoon cornstarch

1 tablespoon finely grated lemon peel

4 extra-large eggs plus 1 extra-large egg yolk, at room temperature

¼ cup plus 1 tablespoon freshly squeezed lemon juice, strained

6 tablespoons unsalted butter, melted and cooled

⅓ cup ground blanched almonds

1 fully baked 9-inch pie shell, made from 1 recipe Flaky Pie Crust (page 21)

One 9-inch pie

When the eggs, sugar, butter, lemon juice, and almonds bake in the pie shell, the filling acquires a soft, jellylike consistency.

To build the lemon flavor, I use Lemon-Scented Granulated Sugar in place of plain sugar. Lemon-scented sugar is a delight to have on hand; it adds zest to pie fillings and to fruit syrups used for poaching fruit. The sugar is quick to make: Strip the peel from 2 lemons. Pour 6 cups granulated sugar into a large, clean jar, add the lemon peel, cover tightly, and shake well. Let stand in a cool pantry for about 1 week, shaking the jar from time to time. After 1 week, discard the lemon peel and add 12 strips of air-dried lemon peel. (To air-dry, leave the strips of peel on a sheet of waxed paper at room temperature for 1 to 2 days.) Cover the jar and store in a cool pantry, where the sugar will keep indefinitely.

Blend sugar and cornstarch in a large mixing bowl. Stir in the lemon peel. Add the eggs and egg yolk, one at a time, beating well after each addition. Stir in the lemon juice, butter, and almonds.

Pour the filling into the baked pie shell. Bake in a preheated 325 degree oven for about 50 minutes, or until the top is a light golden color and the filling has set; a knife inserted 2 to 3 inches from the edge will withdraw clean.

Transfer to a cooling rack. Serve at room temperature.

Lemon Meringue Pie

⅓ cup cornstarch

1½ cups granulated sugar

Pinch of salt

1½ cups water

4 extra-large egg yolks, at room temperature, lightly beaten

¼ cup freshly squeezed lemon juice, strained

2 tablespoons finely grated lemon peel

2 tablespoons unsalted butter, cut into small chunks

1 fully baked 9-inch pie shell, made from 1 recipe Flaky Pie Crust (page 21)

MERINGUE TOPPING:

9 extra-large egg whites, at room temperature

¾ cup granulated sugar

¼ teaspoon cream of tartar

One 9-inch pie

This is the pie my mother made all through my childhood and teenage years. She adapted the recipe from one printed in *McCall's* magazine many years ago. I still make the filling as my mother did, but I use my pie crust and a more voluptuous meringue. Sometimes I use Lemon-Scented Granulated Sugar (page 122) in place of the plain sugar.

Thoroughly blend cornstarch, sugar, and salt in a large, heavy saucepan. Slowly blend in the water, whisking constantly. Bring to the boil over moderately high heat, stirring. Boil 1 minute. Remove from heat. Stir ¼ cup of the hot mixture into the yolks, then add the egg yolk mixture to the hot mixture. Bring to the boil, boil 1 minute, and remove from heat. Stir in lemon juice, peel, and butter, a chunk at a time.

Pour the filling into the pie shell.

For the topping, stir the egg whites and sugar in the top of a double boiler. Set the saucepan containing the whites over a saucepan holding about 1½ inches of barely simmering water. Let the sugar and whites warm over the water for 30 to 35 seconds, stirring. Remove the saucepan, wipe dry, then transfer the whites to a large, deep mixing bowl. Beat the whites on moderately high speed until frothy, add the cream of tartar, and continue beating the whites on high speed until firm but moist peaks are formed.

Spread the meringue on top of the pie filling, enclosing it completely. Peak and swirl the meringue decoratively with a narrow spatula. Bake in a preheated 400 degree oven for about 10 minutes, or until the meringue is lightly browned.

Transfer to a cooling rack. Serve at room temperature.

Vanilla Meringue Pie

¼ cup cornstarch

¾ cup Vanilla-Scented Granulated Sugar (page 219)

¼ teaspoon freshly grated nutmeg

Pinch of salt

2 cups light cream, at room temperature

1 cup heavy cream, at room temperature

4 extra-large egg yolks, at room temperature, lightly beaten

Seed scrapings from the inside of a 3-inch piece of fresh vanilla bean

4 tablespoons unsalted butter, cut into small chunks

2 teaspoons pure vanilla extract

1 fully baked 9-inch pie shell, made from 1 recipe Flaky Pie Crust (page 21)

Cream pies are a joy to make because they rely on only the simplest of things—dairy staples, a heavy pot to make a pudding, and a baked pie shell.

In this pie, the flavor of vanilla comes through in several forms: from liquid extract, Vanilla-Scented Granulated Sugar, and scrapings from a fresh vanilla bean. The creamy, pale yellow filling has specks of vanilla seeds, which look and taste appealing.

The vanilla pudding is covered with a meringue and its soft lightness is a good textural relief from the richness of the pudding.

Thoroughly blend the cornstarch, sugar, nutmeg, and salt in a heavy 2-quart saucepan (preferably made of enameled cast iron). The mixture should look like a fine baby powder. Slowly blend in the light cream, whisking continuously. Blend in the heavy cream. Beat in the egg yolks and seed scrapings from the vanilla bean. Set the saucepan over moderate heat and bring the mixture to a boil, stirring continuously. When the bubbles cannot be stirred down, reduce the heat and let simmer for 2 minutes while stirring.

Remove from the heat. Beat in the chunks of butter, one at a time, adding the next only after the first has melted into the pudding. Beat in the vanilla extract. Pour into a bowl and press a piece of plastic wrap over the surface. Cool the pudding for 30 minutes, then turn it into the baked pie shell.

For the topping, stir together the egg whites and sugar in

MERINGUE TOPPING:

9 extra-large egg whites,
  at room temperature

¾ cup granulated sugar

¼ teaspoon cream of
  tartar

One 9-inch pie

the top of a double boiler. Set the saucepan containing the whites over a saucepan holding about 1½ inches of barely simmering water. Let the sugar and whites warm over the water for 30 to 35 seconds, stirring continuously. Remove the saucepan, wipe dry, then transfer the whites to a large, deep mixing bowl. Beat the whites on moderately high speed until frothy, add the cream of tartar, and continue beating on high speed until the whites have formed firm but moist peaks.

Pile the meringue on top of the pie filling, spreading it to enclose the filling completely. Peak and swirl the meringue decoratively with a narrow spatula.

Bake in a preheated 400 degree oven for 10 minutes, or until the meringue is lightly browned.

Transfer to a cooling rack. Serve at room temperature, preferably no longer than 4 to 5 hours after baking.

❖❖❖❖❖❖❖❖❖❖❖❖❖❖❖❖❖

Lime Cream Pie

5 extra-large egg yolks, at
  room temperature

1 14-ounce can sweetened
  condensed milk

7 tablespoons fresh or
  bottled Key lime juice

1 fully baked 9-inch pie
  shell, made from 1
  recipe Flaky Pie Crust
  (page 21)

WHIPPED CREAM TOPPING:

2 cups cold heavy cream

¼ cup sifted
  confectioners' sugar

4 to 5 tablespoons lightly
  toasted sweetened
  shredded coconut

One 9-inch pie

The filling for this pie uses the tart juice from Key limes,
which, along with sweetened condensed milk and plenty of
egg yolks, makes a delicious sweet-sour filling. When baked
and cooled completely, the lime custard layer is covered with
a thick mantle of lightly sweetened whipped cream and sprinkled with toasted coconut.

The penetrating flavor of the limes makes this a sprightly
pie to serve anytime, but I love to have it on hand for dessert
in early spring to recharge the winter-weary taste buds.

Beat the egg yolks in a medium-size mixing bowl until combined. Blend in the milk and lime juice. Pour the filling into
the baked pie shell. Bake in a preheated 350 degree oven for
15 to 20 minutes, or until it is set and a knife inserted 2 to 3
inches from the edge of the pie will withdraw clean.

Transfer to a cooling rack. Cool to room temperature.

For the whipped cream topping, beat the heavy cream in a
deep, chilled bowl until soft peaks are formed. Sprinkle with
confectioners' sugar and continue beating. Beat until it holds
its shape in firm peaks.

Spoon the cream over the pie filling, spreading it to cover
the filling entirely. With the back of a spoon, make deep swirls
in the cream. Chill in the refrigerator for at least 3 hours. Just
before serving, sprinkle with toasted coconut.

Substitution Note: Bottled Key lime juice is an excellent substitute for fresh limes if they are not available. I particularly like
Nellie and Joe's Key West Lime Juice, available in 16-ounce
bottles.

SWEET AND CREAMY PIE COMPANIONS

Vanilla Pouring Custard, Double Vanilla Ice Cream, and Vanilla-Scented Whipped Cream are lovely accompaniments to a slice of country pie. These may be scooped, puddled, or spooned over and about a helping of pie.

I love the way the pouring custard runs into the juice of a fruit pie filling, faintly tinting the juice a soft pastel color, and the way a puff of sweetened whipped cream plays against the richness of all the nut, chocolate, and mincemeat pies. Pie served à la mode is delicious, too. Vanilla ice cream enhances all of the fruit pies, rich pies such as my Coconut-Walnut-Chocolate-Chip "Candy" Pie (page 86) and the streusel-topped pies—Apple Streusel Pie (page 104), Cinnamon-Pear Pie with Walnut Streusel (page 69), and Peach Streusel Pie (page 38), among them.

Vanilla Pouring Custard

1 small vanilla bean

1¼ cups light cream

3 extra-large egg yolks, at room temperature

1¼ teaspoons arrowroot

3 tablespoons granulated sugar

1 teaspoon pure vanilla extract

Enough pouring custard to accompany one country pie

This is a smooth, cream-enriched custard sauce, lightly thickened with egg yolks and flavored with vanilla.

Serve a pitcher with any of the fruit or mincemeat-filled country pies. I love the way the soft, lightly scented sauce mingles with the juices when poured over each slice.

Slit the vanilla bean down the center (without cutting through the whole bean) to expose the tiny seeds. Pour the cream into a small, heavy saucepan; add the vanilla bean. Scald over moderately high heat, remove from heat, and set aside.

Beat the egg yolks in a large mixing bowl for 1 minute. Add the arrowroot and sugar and continue beating until thick and light.

Remove the vanilla bean from the cream. Add the cream slowly to the egg yolk mixture, whisking all the while. Pour into a heavy saucepan, set over low heat, and cook slowly, stirring continuously with a wooden spoon, until the mixture thickens. The custard is ready when it lightly coats the back of a wooden spoon. Off the heat, stir in the vanilla.

Strain through a fine-meshed sieve into a bowl. If you are not serving the custard warm, sprinkle the top with a fine haze of superfine sugar to keep a skin from forming.

Use the custard warm, at room temperature, or chilled, ladled from a small, deep bowl or poured from a decorative pitcher.

Double Vanilla Ice Cream

1 plump, fat vanilla bean

2 cups light cream

Pinch of salt

¾ cup granulated sugar

5 extra-large egg yolks, at room temperature

1 tablespoon pure vanilla extract

1¾ cups heavy cream, cold

½ cup cold milk

Enough vanilla ice cream to accompany two country pies

Rich and cooling, this vanilla ice cream may bring back to life the nostalgic ritual of hand-cranking ice cream. It's one of those simple pleasures that ought to be revived. Have a favorite country pie on the cooling rack, then gather everyone to churn the following creamy mixture into a frozen delight.

This is a good ice cream for pies, made of sweet cream, plenty of egg yolks, sugar, and vanilla. (I use the tiny seeds scraped out from the inside of the vanilla bean, the scraped-out bean itself, and pure vanilla extract to flavor the ice cream.)

Double Vanilla Ice Cream is a fine plate mate for a slice of any oven-fresh fruit pie—apple, pear, mincemeat, rhubarb, peach, plum, nectarine, blueberry, blackberry, red raspberry, black raspberry, or strawberry.

Slit the vanilla bean down the belly to expose the tiny seeds, using a sharp paring knife. With the tip of a small spoon, scrape the seeds into a heavy, medium-size saucepan. Add the scraped-out bean and the light cream. Scald over moderately high heat. Remove from heat, add the salt, and set aside.

Put the sugar and egg yolks in a large mixing bowl; beat well until slightly thickened. Strain the cream through a fine-meshed sieve. Add to the egg yolk and sugar mixture slowly, a few tablespoons at a time, whisking well. Discard the vanilla bean.

Pour into a medium-size heavy saucepan. Cook slowly, stirring continuously, over low heat until slightly thickened and the custard lightly coats the back of a wooden spoon. Remove from the heat, stir in the vanilla, and let cool to room temperature.

Stir the heavy cream and milk into the custard, pour into a storage container, cover, and refrigerate for about 6 hours, overnight, or until well chilled.

Freeze in a hand-cranked or electric ice cream maker according to the manufacturer's directions.

❖❖❖❖❖❖❖❖❖❖❖❖❖❖❖❖❖

Vanilla-Scented Whipped Cream

1½ cups very cold heavy cream

3 tablespoons sifted confectioners' sugar

1 teaspoon pure vanilla extract

Enough whipped cream to accompany one country pie

This cloud-light dessert sauce is designed to add creaminess to a warm slab of pie. A puff of lightly sweetened whipped cream with a bit of vanilla is a welcome accompaniment to down-home country pies. The sauce marries beautifully with those pies built on apples, pears, peaches, nectarines, plums, and rhubarb; all of autumn's squash and summer's berries; and almost any pie containing chocolate or nuts, pecans in particular.

Pour the cream into a well-chilled, deep bowl. Whip until it begins to mound very lightly. Sprinkle with confectioners' sugar; stir. Stir in the vanilla extract. Continue beating until gentle, floppy peaks are formed. The whipped cream should hold its shape softly in a spoon.

Turn into a bowl and serve dollops alongside a helping of pie.

THE COUNTRY PIE SWAP

*J*ust like a cookie swap, a country pie swap is an informal dessert party where everyone can bring a favorite pie, exchange recipes and gossip, and dip into luscious wedges of freshly baked pie.

Organize a pie swap as a neighborhood party, holiday gathering, or Sunday afternoon tea-and-coffee klatch. Encourage guests to bring their pies nestled in carrying baskets or in deep serving platters. A large bread board is a good base for a pie, as is a round pressed-glass, narrow-lipped cake plate lined with doilies. A Shaker pie carrier, made of interconnected wooden slats, looks beautiful holding a pie. Line it with a crisp, colorful tea towel or antique piece of lace before you set in the pie.

The gathering of pies looks pretty—and tempting—assembled on a table or sideboard, with a selection of iced or hot tea and coffee set up nearby. Offer bowls of whipped cream or ice cream on the side if you like.

If you are hosting the swap, make sure no two pies are alike and try to arrange for a variety of fillings. Gently persuade people to bring a pie they are known for. And remind each pie baker to bring copies of his or her own pie recipe (including both crust and filling) to hand out to the other guests.

Country Pies That Use Fresh Fruits and Vegetables

❖❖❖

Peach Streusel Pie   38
Deep-Dish Gingered Peach Pie   40
Double-Crust Blueberry-Peach Pie   42
Deep-Dish Blueberry Pie   44
Spiced Red Plum Pie   45
Prune Plum Pie   46
Deep-Dish Walnut-Rum-Plum Pie   46
Double-Crust Nectarine Spice Pie   48
Sour Cherry Pie   50
Glazed Yellow Cherry Pie   51
Deep-Dish Blackberry Pie   52
Apple-Raspberry Pie   53
Red Raspberry Pie   54
Fresh Apricot Pie   55
Late-Season Green Tomato Pie   56
Double-Crust Apple Pie   62
Apple-Ginger Mincemeat Pie   63
Apple-Pear Pie with Apple Cider Syrup   66
Pear Mincemeat Pie   68
Cinnamon-Pear Pie with Walnut
    Streusel   69

Spiced Pear-Currant Pie   71
Cranberry-Walnut Mincemeat Pie   72
Pumpkin Custard Pie   76
Pumpkin Crunch Pie   78
Fresh Sugar Pumpkin Pie   80
Apricot-Yam Pie   81
Orange–Butternut Squash Pie   82
Brandied Golden Acorn Squash Pie   84
Banana Cream Pie   100
Spicy Sweet Potato Pie   103
Apple Streusel Pie   104
Glazed Strawberry Pie   112
Deep-Dish Strawberry-Rhubarb Pie   113
Plum-Rhubarb Pie   114
Orange-Rhubarb Pie   115
Mile-High Lemon Cream Pie   118
Lemon Slice Pie   119
Lemon Pudding Pie   121
Lemon-Almond Pie   122
Lemon Meringue Pie   123
Lime Cream Pie   126

Country Pies That Use "Goods on Hand" (Basic Dairy and Pantry Staples)

❖❖❖

Golden Pecan Pie   74

Bourbon Pecan Pie   75

Coconut-Walnut-Chocolate-Chip "Candy" Pie   86

Brown Sugar Pie   87

Vanilla Custard Pie   92

Coconut Custard Pie   93

Maple Cream Pie   94

Maple-Walnut Pie   95

Old-Fashioned Chocolate Fudge Pie   96

Mile-High Coconut Cream Pie   98

Chocolate Silk Pie   102

Buttermilk Pie   106

Coconut "Candy" Pie   116

Shimmery Chocolate Pie   117

Vanilla Meringue Pie   124

OLD-FASHIONED BAKING GOODNESS

Wendy Wheeler

American country cooking is sensuous and forthright, lacking fussiness and rigidity. There's nothing quite like the rich textures and tastes of this home-style kind of cooking: a well-cured ham with its faintly sweet smell, a pot of greens simmering on the stovetop, jars of intensely colored peach preserves and raspberry jam lining the pantry shelf, the picnic cakes, coffee cakes, and keeping cakes—and those irresistible two- and three-layer cakes capped off with a good, homemade frosting.

Soft, meltingly tender cakes made from fresh butter, eggs, flour, leavening, spices, and not much more conjure up childhood memories of happy days: birthdays, Sunday suppers, school or charity bake sales, holidays. These are the cakes that are a very special part of the American cooking tradition; they are vigorously flavored, simple to bake, and easy to devour.

Country cakes are sumptuous everyday cakes, like a triple-layer coconut cake with a fluffy marshmallow frosting or a vanilla pound cake enriched with plenty of egg yolks, butter, and vanilla; a gingerbread cake dotted with blueberries or a one-layer chocolate cake dressed up with a contrasting cream-cheese batter. They are especially pleasing served in the afternoon with tea or after supper for dessert. The cakes, made from dairy and pantry staples (which I like to call "goods on hand"), are made up of all the flavors we know and love. And most of the cake batters in this book can be put together in the time it takes to preheat the oven.

More often than not, the heritage of cake baking evolved from the tradition of a grandmother, mother, or aunt who whipped up cakes on the side while the preserving kettle bubbled away or the bread dough was on the rise. Cakes were eaten almost as soon as they had the chance to cool off from the intense heat of the oven, and they never lasted much longer than the next morning, when farmhands or other early risers finished them off with a second cup of coffee.

The home baking that was accomplished by country cooks long ago was natural, effortless, direct—even though they had to contend with so many unpredictable elements, such as unreliable wood-fired ovens and less-than-foolproof leaveners. Still, all the right instincts of good baking endured and, with those instincts, heirloom-quality recipes; the recipes were then passed on to the next generation of young women, and the next.

My own lifetime of cake baking began in my paternal grandmother's kitchen, watching her make her now-famous hot milk cake, or a white fruit cake, or rich pound cakes baked in loaf tins. As soon as I was old enough to reach the kitchen counter, I took over the task of baking for our family and produced my first hot milk cake. This cake tastes of sweet butter, fresh whole milk, eggs, and vanilla. It is the kind of cake you bake as a part of daily cooking, made as it is from what's on hand in the refrigerator and pantry. You can serve it by the generous slice with a hot cup of coffee or lemon tea or in wedges with a mound of berries and whipped cream. To me, this cake is the essence of country because it is sensible and wholesome, with a clear, pure flavor.

Other country cakes, tender and even textured, contain generous amounts of spices, nuts, coconut, or chocolate, and sometimes shredded or pureed vegetables, berries by the cupful, or sliced ripe fruit. Cake batters are baked in tube pans (sometimes plain straight-sided pans, sometimes fluted ones), loaf pans, springforms, single-layer square pans, ordinary round layer cake pans, or muffin tins. Cakes might be finished off with a simple streusel crumble, a haze of confectioners' sugar, or a light and buttery icing. Many of the cakes are delicious served as is; some of them just beg for a hand-dipped scoop of ice cream to be placed atop a slice.

The cakes in this section are the kind you would love to have at hand: a bourbon-laced pound cake to keep and slice as you like; a spicy apple cake to set out on the back porch midafternoon or evening and gobble up with coffee or tea; small vanilla cakes to serve warm, shortcake-style, with sliced and sugared strawberries and whipped cream; a chocolate pan cake iced with a rich, thick frosting inlaid with chopped pecans—an easy sweet that can be transported in its baking tin to a neighbor's house, school bake sale, or bring-a-dish supper. These are the cakes that never fail to please me and I hope that the recipes for them find a permanent place in your baking file, too.

THE SIMPLE ART
OF COUNTRY CAKES

Wendy Wheeler

The smooth, almost rhythmic mixing of a cake batter is one cooking process that never fails to comfort me. Along with bread baking, it's cake making I turn to when I need to be reminded of the simple pleasures in life.

With only a few exceptions, the cake batters in this book are made in the following way: The fat, usually butter, is beaten for several minutes before a measure of sugar is added in stages and thoroughly combined; eggs and flavoring are then mixed into the batter completely; finally, a sifted or stirred flour mixture, which contains leavening, salt, and any spices being used, is added to the batter alternately with a liquid, such as milk, buttermilk, or cream. Sometimes the batter is further lightened with egg whites beaten to the firm peak stage, such as the cake batter in my Coconut Layer Cake (page 166), or further enriched with nuts, berries, or chocolate chips. Occasionally, the batter is poured over an arrangement of fruit, as for my Peach Upside-Down Cake (page 206), Spiced Nectarine Upside-Down Cake (page 208), and Apple-Ginger Upside-Down Cake (page 210).

Cakes will emerge from the oven picture perfect if you follow the directions to beat, cream, blend, fold, or stir the ingredients together, as set forth in each step of the recipe. Generally, in the first stages of cake making, butter is beaten until soft and malleable; sugar is added, a portion at a time, then vigorously whipped into the butter; eggs (whole or just yolks) are beaten in, one at a time, to strengthen the batter and add volume and richness. After the flavorings are added (extracts, grated citrus rind, and so on), the flour and liquid are added. This final part of the mixing is done slowly and delicately. It is traditional to add the dry and liquid mixtures in alternate batches, beginning and ending with the dry (flour) mixture. This method creates the lightest, most even-grained cakes.

The yeast dough for my Caramel Upside-Down Sticky Cake (page 188) can be made in a large stoneware bowl with a great big wooden spoon and little else except a good pair of hands for kneading the dough.

Some of the little cakes, such as the Ginger Cakes (page 254), Chunky Apple Cakes with Pecans (page 252), and Pear Cakes with Walnuts and Currants (page 262), can be made quickly and easily in one bowl. In each of these recipes, a flour mixture is combined with a whisked liquid mixture to form a light, slightly lumpy batter. The batter is spooned into individual muffin cups and baked straightaway. These cakes take minutes to assemble and well under 30 minutes to bake, so you can always have a little something sweet and fresh on short notice.

All of this, of course, leads up to the time when a cake is pulled from the oven, all fragrant and warm, and you just have to wait impatiently for it to cool before cutting away a big piece, even though no one has yet had the chance to set eyes on it.

———————❖❖❖———————

THE COUNTRY CAKE KITCHEN

"Add a joyful touch of grace!"

Wendy Wheeler

I enjoy filling the house with the sweet aroma of a cake baking and I take pride in serving my guests something made from pure and wholesome ingredients. Since my first love in the whole realm of cooking is baking, I'm always mixing up some batter or another for big cakes and little cakes, dough for cookies and breads, crusts for pies. And I have amassed a pile of recipes and a load of bakeware, old and new, over the years. Still, I always go back to the dog-eared handwritten cake recipes that my mother and grandmother followed and I continue to turn cake batters into the very pans that they used. The pans have a luster that only time and use can bring to them.

Baking a good old-fashioned cake, one that would make you proud, does not require an investment in fancy equipment or odd gadgets. Indeed, most cooks have probably accumulated much of the equipment listed here. I have listed the cake pans used in this book and the handy baking tools that are used constantly in my kitchen, all of which make the preparation of cakes a pleasurable experience.

Notes on equipment, ingredients, and some of my favorite things

For baking, I prefer to use sturdy aluminum cake pans; such pans are readily available in cookware and department stores and in the bakeware section of most well-stocked hardware stores and supermarkets. Baking in aluminum produces layer cakes with an even-grained, light crumb, loaf cakes that rise high and moist, and muffins that turn out plump, tender, and well risen. What's more, aluminum pans are a breeze to clean up. I like Bundt and tube pans that are lined with a nonstick coating and are well constructed. Look for pans with well-meshed seams and tightly rolled edges. The best nonstick pans have interior surface finishes that are bonded on, not simply washed or sprayed on. I still grease and flour the inside of a nonstick pan before filling it with batter, for that little extra bit of insurance; this guards against small patches of cake batter fusing to the side of the pan—the work of a kitchen demon!

For cooking fragile stovetop frostings, such as the Billowy White Frosting in the recipe for Coconut Layer Cake (page 166), I use a good-size double boiler; it's made of ovenproof glassware and has remained in perfect shape for well over 30 years. If you don't have a double boiler, you can improvise one by placing a large, deep heatproof bowl over a simmering pan of water; just make sure that the bowl is anchored well over the pot so that it does not tip over.

A handheld mixer will do a fine job of beating and mixing any of the cake batters in this book, although you must pick it up and put it down frequently when you add a new ingredient or when you need to scrape down the sides of the mixing bowl. If you bake regularly, you will find that a freestanding electric mixer does the mixing, creaming, and beating efficiently and quickly. A mixer whose bowl and beaters both revolve is the kind I would recommend. My mixer is equipped with both small and large bowls; the bowls, which are made of tempered glass, have straight sides and bottoms that curve gently inward. As the beaters beat whatever mixture is in the bowl and the bowl revolves, I can easily push a spatula around the sides to move the contents along; this, I think, is an important feature of the mixer. It may be my imagination, but I believe that this kind of mixer produces light, silky, even-textured batters and cakes that bake up high and moist.

Here are some of the small tools and bakeware that I've come to rely on:

BAKEWARE

Three 9-inch round layer cake pans

One 9-inch tube pan (about 4 inches deep, lined with a nonstick coating)

One 10-inch tube pan (about 4 inches deep, lined with a nonstick coating)

One 9-inch fluted Bundt pan (3¾ to 4 inches deep, lined with a nonstick coating)

One 10-inch fluted Bundt pan (3¾ to 4 inches deep, lined with a nonstick coating)

Two muffin tin trays (each tray holding 12 individual muffin cups; each cup measuring 2¾ inches in diameter)

One 8 x 8 x 2-inch square baking pan

One 10 x 10 x 2-inch square baking pan

One 8-inch round springform pan

One 8-inch round cake pan

One 9-inch round springform pan

One 10 x 3¾ x 3-inch loaf pan

One 9 x 5 x 3-inch loaf pan

One 9 x 13 x 2-inch rectangular baking pan

SMALL TOOLS

Dry measuring cups

Liquid measuring cups

Wire cake racks

Flexible metal and rubber spatulas

Measuring spoons

Waxed paper or parchment paper

Flexible palette knife

Nutmeg grater

Whisk

❖❖❖

A country cake is made up of simple things—flour, fresh butter, spices, leavening, and a flavoring or two. Once the pantry is stocked with staples and the refrigerator with some of the usual dairy goods, you'll be ready to make any cake in this book.

For cake baking, I like to keep a larder well stocked with ingredients, mostly because I love to bake and do so quite often. On the pantry shelf, I store bleached all-purpose flour, which I buy in five-pound sacks, and boxes of bleached cake flour. I have a supply of the sweeteners that I tend to use the most: granulated sugar, light and dark brown sugar, confectioners' sugar, and superfine sugar (a fine, almost powdery sugar, sometimes called dessert or bar sugar, available in one-pound boxes in most markets). I keep the flour and sugar in individual apothecary jars, sealed tight with their glass lids. Every few months I make up a batch of scented sugar, such as vanilla sugar or lemon sugar, for flavoring and sweetening cake batters; I store those along with the other kinds of sugar. I also keep some confectioners' sugar in an old glass shaker so it is always handy for sprinkling over a freshly baked cake.

On another shelf, I arrange tins of baking powder, boxes of baking soda, and numerous bottled extracts, along with jars and tins of ground spices, pouches of nutmeats, tins of sweetened shredded coconut, and glass cylinders stuffed with plump vanilla beans and cinnamon sticks. I keep many kinds of chocolate—regular and miniature chips, bittersweet bars, squares of unsweetened or semisweet chocolate, unsweetened cocoa powder—on hand.

I always use fresh, not previously frozen, unsalted butter. Fresh butter is a delight to work with and it creates a tender, fine-grained cake that rises impressively while baking. Butter imparts a full, rich taste to a cake. I use thick dairy sour cream, with no starch or preservatives added.

I buy all of my eggs, buttermilk, and cream at a local health food store. The eggs are laid by free-ranging hens and the yolks are thick and shiny, a brilliant yellow-orange color. I find these eggs indispensable for baking, sauces, and ice cream. I buy both jumbo and extra-large eggs. Sometimes a batter needs the fullness of jumbo eggs; at other times, extra-large eggs are sufficient for binding and enriching the batter. Each recipe in this book specifies the size of egg to be used. (If you have only large eggs on hand, it's good to know that a large egg is equivalent to about 2 ounces or ¼ cup, an extra-large egg is 2¼ ounces, and a jumbo egg, 2½ ounces. If, for example, a recipe calls for 4 jumbo eggs, you could substitute 5 large eggs. If you are making some of the big pound cakes and think you may be shy an ounce, it's safe to add an additional egg yolk to the batter. This works only for Best Vanilla Pound Cake [page 218], Bourbon Pound Cake [page 224], Spice Pound Cake [page 226], Rich Nut Pound Cake [page 228], and Cream Pound Cake [page 230].)

Good buttermilk is heavy and loaded with curds of butterfat, and the best kind is not treated to ultrapasteurization or stabilizers. Look for dairy-fresh buttermilk at a local health food store or farmers' market or, best of all, a dairy that sells to the general public.

There is one last component of cake baking that is not a piece of equipment and not an ingredient (at least not the kind you buy at the grocery store). It is the sometimes elusive "touch of grace." The poetic phrase "Add a touch of grace" is repeated often in many old "receipt" books, frequently following recipes for breads and cakes. It is a reminder that baking should be done with a loving spirit. So don't forget to add a joyful "touch of grace" to the recipes that follow.

<hr>

About cake plates

Be it sparkling patterned glass or richly colored porcelain, a beautiful cake plate shows off a cake in a wonderful way. Over the years, I've expanded my collection of pressed-glass cake-stands to include platters and plates and I love to choose from the array of softly colored Depression-glass cake plates, flowery china plates, and footed cake-stands, matching the cake to the serving piece.

Footed cake-stands, made out of china or glass, generally measure about five to seven inches high and range from nine to twelve inches in diameter. Most are finished decoratively with a narrow lip or modest fluted or scalloped edge that keeps the crumbs under control and prevents the cake from sliding off.

Antique pressed-glass stands, known as doughnut or tea cake-stands, are somewhat smaller, measuring about four inches high and seven to eight inches in diameter. These were made for serving such sweets as small, three-bite doughnuts, crullers, miniature cupcakes, and little fancy cookies. Any cake-stand looks even lovelier lined with a lacy paper doily or flat, shiny leaves (such as galax or lemon) before the cake is placed on top.

A proper cake plate can range in size from nine to ten inches in diameter to a full twelve to fourteen inches. The larger plates are ideal for big, impressive pound cakes, such as Bourbon Pound Cake (page 224), Spice Pound Cake (page 226), Rich Nut Pound Cake (page 228), or Cream Pound Cake (page 230), or layer cakes. Smaller cake plates are ideal for fresh fruit cakes, such as Plum Cake (page 238), Spicy Apple Cake (page 240), Fresh Peach Cake (page 242), Blueberry Gingerbread (page 246), Peach Upside-Down Cake (page 206), Spiced Nectarine Upside-Down Cake (page 208), or Apple-Ginger Upside-Down Cake (page 210). Once the cake is positioned on the plate, I like to ring the edge with something fresh and pretty, like sprigs of lavender or heather or cherry, apple, or peach blossoms.

BACK PORCH CAKES

Wendy Wheeler

BACK PORCH CAKES

————◆◆◆————

Marbled German Chocolate Cake   156
Black Walnut and Chocolate Pan Cake   158
Orange Cake   160
Buttermilk Cake   162
Buttermilk Chocolate Layer Cake   164
Coconut Layer Cake   166

*R*elaxing on the back porch (or veranda or patio) with a piece of cake and a hot or cold drink is just the thing to do when the living is easy. The porch with its washed-pine, wicker, or painted furniture is also the place for the time-honored rituals of shucking corn and cranking the ice cream maker.

Cakes to be savored midafternoon with a cup of tea should be informal, plain, and rather buttery. For those times, cut into a freshly baked Orange Cake (page 160), Buttermilk Cake (page 162), or Black Walnut and Chocolate Pan Cake (page 158). Reserve the tall iced layer cakes and the fudgy, cheesecake-based Marbled German Chocolate Cake (page 156) for well after dinner, when there's time to linger over and appreciate a toothsome dessert. A pot of hot coffee or a pitcher of iced tea, depending on the weather and your mood, should be served along with the cake.

Back porch cakes look particularly appealing, I think, when presented on old pressed-glass cake-stands or flat, flowery cake plates. Mostly I use the plates and stands from my collection of Depression glass; the pink-, green-, or amber-hued plates seem to show off pieces of cake gloriously. Since the big layer cakes cut into deep, hefty slices, I serve those on large luncheon or dinner plates; smaller dishes can handle daintier cakes.

Marbled German Chocolate Cake

This flavorful square cake is a swirled blend of rich vanilla cheesecake and mellow German chocolate cake. The waves of cheesecake keep the whole cake moist and make each bite taste creamy and silky. My mother baked a Marbled German Chocolate Cake nearly every Saturday morning to serve over the weekend. This is my version of her cake.

Small squares or thick fingers of this cake are delicious served with tall glasses of iced coffee made from freshly ground coffee beans. I serve a little pot of cream and a bowl of superfine sugar with iced coffee.

———— ❖❖❖ ————

FOR THE CREAM-CHEESE MIXTURE:

6 ounces cream cheese, softened at room temperature

4 tablespoons (½ stick) unsalted butter, softened at room temperature

⅓ cup granulated sugar

2 extra-large eggs, at room temperature

2 tablespoons plus 2 teaspoons *sifted* cake flour

2 teaspoons pure vanilla extract

FOR THE GERMAN CHOCOLATE CAKE BATTER:

8 ounces (2 bars) German sweet chocolate, coarsely chopped

½ cup (1 stick) unsalted butter, cut into chunks

1 cup *unsifted* cake flour

Lightly butter and flour a 10-inch square baking pan; set aside. Preheat the oven to 350 degrees.

For the cream-cheese mixture, beat the cream cheese and butter in the small bowl of an electric mixer on moderately high speed for 2 minutes. Beat in the sugar. Blend in the eggs, one at a time, beating well after each one. Add the flour and blend it in on low speed. Blend in the vanilla; set aside. Wash and dry the beaters.

For the German chocolate cake batter, melt the chopped chocolate and butter chunks in a small heavy saucepan over low heat. When the chocolate and butter have melted down completely, remove the saucepan from the heat and stir once or twice; set aside.

Sift together the flour, baking powder, and salt onto a sheet of waxed paper. Beat the eggs in the large bowl of an electric

½ teaspoon baking
powder

½ teaspoon salt

4 extra-large eggs, at
room temperature

1¼ cups Vanilla-Scented
Granulated Sugar
(page 219) or plain
granulated sugar

2 teaspoons pure vanilla
extract

One 10-inch square cake

mixer on moderate speed for 1 minute. Beat in the sugar and vanilla. With the mixer on low speed, blend in the chocolate-butter mixture until combined. Add the sifted dry ingredients in 2 additions, beating just until the particles of flour have been absorbed.

Pour two-thirds of the German chocolate cake batter into the prepared baking pan. Spoon the cream cheese batter on top. Carefully pour the remaining German chocolate cake batter on top of that. Using a plain table knife, marbleize the batters by drawing the knife through all 3 layers in gentle swirls.

Bake the cake on the lower-third-level rack of the preheated oven for 40 to 45 minutes, or until a wooden pick inserted in the center of the cake comes out almost clean (a few moist particles will still cling) and the cake pulls slightly away from the sides of the pan.

Let the cake cool in the pan on a wire rack for 10 minutes. Carefully invert the pan onto a second rack, then invert again to cool right side up.

Serve the cake cut in fingers or squares.

Black Walnut and Chocolate Pan Cake

4 ounces (4 squares) unsweetened chocolate, roughly chopped

1 cup (2 sticks) unsalted butter, cut into chunks

1½ cups *unsifted* cake flour

¼ teaspoon baking powder

½ teaspoon salt

4 jumbo eggs, at room temperature

2 cups Vanilla-Scented Granulated Sugar (page 219)

2 teaspoons pure vanilla extract

1 cup chopped black walnuts

Confectioners' sugar for dusting, optional

One 9-inch round cake

A fudge cake with body and substance, this is best served in thin wedges. The fine, full aroma of chocolate comes through in each slice, as does the distinctive flavor of black walnuts. A scoop of Pure Vanilla Ice Cream (page 266) would make a lovely accompaniment to a slice of this cake, as its subtle, understated taste plays nicely against the deep, dark flavor of the chocolate. Any leftover cake can be broken up into little chunks, mashed slightly with the back of a knife or cleaver, and folded into softened vanilla ice cream. The brownielike bits become embedded in the ice cream. It's a concoction everyone seems to like.

Lightly butter a 9-inch round springform pan. Line the bottom of the pan with a round of waxed paper. Dust the sides of the pan with flour; set aside. Preheat the oven to 375 degrees.

Place the chocolate and butter in a medium-size saucepan, set over low heat and cook slowly until the butter and chocolate have melted down completely. Set aside to cool.

Stir together the flour, baking powder, and salt in a small bowl. Place the eggs in the large bowl of an electric mixer and beat on high speed for 30 seconds. Add the sugar and beat for 30 seconds longer. By hand, whisk together the chocolate-butter mixture and vanilla for a few seconds, then add it to the eggs and sugar. Beat on low speed until the chocolate mixture is incorporated. By hand, stir in the flour, beating slowly with a wooden spoon just until the particles of flour have been absorbed. Fold in half of the walnuts. Spoon the batter into the prepared pan. Spread the batter evenly in the pan. Sprinkle the remaining walnuts evenly over the top.

Bake the cake on the lower-third-level rack of the preheated oven for 45 minutes, or until a wooden pick inserted in the center of the cake comes out barely clean; the cake will just begin to pull away from the sides of the pan.

Let the cake cool in the pan on a wire rack for 30 minutes. Remove the outside hinged ring of the pan and let the cake cool completely. When it has reached room temperature (about 4 to 5 hours), invert it onto a second cooling rack, then invert again so that the cake is right side up. Sift a little confectioners' sugar over the top, if you like.

Serve the cake cut in narrow wedges.

Orange Cake

3½ cups *unsifted* all-purpose flour

1 tablespoon hot water

½ teaspoon baking soda

1 cup buttermilk, at room temperature

1 cup shortening

½ cup (1 stick) unsalted butter, softened at room temperature

2½ cups granulated sugar

4 jumbo eggs, at room temperature

1 tablespoon pure orange extract

1 tablespoon finely grated orange rind

1 tablespoon orange liqueur, such as Cointreau, Grand Marnier, or Triple Sec

FOR THE ORANGE GLAZE:

2 tablespoons finely julienned orange peel (see Note)

½ cup freshly squeezed orange juice

Orange extract, grated orange rind, and orange liqueur perfume this big cake with a heady citrus fragrance. The cake, still warm from the oven, is crowned with a glaze containing thin wisps of orange rind. Pair slices of Orange Cake with a pot of Darjeeling tea for a revitalizing midafternoon treat. I have this special recipe from my good friend Mimi Davidson, who created the cake for a local restaurant several years ago. Mimi likes to have one on hand for weekend guests.

Lightly butter and flour a 10-inch fluted Bundt pan; set aside. Preheat the oven to 350 degrees.

Sift the flour onto a sheet of waxed paper; set aside.

Place the hot water in a small bowl, add the baking soda, and stir to dissolve. Whisk the baking soda mixture into the buttermilk and set aside.

Cream the shortening and butter in the large bowl of an electric mixer on moderately high speed for 3 minutes. Add the sugar in 3 additions, beating thoroughly on moderate speed until light and white-looking after each portion is added. Beat in the eggs, one at a time, beating thoroughly after each one. Scrape down the sides of the mixing bowl often to keep the mixture even textured. With the mixer on low speed, alternately add the flour in 3 additions and the buttermilk in 2 additions, beginning and ending with flour. Beat in the orange extract, orange rind, and orange liqueur. Pour and scrape the batter into the prepared pan. Shake the pan gently from side to side to level the top of the batter.

¾ cup granulated sugar

1½ teaspoons water

1 tablespoon orange
  liqueur (the same as
  that used in the cake
  batter)

One 10-inch Bundt cake

Bake the cake on the lower-third-level rack of the preheated oven for 1 hour and 20 minutes to 1 hour and 30 minutes, or until a wooden pick inserted into the middle of the cake comes out clean and dry and the cake pulls away slightly from the edges of the pan.

While the cake is baking, make the orange glaze. Put the orange peel in a small saucepan of boiling water; boil 1 minute. Drain the peel in a small stainless steel sieve and refresh it under cold running water. Drain on paper toweling. Place the peel, orange juice, sugar, water, and liqueur in a medium-size stainless steel or enameled cast-iron saucepan. Cover the pan and set over low heat; cook slowly until the sugar has dissolved completely. When every last granule of sugar has melted down, uncover the pot and bring the contents of the saucepan to the boil. Boil for 3 minutes and remove from the heat.

Let the cake cool in the pan on a wire rack for 5 minutes. Spoon a third of the syrup (without any peel) over the cake while it is still in the pan. When the syrup has been absorbed, carefully invert the cake onto a second cooling rack. Spoon the remaining syrup, along with the wisps of peel, over the top. Let cool completely.

Serve the cake cut in medium thick slices.

Note: To make finely julienned orange peel, pare long, wide strips from the outer peel of a thick-skinned orange (like a navel orange), square off the ends with a sharp knife, then cut ¹⁄₁₆-inch-wide strips from the sections of peel.

Buttermilk Cake

1 tablespoon finely grated
   lemon rind

1 tablespoon plus
   1 teaspoon pure lemon
   extract

3½ cups *sifted* all-purpose
   flour

¼ teaspoon salt

½ teaspoon baking soda

1 cup buttermilk, at room
   temperature

1½ cups (3 sticks)
   unsalted butter,
   softened at room
   temperature

2½ cups granulated sugar

5 jumbo eggs, at room
   temperature

FOR THE LEMON GLAZE:

⅓ cup freshly squeezed
   and strained lemon
   juice

¾ cup granulated sugar

One 10-inch Bundt cake

The cool and tart flavor of lemon peel adds a zesty—and graceful—note to this cake. I like to let the finely grated lemon peel steep in an ample amount of lemon extract well before it is beaten into the batter so that the peel has the chance to bloom. The lemon glaze is a nice finishing touch, adding as it does a featherlight sweet-and-sour coating. Thick hunks of Buttermilk Cake are wonderful served in summer with piles of fresh berries and mounds of whipped cream. Slender slices of cake, perhaps two to a serving, served with a warm compote of dried fuit, make a marvelous midwinter treat.

Lightly butter and flour a 10-inch fluted Bundt pan; set aside. Preheat the oven to 350 degrees.

Blend the lemon rind and lemon extract together in a small cup; set aside.

Sift together the flour and salt onto a sheet of waxed paper; set aside. Stir the baking soda into the buttermilk; set aside.

Cream the butter in the large bowl of an electric mixer on moderately high speed for 3 minutes. Add the sugar in 3 additions, beating for 1 minute on moderately high speed after each portion is added. Beat in the eggs, one at a time, blending well after each addition. Blend in the lemon rind–extract mixture. Scrape down the sides of the mixing bowl to keep the mixture even textured. With the mixer on low speed, alternately add the flour in 3 additions with the buttermilk in

2 additions, beginning and ending with flour. Pour and scrape the batter into the prepared pan.

Bake the cake on the lower-third-level rack of the preheated oven for about 1 hour and 15 minutes, or until a wooden pick inserted in the center of the cake comes out clean and dry and the cake pulls away slightly from the edges of the pan.

Let the cake cool in the pan on a wire rack for 5 minutes.

To make the glaze, combine the lemon juice and sugar in a small bowl. Invert the cake onto a second cooling rack. Brush the glaze over the top and sides of the hot cake. Let cool completely.

Serve the cake cut in thin slices.

Buttermilk Chocolate Layer Cake

2 cups *sifted* cake flour

1½ teaspoons baking
soda

¼ teaspoon salt

½ cup (1 stick) unsalted
butter, softened at
room temperature

1½ cups granulated sugar

2 extra-large eggs, at
room temperature

1 teaspoon pure vanilla
extract

3 ounces (3 squares)
unsweetened
chocolate, melted and
cooled

1½ cups buttermilk, at
room temperature

FOR THE THIN AND RICH
CHOCOLATE FROSTING:

3 ounces (3 squares)
unsweetened
chocolate, coarsely
chopped

A chocolate layer cake as fine-grained and light as this is typical of the kind you would meet up with at a county fair, church supper, or neighborhood get-together. It is beloved for its intense chocolate flavor, ethereal texture, and rich frosting. This is a good cake to have around to satisfy the teatime sweet tooth. I like to assemble the cake on a pressed-glass cake-stand lined with doilies and serve big pieces on glass plates in the same pattern as the stand.

Lightly butter and flour the inside of two 9-inch round cake pans. Line the bottom of each pan with a circle of waxed paper; set aside. Preheat the oven to 350 degrees.

Resift the flour with the baking soda and salt onto a large sheet of waxed paper. Cream the butter in the large bowl of an electric mixer on moderate speed for 3 minutes. Beat in the sugar in 2 additions, beating well after each portion is added. Beat in the eggs, one at a time, blending well after each one. Blend in the vanilla and melted chocolate and beat on low speed until the mixture is chocolate colored throughout, scraping down the sides of the bowl with a rubber spatula to keep the mixture even textured. With the mixer on low speed, alternately add the sifted flour mixture in 3 additions and the buttermilk in 2 additions, beginning and ending with the flour mixture. Pour and scrape the batter into the prepared pans, dividing it evenly.

Bake the layers on the lower-third-level rack of the preheated oven for 25 to 30 minutes, or until a wooden pick

6 tablespoons (¾ stick) unsalted butter, cut into chunks

½ cup granulated sugar

1 tablespoon cornstarch

¼ cup milk, at room temperature

¼ cup light cream, at room temperature

1 teaspoon pure vanilla extract

One 2-layer 9-inch round cake

inserted in the center of each layer comes out clean and dry and the cake pulls away slightly from the edges of the pan.

Cool the layers in the pans on wire racks for 3 to 5 minutes. Invert the cakes on additional wire racks and peel off the waxed paper if necessary. Let cool completely.

To make the thin and rich frosting, melt the chocolate and butter in a medium-size heavy saucepan. Thoroughly blend together the sugar and cornstarch in a mixing bowl. Combine the milk and light cream and blend into the cornstarch mixture. Off the heat, stir the sugar-milk mixture into the melted butter and chocolate, stirring well. Place the saucepan over moderate heat and bring to a boil, stirring slowly. When the mixture reaches the boil, boil for 1 to 2 minutes, or until moderately thick (the frosting will be thick enough to coat the back of a spoon). Remove from the heat and stir in the vanilla. Let the frosting cool until it reaches a soft spreading consistency, about 15 minutes, depending on the temperature of your kitchen.

Place one of the cake layers on a flat serving dish or cake plate and spread with a little of the frosting. Top with the second cake layer. Spread the remaining frosting over the top and sides of the cake with a flexible palette knife—the frosting will be thin and shiny. (If the frosting is still warm when spread over the cake, it will puddle a bit at the base of the cake; in that case, wait a few minutes for the frosting to firm up, then spread it up against the sides of the cake.) Let the cake sit for about 2 hours to set the frosting.

Serve the cake cut in thick slices.

Coconut Layer Cake

3 cups *sifted* cake flour

2¼ teaspoons baking powder

¼ teaspoon salt

1 cup (2 sticks) unsalted butter, softened at room temperature

1 box (1 pound) confectioners' sugar, *sifted*

4 jumbo egg yolks, at room temperature

2 teaspoons pure vanilla extract

1 teaspoon coconut extract

1 cup milk, at room temperature

1⅓ cups lightly packed sweetened flaked coconut

4 jumbo egg whites, at room temperature

⅛ teaspoon cream of tartar

This light and high three-layer cake is iced with a billowy white frosting; then the frosting is partially concealed by handfuls of shredded coconut covering the top and sides of the cake. It is a cake reminiscent of the kind you used to find at a diner featuring homemade desserts or a charity bake sale. In my kitchen, you'd see the cake standing tall and proud under a great big Depression-glass cake-keeper. I like to serve the cake with a pot of hot coffee at the close of a Sunday supper, but you can certainly offer it with tall glasses of minted iced tea on an early summer afternoon—an indulgence I heartily recommend.

Lightly butter and flour three 9-inch round cake pans. Line the bottom of each pan with a circle of waxed paper; set aside. Preheat the oven to 350 degrees.

Resift the flour with the baking powder and salt onto a large sheet of waxed paper; set aside. Cream the butter in the large bowl of an electric mixer on moderately high speed for 3 minutes. Reduce the speed to moderate and beat in the confectioners' sugar in 4 additions, blending well after each portion is added. Scrape down the sides of the mixing bowl frequently. Continue to cream the butter and sugar on moderately high speed for 3 minutes. Beat in the egg yolks, one at a time, blending well after each one. Blend in the vanilla and coconut extracts. With the mixer on low speed, alternately add the sifted dry ingredients in 3 additions with the milk in 2 additions, beginning and ending with the dry mixture. By hand, fold in the coconut.

4 jumbo egg whites, at
room temperature

¾ cup plus 2 tablespoons
Vanilla-Scented
Granulated Sugar
(page 219) or plain
granulated sugar

Pinch of salt

⅓ cup plus 1½
tablespoons light corn
syrup

1 teaspoon pure vanilla
extract

FOR FINISHING THE CAKE:

About 2⅔ to 3 cups
lightly packed
sweetened flaked
coconut

One 3-layer 9-inch round cake

Beat the egg whites until frothy in a clean, dry mixing bowl. Add the cream of tartar and continue beating until firm—but still moist—peaks are formed. Stir 2 large spoonfuls of white into the cake batter to lighten it, then fold in the remaining whites. Divide the batter among the 3 pans, gently leveling the top by shaking each pan from side to side.

Bake the layers on the upper- and lower-third-level racks of the preheated oven for about 30 to 35 minutes, or until a wooden pick inserted in the center of the cakes comes out clean and dry and the layers begin to pull away from the sides of the pan. To ensure even heat distribution, rotate the pans from lower third to upper third and from front to back halfway through the baking time.

Cool the layers in the pans on wire racks for 2 to 3 minutes. Run a thin, flexible palette knife between each layer and the side of the pan. Invert the layers onto cooling racks. Peel off the waxed paper. Let cool completely.

To make the billowy white frosting, combine the egg whites, sugar, salt, and corn syrup in the top saucepan of a large double boiler. Fill the bottom with about 1½ inches of water and bring to the barest simmer. (The water should come within ½ inch of the bottom of the top pan but not touch it; adjust the water level accordingly.) Set the top pan over the bottom.

Beat the frosting with a handheld electric beater on moderate speed for 6 minutes. Add the vanilla, raise the speed to moderately high, and continue beating for 1 to 2 minutes longer, or until the frosting is shiny and marshmallowlike. Carefully remove the top saucepan from the water bath,

(continued)

wipe off the bottom, and beat for a minute or so to cool the frosting slightly.

Place one cake layer on a flat serving plate and spread with a little frosting. Top with the second layer and spread with a little frosting. Put on the last layer. Peak and swirl the remaining frosting all over the top and sides of the cake. Sprinkle $2\frac{2}{3}$ cups coconut heavily over the top and sides of the cake, using an extra $\frac{1}{3}$ cup if necessary to cover the whole cake generously.

Serve the cake, cut in slices, on big plates.

COFFEE CAKES

Wendy Wheeler

COFFEE CAKES

———————— ❖❖❖ ————————

Cocoa-Nut Swirl Coffee Cake 172
Coconut-Cinnamon Pan Cake 174
Apple-Raisin Coffee Cake 176
Maple-Pumpkin Coffee Cake 178
Walnut–Sweet Potato Coffee Cake 180
Banana-Coconut Coffee Cake 182
Raspberry Coffee Cake 184
Date Coffee Cake 186
Caramel Upside-Down Sticky Cake 188

A just-out-of-the-oven coffee cake, fragrant and inviting, is what homestyle baking is all about. Moist and full of the flavor of good butter, eggs, spices, nuts, and fruit, it is the perfect bit of cake to have around for morning or afternoon snacking. Coffee cake goes down easily with oversized cups of hot coffee, naturally, done right with cream and sugar. Or serve slices of cake with a pitcher of fairly strong iced coffee lightened with cream.

Treat friends or neighbors who stop by your house some afternoon after a round of errands to slices of Apple-Raisin Coffee Cake (page 176), squares of Coconut-Cinnamon Pan Cake (page 174), or fat hunks pulled away from a Caramel Upside-Down Sticky Cake (page 188). To make the coffee and coffee cake hour a more festive event, set out refreshments on a big table spread with a colorful quilt or lacy linen coverlet; arrange napkins, charming plates, silver dessert forks, and spoons in a still life along with a variety of cakes, baskets of seasonal fruit, and wildflowers.

Cocoa-Nut Swirl Coffee Cake

2½ cups *unsifted* all-purpose flour

2½ teaspoons baking powder

½ teaspoon baking soda

¼ teaspoon salt

¾ teaspoon ground cinnamon

1 cup (2 sticks) unsalted butter, softened at room temperature

1½ cups Vanilla-Scented Granulated Sugar (page 219) or plain granulated sugar

3 extra-large eggs, at room temperature

1 teaspoon pure vanilla extract

1 cup sour cream, at room temperature

FOR THE COCOA-NUT SWIRL MIXTURE:

¼ cup granulated sugar

½ cup finely chopped walnuts

This simple butter cake is fussied up with a blend of sugar, walnuts, cocoa powder, and ground cinnamon that meanders through the batter in a curly streak. A close-textured cake, but one that is still quite light, this sweet is a welcome companion to cups of hot coffee or slender glasses of ice-cold lemonade or limeade. Serve thick slices of Cocoa-Nut Swirl Coffee Cake in the morning bread basket, offer thin slices with hot tea on a cool midafternoon, or coat slightly stale slices with a dipping batter of beaten eggs and milk and fry them, French toast-style, and serve at Sunday breakfast.

Lightly butter and flour a plain 9-inch tube pan. Line the bottom of the pan with a circle of waxed paper, trimmed to fit; set aside. Preheat the oven to 325 degrees.

Sift together the flour, baking powder, baking soda, salt, and cinnamon onto a large sheet of waxed paper; set aside.

Cream the butter in the large bowl of an electric mixer on moderately high speed for 2 minutes. Add the sugar in 2 additions, beating thoroughly after each portion is added. Beat for 1 minute on high speed. With the mixer on moderately high speed, blend in the eggs, one at a time. Beat in the vanilla. Scrape down the sides of the mixing bowl and beat the mixture for about 30 seconds longer. With the mixer on low speed, alternately add the sifted dry ingredients in 3 additions and the sour cream in 2 additions, beginning and ending with the dry mixture. Scrape down the sides of the mixing bowl

3 tablespoons *unsifted* unsweetened cocoa powder

1 teaspoon ground cinnamon

Confectioners' sugar for dusting, optional

One 9-inch tube cake

frequently with a rubber spatula to keep the batter even textured.

For the cocoa-nut swirl, combine the sugar, walnuts, cocoa, and cinnamon in a small bowl.

Pour and scrape half the batter into the prepared baking pan. Sprinkle the cocoa-nut swirl mixture evenly over the batter. Pour the rest of the batter on top.

Bake the cake on the lower-third-level rack of the preheated oven for about 50 minutes to 1 hour, or until a wooden pick inserted in the center of the cake comes out clean and dry and the cake pulls away slightly from the edges of the pan.

Let cool in the pan on a wire rack for 4 to 5 minutes. Invert onto a second cooling rack, then invert again to cool right side up. Dust the top of the cake with a little sifted confectioners' sugar, if you like.

Serve the cake cut in medium thick slices.

Coconut-Cinnamon Pan Cake

1½ cups *unsifted* all-purpose flour

2 teaspoons baking powder

¼ teaspoon salt

1 teaspoon ground cinnamon

½ teaspoon freshly grated nutmeg

¼ teaspoon ground allspice

½ cup (1 stick) unsalted butter, softened at room temperature

½ cup granulated sugar

½ cup firmly packed light brown sugar

1 extra-large egg plus 2 extra-large egg yolks, at room temperature

½ cup milk blended with 2 teaspoons pure vanilla extract, at room temperature

Underneath all of the spices and the coconut-butter crumble of this recipe is a very simple formula for a butter cake made in a square pan. I was first taught how to make it in a home economics class at the age of eight. Years later, I made a marvelous little coffee cake out of the main ingredients and since then, I bake the cake often to serve with tea or at brunch. It is delicious cut in squares and served with whipped cream, a bowl of berries, and a pot of herbal tea for a casual midafternoon break. Cake left over to the next day can be warmed and served at breakfast. Or layer a bowl with cubes of cake, custard, and sweetened berries to make a splendid summer pudding.

Lightly butter and flour a 10-inch square cake pan and line the bottom with waxed paper; set aside. Preheat the oven to 350 degrees.

Sift together the flour, baking powder, salt, cinnamon, nutmeg, and allspice onto a large sheet of waxed paper.

Cream the butter in the large bowl of an electric mixer on moderately high speed for 2 to 3 minutes. Beat in the granulated sugar; continue beating for 2 minutes. Add the brown sugar and beat for 1 minute longer. Beat in the egg and egg yolks and blend well. With the mixer on low speed, alternately add the sifted flour mixture in 2 additions with the milk in 1 addition, beginning and ending with flour. Spoon the batter into the prepared pan; spread evenly.

For the coconut-butter crumble, place the butter, brown

FOR THE COCONUT-BUTTER CRUMBLE:

2½ tablespoons cold
   unsalted butter, cut
   into small bits

¼ cup firmly packed light
   brown sugar

1 tablespoon *unsifted*
   all-purpose flour

¾ cup sweetened
   shredded coconut

¼ cup chopped walnuts

One 10-inch square cake

sugar, flour, coconut, and walnuts in a bowl. Mix all of the ingredients together with your fingertips until it looks like a rough streusel, making sure that the butter is broken down into small bits. Sprinkle the crumble evenly over the top of the cake batter.

Bake the cake on the lower-third-level rack of the preheated oven for about 40 minutes, or until a wooden pick inserted into the center of the cake comes out clean and dry and the cake pulls slightly away from the sides of the pan.

Let cool in the pan on a wire rack for 5 to 10 minutes. Carefully invert the cake onto a second cooling rack and peel away the waxed paper; invert again to cool right side up.

Serve the cake warm or at room temperature, cut in squares.

Apple-Raisin Coffee Cake

1¾ cups *unsifted* all-purpose flour

1 teaspoon baking powder

½ teaspoon baking soda

¼ teaspoon salt

1 teaspoon ground cinnamon

¼ teaspoon freshly grated nutmeg

¼ teaspoon ground allspice

¼ cup dark seedless raisins

½ cup (1 stick) unsalted butter, softened at room temperature

¾ cup granulated sugar

2 extra-large eggs, at room temperature

2 teaspoons pure vanilla extract

3 tablespoons light cream, at room temperature

Thin slices cut from this firm-textured, moderately sweet loaf are appealing served at breakfast with coffee or tea. The cake can also be paired with hot mulled cider for a warming snack. Dark seedless raisins, incorporated in the batter along with the shreds of apple, add a pleasant sweetness to each slice. If your raisins are not as moist as they should be, plump them up in hot apple juice or cider. Apple-Raisin Coffee Cake keeps nicely for a week stored in an airtight tin or cake-keeper.

Lightly butter and flour a 10 x 3¾ x 3-inch loaf pan; set aside. Preheat the oven to 350 degrees.

Sift together the flour, baking powder, baking soda, salt, cinnamon, nutmeg, and allspice onto a large sheet of waxed paper. Place the raisins in a small bowl and toss with 1 teaspoon of the sifted mixture.

Cream the butter in the large bowl of an electric mixer on moderately high speed for 2 to 3 minutes. Add the sugar in 2 additions, beating well for 1 to 2 minutes after each portion is added. Beat in the eggs, one at a time, blending well after each one. Scrape down the sides of the bowl with a rubber spatula and beat again for a few seconds. Blend in the vanilla and cream. With the mixer on low speed, add the sifted flour mixture, beating just until the particles of flour have been absorbed. By hand, stir in the apple and raisins. Spoon the batter into the prepared pan.

Bake the cake on the lower-third-level rack of the preheated

1 cup tightly packed
  peeled, cored, and
  shredded tart apple,
  such as Granny Smith

Confectioners' sugar for
  dusting, optional

One 10 x 3¾ x 3-inch loaf cake

oven for about 50 minutes, or until a wooden pick inserted into the center of the cake comes out clean and dry.

Let cool in the pan on a wire rack for 4 to 5 minutes. Invert onto a second cooling rack, then invert again to cool right side up. Dust the cooled loaf with sifted confectioners' sugar, if you like.

Serve the cake cut in medium thick slices.

Maple-Pumpkin Coffee Cake

2 cups *unsifted* all-purpose
flour

2 teaspoons baking
powder

¼ teaspoon baking soda

¼ teaspoon salt

1 teaspoon ground
cinnamon

¼ teaspoon freshly grated
nutmeg

¼ teaspoon ground
allspice

¼ teaspoon ground
ginger

⅛ teaspoon ground
cloves

⅓ cup chopped pecans

¼ cup dark seedless
raisins

4 tablespoons (½ stick)
unsalted butter, melted
and cooled

½ cup firmly packed light
brown sugar

¼ cup granulated sugar

2 extra-large eggs, at
room temperature

This rust-colored loaf cake has a soft texture and fine, delicate crumb. Slices seem made for pairing with hot, strong coffee and a warm fruit compote simmered with whole spices. It is also a good morning cake to serve with butter and jam. I love this cake because it is not too sweet. Sometimes, at Thanksgiving for instance, I sneak triangles of this cake into a bread basket already loaded with corn muffins and biscuits—and watch them disappear.

Lightly butter and flour a 10 x 3¾ x 3-inch loaf pan; set aside. Preheat the oven to 350 degrees.

Sift together the flour, baking powder, baking soda, salt, cinnamon, nutmeg, allspice, ginger, and cloves onto a large sheet of waxed paper. Place the pecans and raisins in a small bowl and toss with 2 teaspoons of the sifted mixture.

Stir together the melted butter, brown sugar, and granulated sugar in a large mixing bowl, using a wooden spoon. Beat in the eggs and vanilla. Blend in the maple syrup–milk mixture and the pumpkin puree. Add the sifted dry ingredients and stir with a wooden spoon. Fold in the floured pecans and raisins. Spoon the batter into the prepared pan.

Bake the cake on the lower-third-level rack of the preheated oven for about 45 minutes, or until the cake is well risen and plump and a wooden pick inserted into the center of the cake comes out clean and dry.

Let cool in the pan on a wire rack for 5 minutes. Invert onto a second cooling rack, then invert again to cool right side up.

2 teaspoons pure vanilla
extract

2 tablespoons pure maple
syrup blended with
2 tablespoons milk

1 cup unsweetened
pumpkin puree, fresh
(at right) or canned

Confectioners' sugar for
dusting, optional

One 10 x 3¾ x 3-inch loaf cake

Dust the top of the cooled cake with sifted confectioners' sugar, if you like.

Serve the cake cut in medium thick slices.

Homemade Pumpkin Puree

Cut a small pumpkin (4 to 5 pounds) in half, using a large knife or cleaver. Scoop out the pumpkin seeds with a spoon and discard them or clean off the filaments and roast the seeds in the oven (they are delicious to snack on). Cut the pumpkin flesh into very large chunks, roughly 3 inches square. Place the chunks in a steamer basket and steam over moderately high heat until the flesh has softened completely, about 15 minutes. Let cool completely. Scrape the flesh from the skin, then puree the flesh with a large pinch of salt in the work bowl of a food processor fitted with the steel knife or with a food mill or potato ricer. Spoon 1-cup quantities of the puree into sturdy storage containers. Press a piece of plastic wrap directly over the top, then seal with the lid. The puree will keep in the refrigerator for up to 1 week or in the freezer for up to 6 months.

Walnut–Sweet Potato Coffee Cake

2 cups *unsifted* all-purpose flour

2 teaspoons baking powder

¼ teaspoon baking soda

½ teaspoon salt

1 teaspoon ground cinnamon

½ teaspoon freshly grated nutmeg

¼ teaspoon ground allspice

¼ teaspoon ground ginger

½ cup chopped walnuts

4 tablespoons (½ stick) unsalted butter, melted and cooled

⅓ cup firmly packed light brown sugar

⅓ cup granulated sugar

2 extra-large eggs, at room temperature

2 tablespoons milk, at room temperature

A butter-rich cinnamon, walnut, and sugar topping caps off this modestly sweetened but amply spiced coffee cake. Serve it in thin slices at teatime, with dollops of cinnamon-flavored whipped cream.

Lightly butter and flour a 10 x 3¾ x 3-inch loaf pan; set aside. Preheat the oven to 350 degrees.

Sift together the flour, baking powder, baking soda, salt, cinnamon, nutmeg, allspice, and ginger onto a large sheet of waxed paper. Place the walnuts in a small bowl and toss with 1 teaspoon of the sifted mixture.

Stir together the melted butter, brown sugar, and granulated sugar in a large mixing bowl, using a wooden spoon or flat paddle. Beat in the eggs, one at a time, blending well after each one. Beat in the milk, cream, vanilla, orange rind, and pureed sweet potatoes. Add the sifted flour mixture and stir. Fold in the floured walnuts. Spoon the batter into the prepared pan.

For the topping, put the butter cubes, walnuts, sugar, and cinnamon in a small mixing bowl. Crumble the mixture together with your fingertips until the butter is broken down into small bits. Sprinkle the topping evenly over the top of the cake.

Bake the cake on the lower-third-level rack of the preheated oven for about 45 minutes, or until a wooden pick inserted into the center of the cake comes out clean and dry and the cake pulls away slightly from the edges of the pan.

- 2 tablespoons light cream, at room temperature
- 1 teaspoon pure vanilla extract
- 2 teaspoons finely grated orange rind
- 1 cup steamed and pureed sweet potatoes, at room temperature

FOR THE CINNAMON-WALNUT TOPPING:

- 2 tablespoons cold unsalted butter, cut into small cubes
- 4 tablespoons chopped walnuts
- 3 tablespoons granulated sugar
- 1 teaspoon ground cinnamon

One 10 x 3¾ x 3-inch loaf cake

Let cool in the pan on a wire rack for 5 minutes. Invert onto a second cooling rack, then invert again to cool right side up. Serve the cake cut in medium thick slices.

Banana-Coconut Coffee Cake

2 cups *unsifted* all-purpose flour

1 teaspoon baking powder

¼ teaspoon baking soda

¼ teaspoon salt

½ teaspoon ground cinnamon

½ teaspoon freshly grated nutmeg

¼ teaspoon ground allspice

¼ cup chopped unsalted pecans

½ cup (1 stick) unsalted butter, softened at room temperature

¾ cup firmly packed light brown sugar

1 extra-large egg plus 2 extra-large egg yolks, at room temperature

1 teaspoon pure vanilla extract

This loaf of many flavors is graced with chopped pecans, mashed bananas, and flaked coconut. Right before the cake is put into the oven to bake, I sprinkle the top with lightly toasted coconut. Banana-Coconut Coffee Cake makes a mighty fine munching cake, a sweet breakfast bread, or a lush tea cake when served with poached fresh fruit.

This is an old, treasured recipe of mine, based on my grandmother's banana-coconut bread. I add a little more butter than she did, and use brown sugar instead of granulated sugar; I also add ground cinnamon with the nutmeg and allspice. Then I like to top the loaf with lightly toasted coconut just before baking. Some twenty years ago, I baked fifty loaves of Banana-Coconut Coffee Cake for a country fair and not a crumb was left. I was inundated with requests for the recipe—so here it is!

Lightly butter and flour a 9 x 5 x 3-inch loaf pan; set aside. Preheat the oven to 350 degrees.

Sift together the flour, baking powder, baking soda, salt, cinnamon, nutmeg, and allspice onto a large sheet of waxed paper. Place the chopped pecans in a small bowl and toss with ½ teaspoon of the sifted flour mixture.

Cream the butter in the large bowl of an electric mixer on moderately high speed for 2 to 3 minutes. Add the brown sugar and continue beating for 1 to 2 minutes. Beat in the egg and egg yolks. Beat in the vanilla. Blend in the mashed bananas. With the mixer on low speed, add the sifted flour mix-

1½ cups mashed ripe
bananas (2 bananas)
½ cup sweetened flaked
coconut

FOR FINISHING THE CAKE:

¼ cup sweetened flaked
coconut, lightly toasted
(see Note)

One 9 x 5 x 3-inch loaf cake

ture in 2 additions, beating just until the particles of flour have been absorbed. By hand, stir in the pecans and shredded coconut. Spoon the batter into the prepared pan.

Sprinkle the top of the batter with the toasted coconut.

Bake the cake on the lower-third-level rack of the preheated oven for 50 to 55 minutes, or until well risen and a wooden pick inserted into the center of the cake comes out clean and dry. The cake will pull away slightly from the edges of the pan when done.

Let cool in the pan on a wire rack for 5 minutes. Invert onto a second cooling rack, then invert again to cool right side up.

Serve the cake cut in medium thick slices.

Note: To toast the coconut, preheat the oven to 350 degrees. Spread out the coconut on a small baking pan and place in the preheated oven. After about 4 to 5 minutes, the coconut should turn golden and fragrant. Remove from the oven and cool completely before using. Alternately, the coconut can be toasted under the broiler: Spread the coconut on a cookie sheet and place 4 inches from the broiler. After 1 minute, the coconut should be toasted. Watch carefully to avoid burning.

Raspberry Coffee Cake

2 cups *unsifted* cake flour

1 teaspoon baking powder

¾ teaspoon baking soda

¼ teaspoon salt

¼ teaspoon ground cinnamon

¼ teaspoon ground nutmeg

Pinch of ground allspice

1¼ cups fresh red raspberries, picked over

½ cup (1 stick) unsalted butter, softened at room temperature

½ cup plus 1 tablespoon Vanilla-Scented Granulated Sugar (page 219) or plain granulated sugar

1 extra-large egg plus 2 extra-large egg yolks, at room temperature

This is a soft, fresh-tasting coffee cake dressed up with red raspberries and energized by a trio of spices. Just before baking, the loaf is topped with a hazy wash of chopped walnuts, sugar, cinnamon, and butter. Serve warm slabs of this cake with English breakfast tea or tall, frosty glasses of iced lemon tea.

Lightly butter and flour a 9 x 5 x 3-inch loaf pan; set aside. Preheat the oven to 350 degrees.

Resift the flour with the baking powder, baking soda, salt, cinnamon, nutmeg, and allspice onto a large sheet of waxed paper. Place the raspberries in a bowl and carefully toss with 1 tablespoon of the sifted mixture.

Cream the butter in the large bowl of an electric mixer on moderately high speed for 2 minutes. Add the sugar and continue beating for 2 minutes longer. Beat in the egg and egg yolks and blend well. Scrape down the sides of the bowl with a rubber spatula, then beat for a moment or two longer. With the mixer on low speed, alternately add the sifted flour mixture in 2 additions and the yogurt-vanilla blend in 1 addition, beginning and ending with flour. By hand, fold in the floured raspberries. Spoon the batter into the prepared loaf pan.

For the topping, place the cold butter cubes, walnuts, sugar, and cinnamon in a mixing bowl. Crumble the mixture together with your fingertips until the butter is reduced to smaller bits. Sprinkle batter evenly with the topping.

¼ cup plain yogurt
  blended with
  2 teaspoons pure
  vanilla extract, at room
  temperature

FOR THE WALNUT TOPPING:

1 tablespoon cold
  unsalted butter, cut
  into small cubes

2½ tablespoons chopped
  walnuts

2 tablespoons granulated
  sugar

½ teaspoon ground
  cinnamon

One 9 x 5 x 3-inch loaf cake

Bake the cake on the lower-third-level rack of the preheated oven for about 45 minutes, or until a wooden pick inserted into the center of the cake comes out without any clinging particles of cake batter (the pick will be tinted pink if you bump into a raspberry).

Let cool in the pan on a wire rack for 4 to 5 minutes. Carefully invert onto a second cooling rack, then invert again to cool right side up.

Serve the cake cut in medium thick slices.

Date Coffee Cake

1¼ cups milk

1¾ cups coarsely
  chopped pitted dates

2½ cups *unsifted*
  all-purpose flour

1¾ teaspoons baking
  soda

¼ teaspoon salt

¾ teaspoon ground
  cinnamon

¼ teaspoon freshly grated
  nutmeg

¼ teaspoon ground
  allspice

¾ cup chopped walnuts

2 jumbo egg yolks, at
  room temperature

3 tablespoons unsalted
  butter, melted and
  cooled

2 teaspoons pure vanilla
  extract

¾ cup granulated sugar

½ cup firmly packed light
  brown sugar

One 9 x 5 x 3-inch loaf cake

A long-keeping, firm-textured coffee cake such as this is a fine thing to have in the cake tin. It combines several textures and tastes: chewy dates and crunchy walnuts, the caramel flavor of brown sugar, and a whiff of cinnamon and nutmeg. The dates —sticky, rich, and sweet—keep this cake moist and fresh-tasting for some time; the cake stores perfectly at room temperature (I keep the loaf in my bread box). Slices of Date Coffee Cake can keep company with large cups of spiced cider, hot coffee, or orange tea.

This recipe is from my Aunt Mamie, who made this loaf every weekend. I have made a few small changes in the original recipe, such as adding a little more brown sugar and cinnamon to the batter. Freshly ground nutmeg, of which she added only a pinch, has been upgraded to ¼ teaspoon.

Lightly butter and flour a 9 x 5 x 3-inch loaf pan; set aside. Preheat the oven to 350 degrees.

Heat the milk in a saucepan until tepid. Place the dates in a large bowl, pour the milk over them, and let stand for 20 minutes. Sift together the flour, baking soda, salt, cinnamon, nutmeg, and allspice onto a large sheet of waxed paper. Place the walnuts in a small bowl and toss with 1 teaspoon of the sifted flour mixture.

Beat together the egg yolks, melted butter, vanilla, and granulated sugar in a large mixing bowl, using a wooden spoon or paddle. Beat in the brown sugar. Stir in the milk-date mixture. Stir in the sifted flour mixture in 2 additions, stirring just until the particles of flour have been absorbed before adding the next batch of flour. Fold in the walnuts. Spoon the batter into the prepared pan.

Bake the cake on the lower-third-level rack of the preheated oven for 50 minutes to 1 hour, or until a wooden pick inserted into the center of the loaf comes out clean and dry. The cake will pull away slightly from the sides of the pan when done.

Let the cake cool in the pan on a wire rack for 4 to 5 minutes. Invert onto a second cooling rack, then invert again to cool right side up.

Serve the cake cut in moderately thin slices.

Caramel Upside-Down Sticky Cake

FOR THE DOUGH:

1 package (1 scant tablespoon) active dry yeast

¼ cup granulated sugar

1 teaspoon salt

3¼ cups *unsifted* all-purpose flour, plus extra flour as necessary

⅓ cup water

⅓ cup light cream

½ cup (1 stick) unsalted butter, cut into chunks

2 extra-large egg yolks, at room temperature

1 teaspoon pure vanilla extract

¼ teaspoon freshly ground nutmeg

FOR THE STICKY MIXTURE:

2 tablespoons unsalted butter

¼ cup light corn syrup

Sticky cake is a light, yeasty cake. Puffy dough is rolled into a large square, slathered with softened butter, and sprinkled with spiced sugar, then rolled into a fat sausage and cut in thick pieces. These soft packages of dough are then laid in a square pan filled with heavy caramel syrup. The syrup is sticky and buttery, and you can scatter such things as chopped pecans, walnuts, or shredded coconut on it before setting in the spirals of dough. The dough for this cake is a pleasure to work with; it's silky to the touch, rolls out magnificently, and can be fashioned into any number of shapes, even freestanding tea rings or twists. A warm piece of sticky cake makes as fine a Sunday morning breakfast treat as anyone could imagine.

For the dough, thoroughly combine the yeast, sugar, salt, and 2 cups of flour in a large mixing bowl. Put water, cream, and butter into a small saucepan and heat until the liquid reaches a temperature of 125 degrees (warm to the touch). Remove from the heat and pour over the flour mixture. Add the egg yolks, vanilla, and nutmeg. Stir everything together with a wooden spoon or paddle. With your hands, work in the remaining flour, a little at a time, to form a soft dough. Turn the dough onto a lightly floured work surface and knead until it is supple and satiny, about 7 to 8 minutes. Place the dough in a buttered bowl, turning several times to coat it lightly in butter. Cover loosely with a sheet of plastic wrap or a tea towel and let rise in a draft-free spot until doubled in bulk, about 1½ to 2 hours.

¼ cup firmly packed light brown sugar

3 tablespoons granulated sugar

FOR THE CINNAMON-SUGAR FILLING:

3 tablespoons unsalted butter, softened at room temperature

½ cup granulated sugar

1 tablespoon firmly packed light brown sugar

1 tablespoon ground cinnamon

¼ teaspoon freshly grated nutmeg

One 10-inch square pull-apart cake

While the dough is rising, make the sticky mixture. Spray a 10-inch square baking pan with vegetable-oil cooking spray; set aside. Place the butter, corn syrup, brown sugar, and granulated sugar in a small, heavy saucepan. Cover the pan and set over low heat. Cook until every granule of sugar has dissolved, about 10 minutes. Uncover the pot, raise the heat to moderately high, and boil for 1½ to 2 minutes, or until lightly thickened. Pour into the prepared baking pan.

Punch down the risen dough in the bowl. Turn it out onto a lightly floured work surface and let it rest for 5 minutes. Using a lightly floured rolling pin, roll out the dough into a rough square, about 13 x 13 inches. Spread the softened butter over the surface of the dough. Combine the granulated sugar, brown sugar, cinnamon, and nutmeg in a small bowl; sprinkle over the butter. Roll up the dough tightly, like a jelly roll. Cut into 9 equal pieces with a sharp knife. Arrange the pieces, cut side up, 3 to a row, in the caramel-lined baking pan. Cover loosely and let rise in a draft-free spot until doubled in bulk, about 1½ to 2 hours. The individual rounds of dough will rise together to form a solid cake.

About 20 minutes before the end of the rising time, preheat the oven to 375 degrees. Bake the cake on the lower-third-level rack of the preheated oven for about 30 minutes, or until golden on top and baked through (a wooden pick inserted into one section of the cake should come out clean).

Let stand in the pan on a cooling rack for 1 minute, then invert the cake onto a serving plate.

Serve the cake warm or at room temperature, sticky side up; let everyone pull apart a portion.

TRAVELING CAKES

Wendy Wheeler

TRAVELING CAKES

———— ❖❖❖ ————

Blueberry–Walnut–Brown Sugar Buckle   194
Chocolate Pan Cake with Chocolate Fudge Frosting   196
Pecan Carrot Cake with Raisins   198
Fudgy Chocolate–Walnut Cake   200

*F*or leisurely bring-a-dish suppers, when guests are encouraged to contribute part of the meal, a delicious cake, made entirely in advance, is just the thing. I call these portable goodies traveling cakes for their ability to withstand bumpy road trips and still look fresh. They are baked in simple square, rectangular, or round baking pans and are left in the pan until cut at serving time. Oftentimes at flea markets and tag sales or antique shows featuring Americana artifacts, you'll come across old baking tins with snap-on lids for traveling; the domed lid, used to cover an iced or uniced cake, protects it during transportation. Traveling cakes are easy to make, they appeal to children and grown-ups alike, and they use ingredients that even casual bakers have on hand. Their rough-and-ready nature makes it possible to transport them easily.

Other cakes that are well suited to packing in a picnic hamper or slicing and tucking into a lunch box are Best Vanilla Pound Cake (page 218), Lemon–Poppy Seed Pound Cake (page 222), Chocolate Pound Cake (page 232), Bourbon Pound Cake (page 224), Spice Pound Cake (page 226), Cream Pound Cake (page 230), Spicy Apple Cake (page 240), Blueberry Gingerbread (page 246), Ginger Cakes (page 254), Blueberry Cakes (page 256), Cream Cheese–Chocolate Chip Cakes (page 258), Vanilla Cakes (page 260), Coconut-Cinnamon Pan Cake (page 174), Apple-Raisin Coffee Cake (page 176), Maple-Pumpkin Coffee Cake (page 178), Banana-Coconut Coffee Cake (page 182), Date Coffee Cake (page 186), and Plum Cake (page 238).

Blueberry–Walnut–Brown Sugar Buckle

1¾ cups *unsifted* all-purpose flour

3 teaspoons baking powder

½ teaspoon salt

½ teaspoon ground cinnamon

¼ teaspoon freshly grated nutmeg

¼ teaspoon ground allspice

⅔ cup blueberries, picked over

½ cup (1 stick) unsalted butter, softened at room temperature

¼ cup firmly packed light brown sugar

¼ cup granulated sugar

2 extra-large eggs, at room temperature

2 teaspoons pure vanilla extract

1 cup milk, at room temperature

This cake tastes of summer: plump blueberries, sweet and fruity, dot a buttery square cake. The batter contains a fair measure of brown sugar, which enhances the taste of blueberries, and a restrained trio of spices. The buckle is best eaten very fresh and still warm, while the sandy topping is still soft. Homemade lemonade is a natural partner.

Lightly butter and flour a 9-inch square baking pan. Line the bottom of the pan with a square of waxed paper; set aside. Preheat the oven to 350 degrees.

Sift together the flour, baking powder, salt, cinnamon, nutmeg, and allspice onto a large sheet of waxed paper. Place the blueberries in a bowl and toss with 1 tablespoon of the sifted mixture.

Cream the butter in the large bowl of an electric mixer on moderately high speed for 2 minutes. Add the brown sugar and granulated sugar; beat for 2 minutes. Beat in the eggs, one at a time, blending well after each one. Scrape down the sides of the bowl with a rubber spatula and beat again for a few moments longer. Blend in the vanilla. With the mixer on low speed, alternately add the sifted dry ingredients in 3 additions and the milk in 2 additions, beginning and ending with the dry mixture. Fold in the blueberries. Spoon the batter into the prepared pan.

To make the crumble, put the butter, walnuts, sugar, and cinnamon in a mixing bowl. Crumble everything together with your fingertips until the butter is reduced to small bits. Sprinkle the crumble evenly over the top of the batter.

FOR THE WALNUT—BROWN
SUGAR CRUMBLE TOPPING:

2 tablespoons cold
  unsalted butter, cut
  into cubes

¼ cup chopped walnuts

3 tablespoons firmly
  packed light brown
  sugar

1 teaspoon ground
  cinnamon

Confectioners' sugar for
  dusting, optional

One 9-inch square cake

Bake the cake on the lower-third-level rack of the preheated oven for 45 to 50 minutes, or until a wooden pick inserted in the center comes out without any particles of cake clinging to it. The cake will shrink slightly from the sides of the pan when done.

Let cool in the pan on a wire rack. Transport the cake as is or invert it onto a second cooling rack, peel away the waxed paper, and invert again onto a serving plate. Dust the top of the cake with a little sifted confectioners' sugar, if you like.

Serve the cake cut in squares.

Chocolate Pan Cake with Chocolate Fudge Frosting

The formula for this cake is really a conspiracy of chocolate. The chocolate cake is light and creamy, and while it is still oven-hot, it is completely covered over with a dense, rich fudge frosting flecked with plenty of chopped pecans. Children love big squares of this cake with a glass of cold milk. The recipe comes from my friend and good cook Alice Romejko, who likes to serve the cake at buffet suppers.

FOR THE CAKE:

1 cup (2 sticks) unsalted butter, cut in rough chunks

4 tablespoons *unsifted* unsweetened cocoa powder

1 cup water

2 cups granulated sugar

2 cups *unsifted* cake flour

1 teaspoon salt

1/2 cup buttermilk blended with 1 teaspoon baking soda, at room temperature

2 extra-large eggs, at room temperature

1 1/2 teaspoons pure vanilla extract

Lightly butter and flour a 9 x 13 x 2-inch cake pan; set aside. Preheat the oven to 400 degrees.

For the cake, place the butter, cocoa, and water in a large saucepan, set over moderately high heat, and bring to a boil. Remove from the heat. Sift together the sugar, flour, and salt into the large bowl of an electric mixer. Whisk together the buttermilk, eggs, and vanilla in a mixing bowl. Pour the hot butter-cocoa-water mixture over the sifted dry mixture and beat on moderate speed until thoroughly blended. Add the whisked egg mixture and continue beating on low speed until the batter is a uniform color, about 1 1/2 minutes. Pour and scrape the batter into the prepared pan.

Bake the cake on the lower-third-level rack of the preheated oven for 20 to 22 minutes, or until a wooden pick inserted into the center of the cake comes out clean and dry and the cake shrinks away slightly from the edges of the pan.

About 10 minutes before the cake is done, make the fudge frosting. Place the butter, chocolate, milk, and cream in a large saucepan, set over low heat, and cook, stirring occasion-

**FOR THE CHOCOLATE
FUDGE FROSTING:**

½ cup (1 stick) unsalted
butter, cut in chunks

2 ounces (2 squares)
unsweetened
chocolate, chopped

5 tablespoons milk, at
room temperature

1 tablespoon light cream,
at room temperature

1 box (1 pound)
confectioners' sugar,
sifted

1 teaspoon pure vanilla
extract

Pinch of salt

1 cup chopped pecans

One 9 x 13-inch cake

ally, until the chocolate has melted down completely. Remove from the heat and beat in the sugar by cupfuls with the vanilla and salt. Blend in the pecans.

As soon as the cake is done, remove it from the oven to a wire cooling rack. Immediately spread the frosting evenly over the top with a flexible palette knife. Let the cake cool in the pan.

For serving, cut the cake in squares directly from the cake pan.

Note: I use 1 teaspoon more vanilla in the cake batter than Alice's recipe calls for and a mixture of milk and light cream in the frosting. For the frosting, you can use all milk (6 tablespoons), if you like.

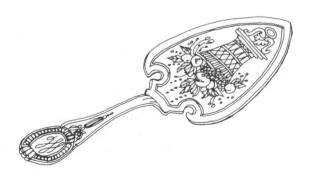

Pecan Carrot Cake with Raisins

1½ cups plus 2 table-
  spoons *unsifted* cake
  flour
1½ teaspoons baking
  powder
1 teaspoon baking soda
¼ teaspoon salt
1½ teaspoons ground
  cinnamon
1 teaspoon freshly grated
  nutmeg
½ teaspoon ground
  allspice
¼ teaspoon ground
  cloves
¾ cup chopped pecans
¾ cup dark seedless
  raisins
½ cup (1 stick) unsalted
  butter, melted and
  cooled
½ cup firmly packed light
  brown sugar
½ cup granulated sugar
1 extra-large egg plus
  2 extra-large egg yolks

Laced with pecans and raisins, this cake is moist and flavorful; the thin carrot shreds virtually melt down in the batter as the cake bakes, creating a crumb that is soft and golden. Cinnamon is the top note of spices, supported by nutmeg, allspice, and cloves. The top of the cake is covered with a thick mantle of simple vanilla cream frosting. Lightly toasted chopped pecans can be sprinkled over the icing once it has set up, if you like.

Lightly butter and flour a 9-inch round springform pan; set aside. Preheat the oven to 350 degrees.

Sift together the flour, baking powder, baking soda, salt, cinnamon, nutmeg, allspice, and cloves into a large mixing bowl. Place the pecans and raisins in a bowl and toss with 1 tablespoon of the sifted mixture.

Whisk together the butter, brown sugar, granulated sugar, egg, egg yolks, vanilla, milk, and cream in a medium-size bowl. Make a large well in the center of the dry ingredients, pour in the whisked mixture, and stir with a wooden spoon until a smooth batter is formed. Fold in the walnuts, raisins, and shredded carrots. Spoon the batter into the prepared pan.

Bake the cake on the lower-third-level rack of the preheated oven for about 45 minutes, or until a wooden pick inserted in the center of the cake comes out clean and dry and the cake pulls away slightly from edges of the pan.

Let the cake cool in the pan on a wire rack.

For the Vanilla Cream Frosting, place the butter, heavy

2 teaspoons pure vanilla
extract

¾ cup milk, at room
temperature

¼ cup light cream, at
room temperature

1½ cups shredded carrots
(about 3 carrots)

FOR THE VANILLA CREAM
FROSTING:

2 tablespoons unsalted
butter, softened at
room temperature

2 tablespoons heavy
cream, at room
temperature

½ teaspoon pure vanilla
extract

About 1½ cups
confectioners' sugar,
sifted, or more as
needed

One 9-inch round cake

cream, vanilla, and ¾ cup of the confectioners' sugar in a small bowl. Beat with a handheld mixer on moderate speed for 2 to 3 minutes. Add the remaining ¾ cup of confectioners' sugar, several tablespoons at a time, beating well after each addition, to make a firm but spreadable frosting. Add up to ¼ cup more confectioners' sugar, if needed, to make the frosting thick and spreadable.

Remove the hinged ring from the cake pan. Swirl the frosting over the top of the cooled cake. To transport the cake, you can replace the ring once the icing has firmed up.

Serve the cake cut in large wedges.

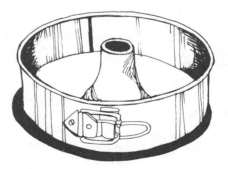

Fudgy Chocolate–Walnut Cake

4 ounces (4 squares) unsweetened chocolate, chopped

½ cup (1 stick) unsalted butter, cut into chunks

⅔ cup *unsifted* cake flour

¼ teaspoon baking powder

½ teaspoon salt

1 jumbo egg plus 2 jumbo egg yolks, at room temperature

2 teaspoons pure vanilla extract

1 teaspoon chocolate extract

1 cup plus 3 tablespoons Vanilla-Scented Granulated Sugar (page 219)

¾ cup chopped walnuts

Confectioners' sugar for dusting, optional

One 8-inch round cake

This thin chocolate cake has been in my cake file for many cake-baking years. I inherited the recipe from my grandmother; she frequently substituted black walnuts for the more subtle English variety. I make this cake often when what I want is a fudgy sweet that's quick to put together. I have served wedges of the cake with many different accompaniments—vanilla custard sauce, red raspberries and whipped cream, vanilla ice cream with hot fudge sauce. Just for fun, try folding in a cup of chopped thin mints (the candy with a mint layer sandwiched between two chocolate layers) or the same amount of diced caramels with the walnuts.

———❖❖❖———

Lightly butter and flour an 8-inch round cake pan. Line the pan with a round of waxed paper; set aside. Preheat the oven to 350 degrees.

Place the chopped chocolate and butter chunks in a small saucepan and set over low heat. Cook, stirring occasionally, until the chocolate and butter have melted down completely. Set aside to cool.

Stir together the flour, baking powder, and salt in a small bowl. Beat the egg and egg yolks with a whisk for 1 minute in a large mixing bowl. Blend in the vanilla and chocolate extracts. Blend in the sugar, beating for 1 minute or until just combined. Stir in the cooled chocolate mixture. Stir in the flour, mixing just until the particles of flour have been absorbed. Fold in ½ cup of the walnuts. Spoon the batter into the prepared pan. Spread the batter evenly in the pan. Sprinkle the remaining ¼ cup of walnuts evenly over the top.

Bake the cake on the lower-third-level rack of the preheated oven for 40 to 45 minutes, until just set; a wooden pick inserted 1 inch from the center will come out damp.

Let cool in the pan on a wire rack until the cake reaches room temperature. Carefully run a thin, flexible palette knife between the edges of the cake and the pan, then invert onto a second cooling rack. Peel away the round of waxed paper. Invert again onto a decorative plate, nut side up. Dust the top of the cake with sifted confectioners' sugar, if you like.

Serve the cake cut in wedges.

TEATIME
UPSIDE-DOWN
CAKES

Wendy Wheeler

TEATIME UPSIDE-DOWN CAKES

————————❖❖❖————————

Peach Upside-Down Cake   206
Spiced Nectarine Upside-Down Cake   208
Apple-Ginger Upside-Down Cake   210

*O*ne of the most enchanting teatimes I can remember was at a cottage hidden in the Virginia countryside. I arrived one late-summer afternoon, just as the hostess was setting up tea and cakes in the garden. It was a rambling kind of garden, full of fruit trees, shade trees, ornamental plantings, and herbs. Tea was offered in pretty floral-patterned china cups, and we tasted a variety of upside-down cakes made from ripe fruit picked just steps away from the kitchen door.

A slice of fresh fruit cake and a cup of hot tea or a tall glass of iced tea can be a marvelous summertime refreshment. And with recipes at hand for Peach Upside-Down Cake (page 206), Spiced Nectarine Upside-Down Cake (page 208), and Apple-Ginger Upside-Down Cake (page 210), you can bring a little bit of the country into your home. Remember that fresh fruit cakes are best eaten warm. That's when the full, sprightly flavor of the fruit comes through best. Fruited upside-down cakes, cut into neat wedges, taste good with dollops of lightly sweetened whipped cream spooned on top.

Peach Upside-Down Cake

FOR PREPARING THE FRUIT:

2 large peaches

1 tablespoon lemon juice

3 tablespoons unsalted butter

¼ cup firmly packed light brown sugar

FOR THE CAKE BATTER:

1½ cups *unsifted* cake flour

1½ teaspoons baking powder

¼ teaspoon salt

½ teaspoon ground cinnamon

½ teaspoon freshly grated nutmeg

½ cup (1 stick) unsalted butter, softened at room temperature

½ cup granulated sugar

1 jumbo egg, at room temperature

2 teaspoons pure vanilla extract

For this cake, a circle of peach slices is placed atop a buttery brown-sugar base, then a batter flavored with ground cinnamon and freshly grated nutmeg gets poured over it all. The texture of the batter is creamy and silky, like a fluid buttercream, so it bakes into a soft, fine-grained cake. Match warm slices of cake with tall glasses of lemonade, minted lemon tea, or cream-lightened iced coffee for a refreshing midsummer teatime snack.

———❖❖❖———

Lightly butter an 8-inch round cake pan; set aside. Preheat the oven to 400 degrees.

Peel the peaches (dip first in boiling water, then in cold water for easier peeling); slice ¾ inch thick. Toss with lemon juice and set aside. Heat the butter and brown sugar in a small saucepan over moderately low heat until the sugar has melted down and the mixture bubbles gently. Pour into the cake pan. Arrange the peach slices on top.

Sift together the flour, baking powder, salt, cinnamon, and nutmeg onto a large sheet of waxed paper. Cream the butter in the large bowl of an electric mixer on moderately high speed for 2 minutes. Add the sugar and continue beating for a minute longer. Beat in the egg, vanilla extract, and almond extract. With the mixer on low speed, alternately add the sifted flour mixture in 2 additions and the milk in 1 addition, beginning and ending with flour. Spoon the batter evenly over the peaches.

Bake the cake on the lower-third-level rack of the preheated

½ teaspoon pure almond
   extract
½ cup milk, at room
   temperature

One 8-inch round cake

oven for about 30 to 35 minutes, or until the cake is golden on top and a wooden pick inserted into the cake comes out clean and dry.

Let cool in the pan on a wire rack for 3 to 4 minutes. Loosen the cake by running a thin, flexible palette knife between the cake and the edge of the pan. Invert onto a shallow, lipped serving plate, fruit side up.

Serve the cake warm, cut in thick wedges.

Note: Two ripe pears, peeled and sliced, may be substituted for the peaches. Leave out the almond extract and add ½ teaspoon ground ginger with the spices.

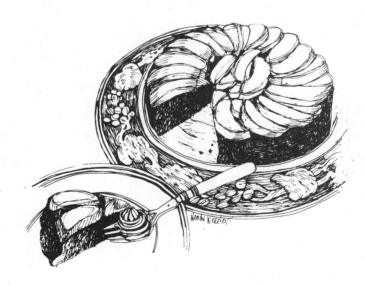

Spiced Nectarine Upside-Down Cake

FOR PREPARING THE FRUIT:

2 tablespoons unsalted butter, melted

⅓ cup granulated sugar blended with ½ teaspoon ground cinnamon

2 large or 3 small ripe nectarines, halved, pitted, and sliced ¾ inch thick, tossed in 1 tablespoon lemon juice

FOR THE CAKE BATTER:

1⅓ cups *sifted* all-purpose flour

½ teaspoon baking soda

¾ teaspoon ground cinnamon

¼ teaspoon ground ginger

¼ teaspoon freshly grated nutmeg

¼ teaspoon salt

This upside-down cake is light and moist, and light molasses gives it a certain depth of color and taste. Molasses and brown sugar make a good combination with spices such as ginger, cinnamon, and nutmeg for cakes that feature fresh fruit like nectarines and peaches. Served with a pitcher of cold lemonade or mint-spiked tea and a bowl of sweetened whipped cream, slices of this cake will get you through the hot, sun-drenched days of summer.

Lightly butter an 8-inch round baking pan. Preheat the oven to 350 degrees. Pour the melted butter on the bottom of the pan and sprinkle evenly with cinnamon sugar. Arrange the nectarine slices over the sugar in a pleasing pattern. Set aside.

Sift the flour with the baking soda, cinnamon, ginger, nutmeg, and salt onto a large sheet of waxed paper. Cream the butter and shortening in the large bowl of an electric mixer on moderately high speed for 2 minutes. Beat in the brown sugar. Blend in the vanilla, egg, and molasses. With the mixer on low speed, alternately add the sifted flour mixture in 2 additions and the buttermilk in 1 addition, beginning and ending with flour. Spoon the batter evenly over the fruit.

Bake the cake on the lower-third-level rack of the preheated oven for 35 to 40 minutes, or until a wooden pick inserted in the cake comes out clean and dry and the cake pulls away slightly from the sides of the baking pan.

2 tablespoons unsalted
butter, softened at
room temperature

2 tablespoons shortening

¼ cup firmly packed light
brown sugar

2 teaspoons pure vanilla
extract

1 extra-large egg, at room
temperature

⅓ cup light molasses

½ cup plus 2 tablespoons
buttermilk, at room
temperature

One 8-inch round cake

Let cool in the pan on a wire rack for 3 to 4 minutes. Loosen the cake by running a thin, flexible palette knife between the cake and the edges of the pan. Invert onto a shallow, lipped serving plate, fruit side up.

Serve the cake warm or tepid, cut in thick wedges.

Apple-Ginger Upside-Down Cake

FOR PREPARING THE FRUIT:

2 tablespoons unsalted butter, melted

¼ cup granulated sugar blended with ¼ teaspoon ground ginger and ¼ teaspoon ground cinnamon

1 large tart cooking apple, peeled, cored, and sliced ¼ inch thick, tossed in 1 tablespoon lemon juice

1 tablespoon chopped ginger preserved in syrup, well drained

FOR THE CAKE BATTER:

1⅓ cups *unsifted* all-purpose flour

¾ teaspoon baking powder

¼ teaspoon salt

½ teaspoon ground ginger

Apples turn soft and satiny when cooked under a blanket of cake batter. In this cake, a spiral of apple slices sits on a bed of cinnamon-ginger sugar and butter, which get absorbed as the cake bakes. During the fall—when crisp cooking apples proliferate at farm markets, country fruit stands, and food cooperatives—I make all kinds of apple desserts (pies, cobblers, and cakes), as well as several different kinds of apple butter. I usually serve this cake after a brisk afternoon of leaf gathering. Warm slices of Apple-Ginger Upside-Down Cake are delicious served together with whipped cream sweetened with apple-cider syrup or maple syrup and spiced with a dash of ground ginger.

———❖❖❖———

Lightly butter an 8-inch round baking pan. Preheat the oven to 350 degrees. Pour the melted butter on the bottom of the pan and sprinkle evenly with the cinnamon-ginger sugar. Arrange the apple slices over the sugar, overlapping them in a spiral pattern. Sprinkle the chopped ginger on top. Set aside.

Sift the flour with the baking powder, salt, ground ginger, nutmeg, cinnamon, and cloves onto a large sheet of waxed paper. Cream the shortening and butter in the large bowl of an electric mixer on moderately high speed for 1 to 2 minutes. Beat in the brown sugar and vanilla. Blend in the egg and maple syrup and beat for 1 minute longer. With the mixer on low speed, alternately add the sifted flour mixture in 2 additions and the milk in 1 addition, beginning and ending with the flour. Spoon the batter evenly over the apples.

¼ teaspoon freshly grated nutmeg

¼ teaspoon ground cinnamon

Pinch of ground cloves

3 tablespoons shortening

1 tablespoon unsalted butter, softened at room temperature

¼ cup firmly packed light brown sugar

2 teaspoons pure vanilla extract

1 extra-large egg, at room temperature

½ cup maple syrup

½ cup plus 1 tablespoon milk, at room temperature

One 8-inch round cake

Bake the cake on the lower-third-level rack of the preheated oven for 35 to 40 minutes, or until a wooden pick inserted in the cake comes out clean and dry and the cake pulls away slightly from the sides of the pan.

Let cool in the pan on a wire rack for 3 to 4 minutes. Loosen the cake by running a thin, flexible palette knife between the cake and edges of the pan. Invert onto a shallow, lipped serving plate, fruit side up.

Serve the cake warm, cut in thick wedges.

POUND
CAKES

Wendy Wheeler

POUND CAKES

————◈◈◈————

Best Vanilla Pound Cake   218
Grandma Lilly's Hot Milk Cake   220
Lemon–Poppy Seed Pound Cake   222
Bourbon Pound Cake   224
Spice Pound Cake   226
Rich Nut Pound Cake   228
Cream Pound Cake   230
Chocolate Pound Cake   232

The pound cakes I love to make are those spiced and flavored butter cakes that taste so good with berries, sliced fruit in season, stewed fruit compotes, a scoop or two of homemade ice cream, or a hot, sweet sauce, such as lemon or chocolate. For these cakes especially, I use farm-fresh eggs from free-ranging hens; the orange-yellow yolks turn the batter a golden color and add to the rich taste of the baked cake.

My pound cakes, or keeping cakes, are made with pure extracts, the seed scrapings from vanilla beans, good baking chocolate, and fresh nuts. The batters are leavened by many eggs, as well as baking powder or baking soda or both. The baking powder and soda, I have discovered over the years, keep the batter light, even with the large amount of butter that is used to enrich the cake. I like my pound cakes to be substantial, yet fine-grained, with a tender, delicate crumb, and I have modified many of the old recipes in my file to achieve that effect.

Pound cake is a joy to have on hand in the cake-keeper, ready to be sliced and served. I think that some of my pound cakes, especially the Best Vanilla Pound Cake (page 218), Spice Pound Cake (page 226), and Cream Pound Cake (page 230), thinly sliced, also make a luxurious addition to the breakfast bread basket.

Whenever I serve pound cake, I always seem to have a bowl of fruit and some whipped cream nearby. The buttery flavor of the cake does blend nicely with the tangy, sweet-sour taste of most any kind of fruit—a mound of mixed berries, lightly poached and spiced pears, cinnamon-seasoned apple wedges sautéed in butter and moistened with spoonfuls of apple cider, or a toss of perfectly ripe sliced peaches, nectarines, and plums.

A syrup spiked with citrus juice is a good thing to keep in the refrigerator for enhancing summer fruits. It goes beautifully with chunks of melon, whole berries, and sliced fruit, adding a sweet, glossy finish. The syrup is simple to make and, stored in the refrigerator, remains fresh-tasting for up to six months.

Fresh Fruit Splash

To make the splash, place 1 cup water and ¾ cup granulated sugar in a small stainless steel saucepan. Cover the pan, set over low heat, and cook until every last granule of sugar has dissolved. Uncover the pan, raise the heat to moderately high, and bring the liquid to a boil. Boil for 10 minutes. Stir in 1 teaspoon finely grated orange peel, ½ teaspoon finely grated lemon peel, ¼ cup freshly squeezed orange juice, and 2 tablespoons freshly squeezed lemon juice. Simmer for 10 minutes. Stir in ¼ cup Grand Marnier and 2 tablespoons Cointreau. Boil 1 minute, then remove from heat. Let cool to room temperature. Pour the cooled syrup into a storage container and seal tightly.

Spoon Fresh Fruit Splash over ripe peach slices and serve with slices of Best Vanilla Pound Cake (page 218); moisten a heap of red raspberries with a few tablespoons of splash and serve with thick slices of Chocolate Pound Cake (page 232); or combine blueberries, blackberries, raspberries, and black raspberries with several spoonfuls of splash and serve with slices of Cream Pound Cake (page 230).

Best Vanilla
Pound Cake

3 cups *unsifted* all-purpose
flour

½ teaspoon baking
powder

¾ teaspoon salt

1½ cups (3 sticks)
unsalted butter,
softened at room
temperature

2¾ cups Vanilla-Scented
Granulated Sugar (see
recipe below)

Seed scrapings from
1 vanilla bean

5 jumbo eggs, at room
temperature

1½ tablespoons pure
vanilla extract

1 cup milk, at room
temperature

Confectioners' sugar for
dusting, optional

One 10-inch tube cake

What is more inviting than the scent of a freshly baked pound cake, pure gold and rich in eggs and butter? My finest pound cake recipe, this one, is flavored with pure vanilla extract and the seeds scraped out of a plump vanilla bean. The minuscule vanilla seeds dot the baked cake. Slices of Best Vanilla Pound Cake taste heavenly when served with poached fruit, pears or peaches, for example, or with a heap of fresh berries seasoned with a little fresh fruit syrup—or with cool dips of Coconut Ice Cream (page 271). Don't forget to hide away a quarter of the pound cake to savor at breakfast, thinly sliced and lightly toasted, then slathered with jam. It's perfect with your morning coffee.

———❖❖❖———

Lightly butter and flour a plain 10-inch tube pan or a 10-inch fluted Bundt pan; set aside. Preheat the oven to 325 degrees.

Resift the flour with the baking powder and salt onto a large sheet of waxed paper. Cream the butter in the large bowl of an electric mixer on moderately high speed for 3 minutes. Beat in the sugar in 3 additions, beating for 1 minute after each portion has been added. Blend in the vanilla bean scrapings. Beat on high speed for 1 to 2 minutes. With the mixer on moderate speed, beat in the eggs, one at a time, blending well after each one; scrape down the sides of the mixing bowl frequently to keep the mixture even textured. With the mixer on low speed, alternately add the flour mixture in 3 additions and the milk in 2 additions, beginning and ending with flour. Pour and scrape the batter into the pre-pared pan.

Bake the cake on the lower-third-level rack of the preheated oven for 1 hour and 10 minutes to 1 hour and 15 minutes, or until golden on top and a wooden pick inserted in the middle of the cake comes out clean and dry.

Let cool in the pan on a wire rack for 10 minutes. Gently loosen the sides of the cake from the pan with a thin, flexible palette knife. Invert onto a second cooling rack, then invert again to cool right side up. Dust the top of the cake with sifted confectioners' sugar, if you like.

Serve the cake cut in thin slices.

Note: To get the seeds from the bean, slash it lengthwise with a sharp paring knife, then run the tip of a teaspoon down the middle of each half to scoop out the seeds.

Vanilla-Scented Granulated Sugar or Vanilla-Scented Confectioners' Sugar

Slit 3 vanilla beans lengthwise to expose the tiny seeds. Bury the beans in 3 pounds of granulated or confectioners' sugar in a large glass jar. Make sure that the sugar covers the beans completely. Let the beans steep in the sugar for at least 1 week before using it to sweeten cake batters, cookie dough, or ice cream mixtures. Store the sugar, covered airtight, at cool room temperature.

Grandma Lilly's Hot Milk Cake

½ cup (1 stick) unsalted butter

1 cup milk

2 cups *unsifted* cake flour

¼ teaspoon salt

4 extra-large eggs, at room temperature

2 cups granulated sugar

1 teaspoon pure vanilla extract

1 teaspoon baking powder

Confectioners' sugar for dusting, optional

_____

One 9-inch tube cake

My grandmother was famous for this cake. She baked it every week in her Georgetown kitchen and served it with things like sweetened raspberries and strawberries, caramelized apples and pears, or homemade ice cream with hot fudge sauce. As cake recipes go, the procedure for this one may strike you as strange. The method is a bit unconventional, but it does work. The milk and butter are heated to boiling hot and added almost at the end of the recipe; then the baking powder is added all by itself. As soon as it is beaten into the batter, the whole lot is poured into the pan and rushed into the oven. What emerges is a light and buttery cake, with a fine, exceptionally moist crumb.

One word of nostalgic advice: It was always considered bad luck in our family to rattle anything in the kitchen while this cake was baking, lest it sink mysteriously. I still always leave the kitchen for the first 40 minutes, at least, of baking time. Not that I'm superstitious, of course.

———❖❖❖———

Lightly butter and flour a plain 9-inch tube pan. (Do not use a tube pan with a removable bottom; the cake batter will seep out.) Set aside. Preheat the oven to 350 degrees.

Place the butter and milk in a large saucepan and bring to the boil over moderate heat. Sift the cake flour with the salt onto a large sheet of waxed paper. Beat the eggs in the large bowl of an electric mixer on moderately high speed for 2 to 3 minutes. With the mixer on moderate speed, beat in the sugar in 3 additions, beating well after each portion is added. With the mixer on low speed, blend in the vanilla. Beat in the flour in 2 additions. When the butter and milk mixture has reached a full, rolling boil, remove it from the heat and pour it into the flour mixture as it revolves in the mixer. The beaters must be turning and the bowl moving while the milk is being added. Scrape down the sides of the mixing bowl to make an even-textured batter. Lastly, add the baking powder and beat for 1 minute at moderate speed. Quickly pour and scrape the batter into the prepared pan.

Bake the cake on the lower-third-level rack of the preheated oven for 1 hour, or until nicely risen and golden on top; a wooden pick inserted into the center of the cake should come out clean and dry.

Let cool in the pan on a wire rack for 5 to 6 minutes, then invert onto a second cooling rack. Invert again to cool right side up. Dust the top of the cake with sifted confectioners' sugar, if you like.

Serve the cake cut in medium thick slices.

Lemon–Poppy Seed Pound Cake

2 tablespoons finely grated lemon peel

1 tablespoon pure lemon extract

3 cups *unsifted* all-purpose flour

³⁄₄ teaspoon baking soda

¹⁄₂ teaspoon baking powder

¹⁄₂ teaspoon salt

1 cup (2 sticks) unsalted butter, softened at room temperature

2 cups Lemon-Scented Granulated Sugar (page 122) or plain granulated sugar

3 jumbo eggs plus 2 jumbo egg yolks, at room temperature

1 cup buttermilk, at room temperature

¹⁄₄ cup poppy seeds

This pound cake is tender and moist and speckled with crunchy poppy seeds that play wonderfully against the subtle lemon flavoring in the cake batter. Although I have served and enjoyed this cake for many years, I only recently added a lemon glaze. I now spoon the glaze over the top and sides of the cake while it is still oven-hot. As the cake cools and the glaze sinks in, the top and sides look faintly sugar encrusted. The glaze makes this pound cake an extra-good keeper.

Lightly butter and flour a 10-inch fluted Bundt pan; set aside. Preheat the oven to 350 degrees.

Mix together the lemon peel and extract in a small bowl; set aside. Sift together the flour, baking soda, baking powder, and salt onto a large sheet of waxed paper. Sift the flour mixture again. Cream the butter in the large bowl of an electric mixer on moderately high speed for 3 minutes. Add the sugar in 3 additions, beating thoroughly after each portion is added. Beat in the eggs, one at a time, blending well after each one; beat in the egg yolks. Scrape down the sides of the mixing bowl. With the mixer on low speed, alternately add the sifted flour mixture in 3 additions and the buttermilk in 2 additions, beginning and ending with the flour. Scrape down the sides of the bowl frequently as the ingredients are added to keep the batter even textured. With the mixer on low speed, blend in the lemon peel–extract mixture and the poppy seeds. Pour and scrape the batter into the prepared pan. Shake the pan gently from side to side to level the top of the batter.

FOR THE LEMON-SUGAR
GLAZE:

⅓ cup freshly squeezed
   lemon juice
⅓ cup Lemon-Scented
   Granulated Sugar or
   plain granulated sugar

One 10-inch Bundt cake

Bake the cake on the lower-third-level rack of the preheated oven for 1 hour to 1 hour and 10 minutes, or until the top of the cake is golden and a wooden pick inserted into the center of the cake comes out clean and dry. The cake will pull away slightly from the sides of the pan when done.

Let cool in the pan on a wire rack for 5 minutes. While the cake is cooling, make the glaze. Combine the lemon juice and the Lemon-Scented Granulated Sugar in a small bowl. Invert the cake onto a second cooling rack. Spoon the glaze over the top and sides of the cake. Let cool completely.

Serve the cake cut in medium thick slices.

Bourbon Pound Cake

3½ cups *unsifted* cake flour

1¼ teaspoons baking powder

½ teaspoon salt

1 teaspoon ground cinnamon

¾ teaspoon freshly grated nutmeg

¼ teaspoon ground allspice

¼ teaspoon ground ginger

1½ cups (3 sticks) unsalted butter, softened at room temperature

3 cups firmly packed light brown sugar

½ cup granulated sugar

4 jumbo eggs plus 2 jumbo egg yolks, at room temperature

¾ cup light cream blended with 2 teaspoons pure vanilla extract, at room temperature

The crumb of this pound cake is a beautiful amber color, owing to the three cups of brown sugar that colors the batter. The faint caramel flavor is reinforced by a good slug of bourbon and tinged by a quartet of spices (cinnamon, nutmeg, allspice, and ginger). I happen to love what the mingling of spices does to uplift the flavor of the cake, playing against the bourbon as they do. You can substitute rum for the bourbon, with excellent results; in that case, I'd use a good Barbados rum, like Mount Gay. A chunky fruit compote is refreshing with a slice of Bourbon Pound Cake. And paired with cool glasses of minted iced tea, slices of the pound cake make an ideal midafternoon treat.

This recipe, originally my mother's, has been through many changes in my hands. My mother used more brown sugar and less vanilla than I do and she replaced part of the butter with shortening, but I find my proportions more appealing. This has become the version I've made at home for years.

Lightly butter and flour a 10-inch fluted Bundt pan; set aside. Preheat the oven to 350 degrees.

Resift the flour with the baking powder, salt, cinnamon, nutmeg, allspice, and ginger onto a large sheet of waxed paper. Cream the butter in the large bowl of an electric mixer on moderately high speed for 3 minutes. Beat in the brown sugar in 3 additions, beating well after each portion. Beat in the granulated sugar. Beat in the eggs, one at a time, blending well after each one. Beat in the egg yolks. Scrape down the

¼ cup good bourbon

Confectioners' sugar for
dusting, optional

One 10-inch Bundt cake

sides of the mixing bowl frequently with a rubber spatula to keep the mixture even textured. Combine the vanilla-cream mixture and bourbon in a small pitcher. With the mixer on low speed, alternately add the sifted dry ingredients in 3 additions and the bourbon-cream mixture in 2 additions, beginning and ending with the dry mixture. Pour and scrape the batter into the prepared baking pan. Shake the pan gently from side to side to level the top of the batter.

Bake the cake on the lower-third-level rack of the preheated oven for 1 hour and 15 minutes to 1 hour and 20 minutes, or until a wooden pick inserted in the center of the cake comes out clean and dry and the cake pulls away slightly from the edge of the pan.

Let cool in the pan on a wire rack for 3 to 4 minutes. Invert onto a second cooling rack. Dust the top of the cake with sifted confectioners' sugar, if you like.

Serve the cake cut in medium thick slices.

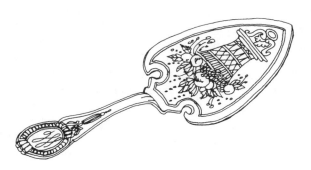

Spice Pound Cake

3 cups plus 2 tablespoons *sifted* cake flour

2 teaspoons baking powder

1/2 teaspoon baking soda

3/4 teaspoon salt

2 teaspoons ground cinnamon

1 teaspoon freshly grated nutmeg

1 teaspoon ground ginger

1/2 teaspoon ground allspice

1/4 teaspoon ground cloves

1 cup (2 sticks) unsalted butter, softened at room temperature

2 3/4 cups superfine sugar

5 extra-large eggs plus 2 extra-large egg yolks, at room temperature

1 tablespoon pure vanilla extract

This cake is a teatime favorite of many people I know. Some serve it with a hot lemon sauce, others present thin slices with raspberries and whipped cream or sugared sliced strawberries. I like the cake with a mix of sliced ripe peaches, nectarines, and plums, doused in a little plum syrup to moisten the slices of fruit so that they shine on the plate.

Lightly butter and flour a plain 10-inch tube pan; set aside. Preheat the oven to 350 degrees.

Resift the flour with the baking powder, baking soda, salt, cinnamon, nutmeg, ginger, allspice, and cloves onto a large sheet of waxed paper. Cream the butter in the large bowl of an electric mixer on moderately high speed for 3 minutes. Add the sugar mixture in 3 additions, beating well after each portion has been added. Beat in the eggs, one at a time, blending well after each one. Beat in the egg yolks. Scrape down the sides of the mixing bowl frequently with a rubber spatula to keep the batter even textured. Beat in the vanilla extract. With the mixer on low speed, alternately add the sifted dry ingredients in 3 additions and the sour cream in 2 additions, beginning and ending with flour. Pour and scrape the batter into the prepared pan; shake the pan gently from side to side to level the top.

Bake the cake on the lower-third-level rack of the preheated oven for about 1 hour and 25 minutes to 1 hour and 30 minutes, or until a wooden pick inserted in the middle of the cake

1 cup sour cream, at
    room temperature
Confectioners' sugar for
    dusting, optional

One 10-inch tube cake

comes out clean and dry and the cake pulls away slightly from the sides of the pan.

Let cool in the pan on a wire rack for 4 to 5 minutes, then invert onto a second cooling rack. Invert again to cool right side up. Dust the top of the cake with a little sifted confectioners' sugar, if you like.

Serve the cake cut in medium thick slices.

Rich Nut Pound Cake

3½ cups *unsifted* all-purpose flour

2¼ teaspoons baking powder

¾ teaspoon salt

1 teaspoon freshly grated nutmeg

¼ teaspoon ground mace

½ teaspoon ground ginger

¼ teaspoon ground allspice

1½ cups (3 sticks) unsalted butter, softened at room temperature

2 cups Vanilla-Scented Granulated Sugar (page 219)

5 jumbo eggs plus 2 jumbo egg yolks, at room temperature

1 tablespoon pure vanilla extract

½ cup milk blended with ½ cup light cream, at room temperature

The collection of nuts used for this pound cake can be varied according to what looks attractive or what kind you are willing to crack open yourself. I do prefer the way the cake tastes when freshly cracked and chopped nuts are used in the batter. I almost always make this cake at Thanksgiving, when I can buy whole nuts at the market. Because this cake is so dense and rich with nuts, it should be sliced quite thin. Serve the slices with a hot pot of lemon tea or freshly brewed coffee.

Lightly butter and flour a plain 10-inch tube pan. Line the bottom of the pan with a circle of waxed paper cut to fit; set aside. Preheat the oven to 325 degrees.

Sift together the flour, baking powder, salt, nutmeg, mace, ginger, and allspice onto a large sheet of waxed paper. Cream the butter in the large bowl of an electric mixer on moderately high speed for 3 to 4 minutes. Add the sugar in 3 additions, beating thoroughly for 1 minute after each portion is added. Beat in the eggs, one at a time, blending well after each one. Beat in the egg yolks. Blend in the vanilla. With the mixer on low speed, alternately add the sifted dry ingredients in 3 additions and the milk-cream mixture in 2 additions, beginning and ending with the dry mixture. By hand, stir in the walnuts, pecans, almonds, Brazil nuts, and black walnuts. Spoon the batter into the prepared pan. Shake the pan gently from side to side to level the top.

Bake the cake on the lower-third-level rack of the preheated oven for about 1 hour and 30 minutes to 1 hour and 40 min-

1 cup coarsely chopped
  walnuts
1 cup coarsely chopped
  pecans
½ cup lightly toasted and
  coarsely chopped
  blanched and skinned
  almonds
½ cup coarsely chopped
  Brazil nuts
¼ cup coarsely chopped
  black walnuts

One 10-inch tube cake

utes, or until a wooden pick inserted into the center of the cake comes out clean and dry and the cake pulls away slightly from the sides of the baking pan.

Cool in the pan on a wire rack for about 4 to 5 minutes, then invert onto a second cooling rack. Peel away the waxed paper if it has stuck to the bottom of the cake. Invert again to cool right side up.

Serve the cake cut in thin slices.

Cream Pound Cake

4 cups *unsifted* all-purpose
flour

3 teaspoons baking
powder

¾ teaspoon salt

2 cups (4 sticks) unsalted
butter, softened at
room temperature

3 cups Vanilla-Scented
Granulated Sugar
(page 219)

5 jumbo eggs plus
2 jumbo egg yolks, at
room temperature

2 tablespoons pure
vanilla extract

1 cup heavy cream
blended with the seed
scrapings from 1 vanilla
bean, at room
temperature

Confectioners' sugar for
dusting, optional

One 10-inch tube cake

Heavy cream, plenty of eggs, butter, and vanilla-flavored sugar go into this mighty pound cake. It is a fine cake to have on hand at any time of year—to serve with summer's sun-kissed berries, the mellow pears of winter (poached in wine), or ruby red strawberries in spring. I often present a Cream Pound Cake on a big flowered china plate and ring the edges with fresh lavender.

Lightly butter and flour a plain 10-inch tube pan and line the bottom of the pan with a circle of waxed paper cut to fit; set aside. Preheat the oven to 350 degrees.

Sift the flour with the baking powder and salt onto a large sheet of waxed paper. Cream the butter in the large bowl of an electric mixer on moderately high speed for 4 minutes. Beat in the sugar in 4 additions, beating for 1 minute after each portion is added. Blend in the eggs, one at a time, beating well after each one. Scrape down the sides of the mixing bowl frequently with a rubber spatula to keep the batter even textured. Beat in the egg yolks. Blend in the vanilla extract. With the mixer on low speed, alternately add the sifted dry ingredients in 3 additions and the cream in 2 additions, beginning and ending with the dry mixture. Scrape down the sides of the mixing bowl with a rubber spatula, then blend again to ensure an even-textured batter. Pour and scrape the batter into the prepared pan. Shake the pan gently from side to side to level the top of the batter.

Bake the cake on the lower-third-level rack of the preheated

oven for 1 hour to 1 hour and 15 minutes, or until the cake is golden on top and a wooden pick inserted in the center of the cake comes out clean and dry. The cake will pull slightly away from the sides of the pan when done.

Let cool in the pan on a wire rack for 4 to 5 minutes, then invert onto a second cooling rack. Peel away the waxed paper if it has stuck to the bottom of the cake. Invert again to cool right side up. Dust the top of the cake with sifted confectioners' sugar, if you like.

Serve the cake cut in thin slices.

Chocolate Pound Cake

3 cups plus 2 tablespoons *sifted* all-purpose flour

3 teaspoons baking powder

1 teaspoon salt

1 cup *unsifted* unsweetened cocoa powder

1 cup (2 sticks) unsalted butter, softened at room temperature

3 cups Vanilla-Scented Granulated Sugar (page 219)

3 jumbo eggs, at room temperature

2 teaspoons pure vanilla extract

2 teaspoons chocolate extract

1½ cups milk blended with the seed scrapings from 1 vanilla bean, at room temperature

My most requested cake recipe by far, this pound cake is full of the aroma of chocolate. The batter is charged with a good shot of vanilla—in the form of vanilla extract, vanilla-flavored sugar, and the seed scrapings from a vanilla bean—which enhances the flavor of the chocolate. The batter is ample and it bakes up into a generous cake; for that reason you must use a large 10-inch tube pan. Slices of pound cake, topped off with a sprinkling of confectioners' sugar, are delicious together with dips of Pure Vanilla Ice Cream (page 266) or Coconut Ice Cream (page 271).

This recipe was handed down to me from my grandmother, who liked to bake this cake on Saturday afternoon and serve it after dinner with vanilla ice cream. Everyone always came by her house for dessert on Saturday night, knowing that this cake would be freshly baked and under her stainless steel cake-keeper. I have made small changes in the original recipe, such as using vanilla sugar in place of fine granulated sugar and increasing the amount of cocoa just a bit.

Lightly butter and flour a plain 10-inch tube pan; line the bottom of the pan with a circle of waxed paper cut to fit and butter the paper. Set aside. Preheat the oven to 325 degrees.

Resift the flour with the baking powder, salt, and cocoa onto a large sheet of waxed paper. Cream the butter in the large bowl of an electric mixer on moderately high speed for 3 minutes. Beat in the sugar in 3 additions, blending well after each portion. Beat in the eggs, one at a time, beating

¼ cup light cream, at
  room temperature
Confectioners' sugar for
  dusting, optional

One 10-inch tube cake

thoroughly after each one. Blend in the vanilla and chocolate extracts. With the mixer on low speed, alternately add the sifted dry ingredients in 3 additions and the milk-vanilla blend in 2 additions, beginning and ending with the dry mixture. Pour in the light cream and beat for 4 minutes on low speed. Carefully pour and scrape the batter into the prepared pan. Shake the pan gently from side to side to level the top.

Bake the cake on the lower-third-level rack of the preheated oven for 1 hour and 15 minutes to 1 hour and 30 minutes, or until the cake is well risen and a wooden pick inserted in the center comes out clean and dry. The cake will pull slightly away from the sides of the baking pan when done.

Let cool in the pan on a wire rack for 4 to 5 minutes. Carefully invert onto a second cooling rack. Peel away the waxed paper if it has stuck to the bottom of the cake. Invert once more to cool right side up. Dust the top of the cake with a little sifted confectioners' sugar, if you like.

Serve the cake cut in thick slices.

FRESH FRUIT PICNIC CAKES

Wendy Wheeler

FRESH FRUIT PICNIC CAKES

——————◆◆◆——————

Plum Cake   *238*
Spicy Apple Cake   *240*
Fresh Peach Cake   *242*
Nectarine Cake   *244*
Blueberry Gingerbread   *246*

*F*ruit cakes are simple, single-layer concoctions that taste country fresh. Making them is a handy—and economical—way to use up just a few peaches, an apple or two, a cupful of berries, or a big handful of petite blue plums. Some cakes are made from creamed batters that enclose whole berries, sliced fruit, or a tangle of shredded fruit, while others are made from thick and soft buttery doughs that form a pillowlike base for a layer of cut-up fruit. These cakes are a snap to make and provide just the right sweet fillip to the end of a meal.

For traveling ease, the cakes are baked in 8- or 9-inch springform pans. A springform pan has a wide hinged band that clasps to the bottom of the cake pan. Leave the band attached while the cake is being transported to protect it while you are on the road. When you are ready to serve dessert, just remove the band and cut the cake in wedges.

If you bake one of these fragrant cakes to serve at home, offer a flavored whipped cream to serve on the side. The whipped cream can be sweetened with fresh fruit syrup or confectioners' sugar. Apple cider–scented whipped cream, for example, would make a light, creamy partner to a slice of Spicy Apple Cake (page 240). And Fresh Peach Cake (page 242) is just wonderful with a dollop of peach-flavored whipped cream. Generally, I blend 2 to 3 tablespoons of syrup into 2 cups of lightly whipped cream.

Plum Cake

1¼ cups *sifted* cake flour

¼ teaspoon baking powder

⅛ teaspoon salt

½ teaspoon ground cinnamon

¼ teaspoon freshly grated nutmeg

⅛ teaspoon ground allspice

½ cup (1 stick) unsalted butter, softened at room temperature

½ cup plus 1 tablespoon Vanilla-Scented Granulated Sugar (page 219) or plain granulated sugar

1 tablespoon firmly packed light brown sugar

2 teaspoons pure vanilla extract

2 jumbo eggs, at room temperature, separated

Pinch of cream of tartar

10 small fresh purple prune plums, halved, pitted, and quartered

This delicately spiced cake is light and soft, with quarters of small prune plums scattered on top helter-skelter. The cake bakes to a moist, fruity conclusion. Plum cake can be served plain or fancy, as you like, with scoops of homemade ice cream, a pitcher of custard sauce, or a bowl of whipped cream. If you are picnic-bound, bring a shaker of confectioners' sugar along and sprinkle a haze of it on top just before serving.

———❖❖❖———

Lightly butter and flour a 9-inch round springform pan; set aside. Preheat the oven to 375 degrees.

Resift the flour with the baking powder, salt, cinnamon, nutmeg, and allspice onto a large sheet of waxed paper. Beat the butter in the large bowl of an electric mixer on moderately high speed for 2 to 3 minutes. Add ½ cup of the granulated sugar and all of the brown sugar; continue beating for 1 to 2 minutes longer. Blend in the vanilla extract and egg yolks, beating well. On low speed, add the sifted dry ingredients, beating just until the particles of flour have been absorbed.

Beat the egg whites in a clean mixing bowl until frothy. Add cream of tartar and continue beating until soft peaks are formed. Sprinkle with the remaining tablespoon of granulated sugar and continue beating until firm but not stiff peaks are formed. Vigorously stir a quarter of the egg whites into the prepared batter, then fold in the remaining whites. Carefully spoon the batter into the prepared baking pan. Place the plum quarters here and there on top of the batter, flesh side up.

- 1 tablespoon granulated sugar blended with ⅛ teaspoon ground cinnamon
- 2 teaspoons unsalted butter, cut into bits
- Confectioners' sugar for dusting, optional

One 9-inch round cake

Sprinkle the sugar-cinnamon blend on top of the plums and dot with butter bits.

Bake the cake on the lower-third-level rack of the preheated oven for about 35 minutes, or until a wooden pick inserted into the cake comes out clean and dry (test between pieces of fruit). The cake will pull away slightly from the sides of the baking pan when done.

Let cool in the pan on a wire rack for 10 minutes, then remove the hinged ring of the pan. Let cool completely. (If you are transporting this cake to a picnic, leave the outer band on for traveling.) Dust the top of the cake with a little confectioners' sugar, if you like.

Serve the cake cut in wedges.

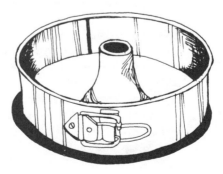

Spicy Apple Cake

1½ cups *unsifted* cake
flour

1 teaspoon baking
powder

½ teaspoon baking soda

¼ teaspoon salt

½ teaspoon ground
cinnamon

½ teaspoon freshly grated
nutmeg

¼ teaspoon ground
allspice

¼ teaspoon ground
ginger

⅛ teaspoon ground
cloves

½ cup (1 stick) unsalted
butter, softened at
room temperature

¾ cup granulated sugar

3 tablespoons firmly
packed light brown
sugar

1 extra-large egg plus
2 extra-large egg yolks,
at room temperature

Loaded with spices and flavored with brown sugar, this simple cake contains shreds of tart apple that keep it very moist and soft. Pack up an apple cake in the autumn picnic hamper with thermoses of hot apple cider or mulled wine.

Lightly butter and flour a 9-inch round springform pan; set aside. Preheat the oven to 350 degrees.

Sift the flour with the baking powder, baking soda, salt, cinnamon, nutmeg, allspice, ginger, and cloves onto a large sheet of waxed paper. Cream the butter in the large bowl of an electric mixer on moderately high speed for 1 minute. Beat in the granulated sugar and brown sugar and continue beating for 2 minutes. Beat in the egg. Beat in the egg yolks. Blend in the milk-vanilla mixture and beat for 1 minute. With the mixer on low speed, add the sifted flour mixture in 2 additions, beating until the particles of flour from the first portion have been absorbed before adding the next. By hand, fold in the shredded apples. Spoon the batter into the prepared pan. Using a small spatula, push about ½ inch of batter up the sides of the baking pan to keep the batter level as it rises and bakes.

Bake the cake on the lower-third-level rack of the preheated oven for about 40 to 45 minutes, or until a wooden pick inserted in the center of the cake comes out clean and dry. The cake will pull away slightly from the edges of the pan when done.

Let cool in the pan on a wire rack for 10 minutes, then

¼ cup milk blended with 2 teaspoons pure vanilla extract, at room temperature

1½ cups peeled, cored, and shredded tart cooking apples

Confectioners' sugar for dusting, optional

One 9-inch round cake

remove the hinged ring of the pan. Let cool completely. (If you are transporting this cake to a picnic, leave the outer band on for traveling.) Dust the top of the cake with a little confectioners' sugar, if you like.

Serve the cake cut in wedges.

Fresh Peach Cake

2 small ripe peaches

1 tablespoon lemon juice

1½ cups *unsifted* cake flour

1½ teaspoons baking powder

¼ teaspoon salt

½ teaspoon ground cinnamon

¼ teaspoon freshly grated nutmeg

¼ teaspoon ground ginger

½ cup (1 stick) unsalted butter, softened at room temperature

½ cup less 2 tablespoons Vanilla-Scented Granulated Sugar (page 219) or plain granulated sugar

2 tablespoons firmly packed light brown sugar

2 extra-large egg yolks, at room temperature

1 teaspoon pure vanilla extract

This is a simple cake for busy days, when what you want is something sweet and fruity that's quickly made. Fresh peach slices are trapped in a faintly spiced batter as it rises. Peach cake makes a good dessert for a family dinner. It is a divine cake for toting to a bring-a-dish supper. I've even packed this cake to take along on a picnic that featured fried chicken and cole slaw. Delicious!

———❖❖❖———

Lightly butter and flour an 8-inch round springform pan; set aside. Preheat the oven to 400 degrees.

Peel the peaches (dip first in boiling water, then in cold water for easier peeling); slice ¾ inch thick. Toss with lemon juice and set aside.

Sift together the flour, baking powder, salt, cinnamon, nutmeg, and ginger onto a large sheet of waxed paper. Beat the butter in the large bowl of an electric mixer on moderately high speed for 2 minutes. Beat in the granulated sugar and brown sugar; beat for 2 minutes. Beat in the egg yolks and vanilla. With the mixer on low speed, alternately add the sifted dry ingredients in 2 additions and the milk-cream blend in 1 addition, beginning and ending with the dry mixture. Spread the batter evenly into the prepared pan. Arrange the peach slices in a pattern on top of the batter.

Bake the cake on the lower-third-level rack of the preheated oven for about 30 minutes, or until a wooden pick inserted into the center of the cake comes out without any particles of cake batter clinging to it. The cake will pull away slightly from the sides of the pan when done.

¼ cup milk blended with
  ¼ cup light cream, at
  room temperature, or
  ½ cup half and half, at
  room temperature
Confectioners' sugar for
  dusting, optional

One 8-inch round cake

Let cool in the pan on a wire rack for 10 minutes, then remove the hinged ring of the pan. Let cool completely. (If you are transporting this cake to a picnic, leave the outer band on for traveling.) Dust the top of the cake with a little confectioners' sugar, if you like.

Serve the cake cut in thick wedges.

Nectarine Cake

2 cups *unsifted* all-purpose
flour

½ cup granulated sugar

1 teaspoon baking
powder

¼ teaspoon salt

½ teaspoon ground
cinnamon

¼ teaspoon freshly grated
nutmeg

¾ cup (1½ sticks) cold
unsalted butter, cut
into chunks

2 tablespoons light
cream blended with
2 teaspoons pure
vanilla extract, at
room temperature

1 jumbo egg, at room
temperature

3 small nectarines,
halved, pitted, and
sliced ¾ inch thick,
tossed in 1 tablespoon
lemon juice

Sliced nectarines are topped here with a sugar and spice crumble. Ripe peaches, peeled and sliced the same way, would also be good to use in this cake. It is the perfect little cake to serve on a lazy summer afternoon with frosty goblets of tea or to carry along to a barbecue or other out-of-doors event.

Lightly butter and flour a 9-inch round springform pan; set aside. Preheat the oven to 400 degrees.

Thoroughly blend together the flour, sugar, baking powder, salt, cinnamon, and nutmeg in a large mixing bowl. Scatter the cold chunks of butter on top and, using 2 table knives, cut the butter into the flour mixture until the pieces of butter have been reduced to pea-size bits. With your fingertips, further reduce the butter to small flakes by reaching down into the flour mixture and crumbling it between your fingertips. Whisk together the vanilla-cream blend with the egg and pour it over the butter-flour mixture. Stir everything together to form a relatively firm batter. Spread the batter on the bottom and about 1¼ inches up the sides of the prepared baking pan, forming a shallow center.

Arrange the nectarine slices on top of the batter, right up to but not touching the sides. In a small bowl, crumble the sugar-spice-flour blend with the cold bits of butter and sprinkle this mixture over the nectarines.

Bake the cake on the lower-third-level rack of the preheated oven for about 30 minutes, or until the cake has risen, is a light golden color, and pulls away slightly from the sides of the baking pan.

3 tablespoons granulated
sugar blended with
1½ tablespoons
unsifted all-purpose
flour, ½ teaspoon
ground cinnamon,
and ¼ teaspoon freshly
grated nutmeg

2 teaspoons cold unsalted
butter, cut into bits

Confectioners' sugar for
dusting, optional

One 9-inch round cake

Let cool in the pan on a wire rack for 10 minutes, then
remove the hinged ring of the pan. Let cool completely. (If
you are transporting this cake to a picnic, leave the outer
band on for traveling.) Dust the top of the cake with a little
confectioners' sugar, if you like.

Serve the cake cut in wedges.

Blueberry Gingerbread

1½ cups *unsifted* cake flour

1 teaspoon baking powder

¼ teaspoon baking soda

¼ teaspoon salt

2 teaspoons ground ginger

1½ teaspoons ground cinnamon

½ teaspoon freshly grated nutmeg

¼ teaspoon ground allspice

⅔ cup fresh blueberries, picked over

½ cup (1 stick) unsalted butter, softened at room temperature

½ cup plus 3 tablespoons Vanilla-Scented Granulated Sugar (page 219) or plain granulated sugar

5 tablespoons light molasses

Strongly flavored with ginger and molasses, this cake is distinctively spicy and dark, but its texture is light and soft. Fresh blueberries are folded through the batter at the last moment. If you leave out the berries, all kinds of other things can be added, such as currants or golden raisins, chopped walnuts, chopped crystallized ginger, or chopped ginger preserved in syrup. This is a wonderful cake to take to a picnic because it slices into neat wedges, and it combines fruit and cake all in one dessert. If you are serving the cake at home, I'd encourage you to accompany it with little mounds of Pure Vanilla Ice Cream (page 266), Lemon Ice Cream (page 270), or unsweetened whipped cream with some thick lemon curd folded into it.

This happens to be my favorite recipe for gingerbread and it has been in my family for years and years. My grandmother used more molasses and less sugar and my mother used vanilla-flavored yogurt in place of sour cream. I have made my own changes: I add more cinnamon and nutmeg, use vanilla-flavored sugar, and add some fruit to the batter.

———❖❖❖———

Lightly butter and flour an 8-inch round springform pan; set aside. Preheat the oven to 350 degrees.

Sift the flour with the baking powder, baking soda, salt, ginger, cinnamon, nutmeg, and allspice onto a large sheet of waxed paper. Put the blueberries in a bowl and toss with 1 tablespoon of the sifted mixture.

Beat the butter in the large bowl of an electric mixer on

1 extra-large egg plus
   2 extra-large egg yolks,
   at room temperature

½ cup sour cream, at
   room temperature

Confectioners' sugar for
   dusting, optional

One 8-inch round cake

moderately high speed for 2 minutes. Beat in the sugar; beat for 2 minutes. Beat in the molasses. Add the egg and beat it in; beat in the egg yolks. With the mixer on low speed, alternately add the sifted dry ingredients in 2 additions and the sour cream in 1 addition, beginning and ending with the dry ingredients. By hand, fold in the floured blueberries. Spoon the batter into the prepared pan. Gently push the batter about ¾ inch up the sides of the baking pan with a small spatula to help the batter rise evenly as the cake bakes.

Bake the cake on the lower-third-level rack of the preheated oven for about 40 to 45 minutes, or until a wooden pick inserted in the center of the cake comes out without any particles of cake clinging to it. The cake will pull away slightly from the sides of the pan when done.

Let cool in the pan on a wire rack for 10 minutes, then remove the hinged ring of the pan. Let cool completely. (If you are transporting the cake to a picnic, leave the outer band on for traveling.) Dust the top of the cake with a little confectioners' sugar, if you like.

Serve the cake cut in wedges.

Note: If you do not have any Vanilla-Scented Granulated Sugar on hand, add 1 teaspoon pure vanilla extract to the batter along with the light molasses.

LITTLE CAKES

Wendy Wheeler

LITTLE CAKES

———————◆◆◆———————

Chunky Apple Cakes with Pecans   252
Ginger Cakes   254
Blueberry Cakes   256
Cream Cheese–Chocolate Chip Cakes   258
Vanilla Cakes   260
Pear Cakes with Walnuts and Currants   262

*B*aked in individual muffin tins, little cakes are those small cushions of cake that emerge from the oven well risen and plump. They are easy to serve— and all too easy to eat. You'll find them here in many flavors, such as vanilla, cream cheese and chocolate chip, ginger, apple, blueberry, and pear. You can bake the cakes in standard muffin tins (about 2³/₄ inches in diameter) or make smaller tea cakes or larger, whopping Texas-size cakes; sometimes I bake the cakes in individual tins shaped like sea shells.

Except for the Cream Cheese–Chocolate Chip Cakes (page 258), which are perfect for satisfying midnight chocolate cravings and for packing up for a picnic dessert or school bake sale, all of these cakes are particularly good warm from the oven, split and served shortcake-style, with lightly sugared fresh fruit and light mounds of sweetened whipped cream. The Vanilla Cakes (page 260) taste especially luscious split and served with sweetened raspberries, a splash of raspberry syrup, and whipped cream.

Chunky Apple Cakes with Pecans

2¼ cups *sifted* cake flour

¾ teaspoon baking powder

¼ teaspoon salt

½ teaspoon ground cinnamon

¼ teaspoon freshly grated nutmeg

¼ teaspoon ground allspice

½ cup vegetable oil

4 tablespoons (½ stick) unsalted butter, melted and cooled

¾ cup granulated sugar

1 extra-large egg plus 2 extra-large egg yolks, at room temperature

1½ teaspoons pure vanilla extract

1¼ cups peeled, cored, and chopped tart

Chopped apples and pecans punctuate a spice-laden batter to create little cakes that taste earthy and robust. They are quickly mixed together in a bowl, and as they bake they perfume the whole house with the aroma of apples and spices. Warm apple cakes are wonderful together with apple slices that have been sautéed in butter with sugar and spices or with applesauce made with fresh cider—and softly whipped heavy cream.

This old-time recipe comes from my grandmother's sister, Aunt Mamie, who really wasn't widely known for her baking abilities. Except for these small cakes and some outrageously delicious chiffon and angel food cakes and a few loaf cakes, Aunt Mamie rarely filled the house with sweet baking scents. For these cakes, my aunt used to crack her own pecans, so that the nutmeats would be oily and snappy-crisp—a practice I heartily recommend. On some occasions, she'd add a large handful (about ⅓ cup) of golden raisins to the batter along with the apples and pecans.

———— ❖❖❖ ————

Lightly butter and flour sixteen 2¾-inch muffin tins; set aside. Preheat the oven to 400 degrees.

Thoroughly stir together the flour, baking powder, salt, cinnamon, nutmeg, and allspice in a large mixing bowl. Whisk together the oil, melted butter, sugar, egg, egg yolks, and vanilla in a medium-size bowl. Make a large well in the center of the dry ingredients, pour in the whisked mixture, and add the chopped apples and pecans. Stir everything together with a wooden spoon, using a few swift strokes (the batter should

cooking apples, such as Granny Smith

¾ cup chopped pecans

About sixteen 2¾-inch cakes

stay slightly lumpy). Fill each muffin cup two-thirds full with batter.

Bake the cakes on the lower-third-level rack of the preheated oven for about 20 minutes, or until a wooden pick inserted into the center of a cake comes out clean and dry.

Let the cakes stand in the tins on a wire rack for 1 minute, then remove them to a second cooling rack.

Serve the cakes warm.

Ginger Cakes

1 cup plus 1 tablespoon
  unsifted cake flour

¾ cup *unsifted*
  stone-ground whole
  wheat flour

⅓ cup firmly packed light
  brown sugar

⅓ cup superfine sugar

¾ teaspoon baking soda

½ teaspoon baking
  powder

¼ teaspoon salt

2 teaspoons ground
  ginger

2 teaspoons ground
  cinnamon

¼ teaspoon ground
  allspice

¼ teaspoon freshly grated
  nutmeg

⅛ teaspoon ground
  cloves

1 extra-large egg plus
  2 extra-large egg yolks,
  at room temperature

½ cup (1 stick) unsalted
  butter, melted and
  cooled

These plump cakes are moist and full of the good taste of ginger, cinnamon, brown sugar, molasses, and buttermilk. Adding whole wheat flour to cake flour gives the cakes a subtle graham-cracker-like flavor, which I happen to love. These light cakes are marvelous warm from the oven, split in half and covered with spoonfuls of fresh fruit and clouds of whipped cream. Over the years, I've paired these cakes with nectarine slices bathed in a spiced sugar syrup, with sliced strawberries tossed in a little fresh strawberry syrup, and with blueberries tossed in blueberry syrup enhanced with fresh lemon juice and bits of finely grated lemon rind.

This recipe has been through many changes over the years. I got the original recipe from the side of a bag of whole wheat flour purchased at a mill in the Maryland countryside. (Sadly, the mill went the way of a superhighway some years ago.) Many refinements later, I've settled on the formula below.

Lightly butter and flour fourteen 2¾-inch muffin cups; set aside. Preheat the oven to 400 degrees.

Sift together the cake flour, whole wheat flour, brown sugar, superfine sugar, baking soda, baking powder, salt, ginger, cinnamon, allspice, nutmeg, and cloves into a large mixing bowl. Whisk the whole egg, egg yolks, melted butter, buttermilk, cream, molasses, and vanilla in a medium-size bowl. Pour the liquid ingredients over the flour mixture, add the minced ginger (or crystallized ginger), and stir everything together with a wooden spoon, using a few swift strokes (the batter

½ cup buttermilk, at room temperature

¼ cup heavy cream, at room temperature

3 tablespoons light molasses

2 teaspoons pure vanilla extract

2 tablespoons minced ginger preserved in syrup, well drained, or the same amount of chopped crystallized ginger

FOR FINISHING THE CAKES:

2 tablespoons granulated sugar blended with 2 teaspoons ground ginger

---

About fourteen 2¾-inch cakes

should be slightly lumpy). Fill each muffin cup two-thirds full with batter. Sprinkle the tops with the ginger-flavored sugar.

Bake the cakes on the lower-third-level rack of the preheated oven for 15 minutes, or until a wooden pick inserted in the center of a cake comes out clean and dry.

Let the cakes stand in the tins on a wire rack for 1 minute, then remove them to a second cooling rack.

Serve the cakes warm.

Blueberry Cakes

2 cups *unsifted* all-purpose
flour

2 teaspoons baking
powder

¼ teaspoon salt

½ teaspoon ground
cinnamon

¼ teaspoon freshly grated
nutmeg

⅛ teaspoon ground
allspice

¾ cup blueberries,
picked over

7 tablespoons unsalted
butter, softened at
room temperature

⅔ cup superfine sugar

2 extra-large eggs, at
room temperature

1 teaspoon pure vanilla
extract

⅔ cup milk, at room
temperature

3 tablespoons granulated
sugar blended with
¼ teaspoon ground
cinnamon, optional

About twelve 2¾-inch cakes

These buttery cakes are chockablock with blueberries. The crumb is soft and cakelike and it barely supports the fresh berries. I love warm blueberry cakes served with a ladleful of poached blueberries and a spoonful of whipped cream or vanilla custard sauce. These cakes also make good miniature tea cakes (use muffin tins about 1¾ inches in diameter). Pile the cakes in a basket and serve them with a pitcher of iced tea, lemonade, or limeade.

Lightly butter and flour twelve 2¾-inch muffin tins; set aside. Preheat the oven to 400 degrees.

Sift together the flour, baking powder, salt, cinnamon, nutmeg, and allspice onto a large sheet of waxed paper. Put the blueberries in a bowl and toss with 1 tablespoon of the sifted mixture. Beat the butter in the large bowl of an electric mixer on moderately high speed for 1 minute. Add the sugar and beat for 2 minutes. Blend in the eggs, one at a time, beating well after each one. Blend in the vanilla. With the mixer on low speed, alternately add the sifted flour mixture in 2 additions and the milk in 1 addition, beginning and ending with the flour. Fold in the floured blueberries. Fill each muffin cup two-thirds full with batter. If you are not going to serve the cakes with extra fruit, sprinkle the tops with cinnamon sugar just before putting the cakes in the oven to bake.

Bake the cakes on the lower-third-level rack of the preheated oven for 15 to 20 minutes, or until well risen and plump; a wooden pick inserted into the center of a cake should come out clean and dry.

Let the cakes stand in the tins on a wire rack for 1 minute, then remove them to a second cooling rack.

Serve the cakes warm.

Cream Cheese–
Chocolate Chip
Cakes

FOR THE CHOCOLATE BATTER:

1½ cups *unsifted* all-purpose flour

1 cup plus 2 tablespoons granulated sugar

¼ cup *unsifted* unsweetened cocoa powder

½ teaspoon salt

1 teaspoon baking soda

1 cup water, at room temperature

⅓ cup vegetable oil

2 teaspoons pure vanilla extract

2¼ teaspoons distilled white vinegar

FOR THE CREAM CHEESE– CHOCOLATE CHIP TOPPING:

1 package (8 ounces) cream cheese, softened at room temperature

Everybody seems to love these dark, moist cakes. The chocolate cake provides an ample base for the rich cream cheese and chocolate chip topping. The cheesecakelike topping bakes right into the cake. You can bake these as tea cakes (use miniature muffin tins that measure about 1¾ inches in diameter) for tasty little mouthfuls to serve with fresh fruit salad. The tea cakes are also nice for school bake sales.

Lightly butter and flour eighteen 2¾-inch muffin cups or line them with paper liners; set aside. Preheat the oven to 350 degrees.

Sift together the flour, sugar, cocoa, salt, and baking soda into a large mixing bowl. Whisk together the water, oil, vanilla, and vinegar in a small bowl. Make a large well in the center of the dry ingredients, pour in the liquid ingredients, and stir both together with a whisk until a batter is formed. Fill each muffin cup a little more than half full with batter.

For the topping, beat the softened cream cheese with the egg, sugar, and vanilla in a small bowl, using a handheld beater. Blend well for 2 minutes, then stir in the chocolate chips. Spoon a heaping tablespoon of topping on top of each cup of chocolate batter.

Bake the cakes on the lower-third-level rack of the preheated oven for 25 minutes, or until nicely risen; a wooden pick inserted into the center of a cake should come out clean and dry.

1 extra-large egg, at room
  temperature
$\frac{1}{4}$ cup granulated sugar
$\frac{1}{2}$ teaspoon vanilla
  extract
$\frac{1}{2}$ cup miniature
  semisweet chocolate
  chips

About eighteen 2¾-inch cakes

Let the cakes stand in the tins on a wire rack for 1 minute,
then remove them to a second cooling rack.

Serve the cakes at room temperature.

Vanilla Cakes

2 cups *unsifted* cake flour

½ teaspoon baking soda

¼ teaspoon salt

¼ teaspoon freshly grated nutmeg

7 tablespoons unsalted butter, softened at room temperature

2 tablespoons shortening

1 cup Vanilla-Scented Granulated Sugar (page 219)

⅔ cup sour cream blended with 2 teaspoons pure vanilla extract

½ teaspoon pure lemon extract

1 teaspoon finely grated lemon rind

1 extra-large egg plus 2 extra-large egg yolks, at room temperature

My grandmother loved pound cakes in all forms, especially in the smaller, cupcake size. This recipe for Vanilla Cakes is hers and I have changed it only slightly—I use vanilla-flavored sugar in the batter. These cakes are reminiscent of the lightest of pound cakes; the batter, soft and velvety, bakes up with the traditional pound cake finish, a tawny brown, speckled top crust. Vanilla Cakes are absolutely delicious taken warm from the oven, split, and covered with sugared strawberries (or raspberries) and a mound of whipped cream.

Lightly butter and flour sixteen 2¾-inch muffin cups; set aside. Preheat the oven to 400 degrees.

Resift the flour with the baking soda, salt, and nutmeg onto a large sheet of waxed paper. Beat the butter and shortening in the large bowl of an electric mixer on moderately high speed for 2 minutes. Add the sugar in 2 additions, beating for 1 minute after each portion is added. Blend in the sour cream–vanilla mixture, lemon extract, and lemon rind. Blend in the egg, beat for 1 minute, then blend in the egg yolks. Beat for 1 minute longer, scraping down the sides of the mixing bowl to keep the batter even textured. With the mixer on low speed, add the sifted flour mixture in 2 additions, beating just until the particles of flour have been absorbed. The batter should have a creamy, silken texture. Fill each muffin cup just over half full with batter. Sprinkle a little of the spiced sugar over the top of each cake.

Bake the cakes on the lower-third-level rack of the pre-

FOR FINISHING THE CAKES:

2 tablespoons
   Vanilla-Scented
   Granulated Sugar
   (page 219) blended
   with ⅛ teaspoon
   freshly grated nutmeg

About sixteen 2¾-inch cakes

heated oven for 20 to 22 minutes, or until well risen and plump; a wooden pick inserted into the center of a cake should come out clean and dry.

Let the cakes stand in the tins on a wire rack for 1 minute, then carefully remove them to a second cooling rack.

Serve the cakes warm or at room temperature.

Pear Cakes with Walnuts and Currants

1³/₄ cups *unsifted*
  all-purpose flour

¹/₃ cup granulated sugar

2 teaspoons baking
  powder

¹/₂ teaspoon baking soda

¹/₄ teaspoon salt

¹/₂ teaspoon ground
  cinnamon

¹/₄ teaspoon freshly grated
  nutmeg

¹/₈ teaspoon ground
  allspice

³/₄ cup buttermilk, at
  room temperature

¹/₃ cup vegetable oil

1 extra-large egg, at room
  temperature

1 teaspoon pure vanilla
  extract

³/₄ cup peeled, cored, and
  diced ripe pears

¹/₂ cup chopped walnuts

¹/₄ cup dried currants

About eleven 2³/₄-inch cakes

Mildly sweet and nutty, these pear cakes could be popped into the breakfast bread basket, made in miniature, and served with whole poached pears or simply served warm from the oven with a mound of spiced and sweetened whipped cream.

————❖❖❖————

Lightly butter and flour eleven 2³/₄-inch muffin cups; set aside. Preheat the oven to 425 degrees.

Thoroughly combine the flour, sugar, baking powder, baking soda, salt, cinnamon, nutmeg, and allspice in a large mixing bowl. Whisk together the buttermilk, oil, egg, and vanilla in a small bowl. Make a large well in the center of the dry ingredients, pour in the whisked mixture, and scatter the diced pears, walnuts, and currants on top. Stir everything together with a wooden spoon, using a few swift strokes (the batter should be slightly lumpy). Fill each muffin cup two-thirds full with batter.

Bake the cakes on the lower-third-level rack of the preheated oven for 15 to 20 minutes, or until well risen; a wooden pick inserted in the center of a cake should come out clean and dry.

Let the cakes stand in the tins on a wire rack for 1 minute, then remove them to a second cooling rack.

Serve the cakes warm.

CAKE AND ICE CREAM

Wendy Wheeler

CAKE AND ICE CREAM

————————— ❖❖❖ —————————

Pure Vanilla Ice Cream   266
Cinnamon Ice Cream   268
Lemon Ice Cream   270
Coconut Ice Cream   271

*E*ven after a warming, stick-to-your-ribs meal, there's always some room left for cake and ice cream. Although good cake is certainly good all by itself, ice cream makes it even better: the cold, rich creaminess of handmade ice cream is a cake's best friend.

These are the ice creams I've been turning out for years—vanilla, coconut (a family favorite), lemon, and cinnamon. For the ice cream base, I use a combination of milk, light cream, and heavy cream, in addition to sugar and bright yellow egg yolks from free-ranging hens. The result is a silky smooth ice cream that complements a slice of cake splendidly.

The ice cream base is made in easy stages. First, you beat a scalded mixture of milk and cream together with egg yolks and sugar; then you cook the custard slowly on the stovetop until it coats the back of a wooden spoon. In the second stage, you stir a goodly amount of heavy cream into the custard and place it in the refrigerator for a thorough chilling. Finally, you transform the custard into a frozen delight.

Ice cream that is made from a stirred-custard base stores nicely in the freezer for several days.

Pure Vanilla Ice Cream

2 vanilla beans

1 cup milk

1 cup light cream

4 jumbo egg yolks, at
room temperature

¾ cup Vanilla-Scented
Granulated Sugar
(page 219) or plain
granulated sugar

Pinch of salt

2 cups cold heavy cream

About 1 quart

Vanilla ice cream is to cake what mashed potatoes are to fried chicken—each is good on its own, but together they make a magical combination. Creamy rich Pure Vanilla Ice Cream, formed into scoops, can top fruit cakes like Peach Upside-Down Cake (page 206), Spiced Nectarine Upside-Down Cake (page 208), or Apple-Ginger Upside-Down Cake (page 210); any of the chocolate cakes, such as Fudgy Chocolate-Walnut Cake (page 200), Chocolate Pan Cake with Chocolate Fudge Frosting (page 196), or Buttermilk Chocolate Layer Cake (page 164); or a pound cake like Rich Nut Pound Cake (page 228) or Best Vanilla Pound Cake (page 218).

———❖❖❖———

Slit the vanilla beans down the center with a sharp paring knife. Place the vanilla beans, milk, and light cream in a medium-size saucepan. Set the pan over moderate heat and scald the liquid; once scalded, remove from the heat and let cool for 10 minutes. Remove the vanilla beans and scrape out the seeds into the milk and cream mixture. Discard the beans.

Beat the egg yolks, sugar, and salt together in a medium-size saucepan with a handheld mixer until light and creamy, about 3 minutes. Add the milk-cream mixture in a slow, steady stream, stirring constantly. Place the saucepan over low heat and cook, stirring all the while, until a light custard is formed, about 10 to 12 minutes, or until the custard coats the back of a wooden spoon. Remove from the heat and pour into a bowl. Cool slightly. Stir in the heavy cream.

Thoroughly chill the ice cream base, covered, in the refrigerator; the base should be chilled for at least 6 hours or, preferably, overnight.

Churn the ice cream mixture in a machine, following directions supplied by the manufacturer. Turn the ice cream into a sturdy storage container, cover, and freeze for at least 1 to 2 hours before serving so that it has a chance to mellow.

Cinnamon Ice Cream

6 whole cinnamon sticks

1 cup milk

1 cup light cream

4 jumbo egg yolks, at room temperature

¾ cup Vanilla-Scented Granulated Sugar (page 219) blended with 1½ teaspoons ground cinnamon

2 cups cold heavy cream

2 teaspoons pure vanilla extract

About 1 quart

This pale tea-colored ice cream, amply flavored with cinnamon, is a delicious partner to slices of Peach Upside-Down Cake (page 206), Best Vanilla Pound Cake (page 218), Bourbon Pound Cake (page 224), Spice Pound Cake (page 226), Rich Nut Pound Cake (page 228), or Spicy Apple Cake (page 240). Baby scoops can accompany the little cakes—most notably, Chunky Apple Cakes with Pecans (page 252), Blueberry Cakes (page 256), Pear Cakes with Walnuts and Currants (page 262), or Vanilla Cakes (page 260).

Place the whole cinnamon sticks, milk, and light cream in a medium-size saucepan. Set the pan over moderate heat and scald the liquid; once scalded, remove from the heat and let cool to room temperature. Discard the cinnamon sticks.

Beat the egg yolks and cinnamon sugar together in a medium-size saucepan with a handheld mixer until light and creamy, about 3 minutes. Slowly add the cinnamon-milk-cream mixture, stirring all the while. Place the pot over low heat and cook, stirring, until a light custard is formed, about 10 to 12 minutes, or until the custard coats the back of a wooden spoon. Remove from the heat and pour into a bowl. Cool slightly, then pour in the heavy cream and vanilla; stir well.

Thoroughly chill the ice cream base, covered, in the refrigerator; the base should be chilled for at least 6 hours or, preferably, overnight.

Churn the ice cream mixture in a machine, following directions supplied by the manufacturer. Turn the ice cream into a sturdy storage container, cover, and freeze for at least 1 to 2 hours before serving so that it has a chance to mellow.

❖❖❖❖❖❖❖❖❖❖❖❖❖❖❖❖❖❖❖

Lemon Ice Cream

1 cup milk

1 cup light cream

5 jumbo egg yolks, at
   room temperature

1 cup Lemon-Scented
   Granulated Sugar
   (page 122) or plain
   granulated sugar

3 tablespoons finely
   grated lemon peel

2 teaspoons pure lemon
   extract

2 cups cold heavy cream

About 1 quart

Because lemon ice cream is creamy with a soft citrus tang, it is a good plate mate to slices of Plum Cake (page 238) or Buttermilk Cake (page 162). Miniature scoops are great teamed up with little cakes like Ginger Cakes (page 254), Blueberry Cakes (page 256), or Vanilla Cakes (page 260).

Place the milk and cream in a medium-size saucepan. Set the pan over moderate heat and scald the liquid; once scalded, remove from the heat and let cool to room temperature.

Beat the egg yolks, sugar, and lemon peel together in a medium-size saucepan with a handheld mixer until light and creamy, about 3 minutes. Slowly add the scalded milk-cream, stirring. Place the pan over low heat and cook, stirring, until a light custard is formed, about 10 to 12 minutes, or until the custard coats the back of a wooden spoon. Remove from the heat and pour into a bowl. Stir in the lemon extract. Cool slightly, then stir in the heavy cream.

Thoroughly chill the ice cream base, covered, in the refrigerator; the base should be chilled for at least 6 hours or, preferably, overnight.

Churn the ice cream mixture in a machine, following directions supplied by the manufacturer. Turn the ice cream into a sturdy storage container, cover, and freeze for at least 1 to 2 hours so that it has a chance to mellow.

Coconut Ice Cream

1 cup canned cream of
coconut

½ cup light cream

½ cup milk

5 jumbo egg yolks, at
room temperature

¾ cup granulated sugar

Pinch of salt

2 cups cold heavy cream

2 teaspoons pure vanilla
extract blended with
2 teaspoons coconut
extract

1½ cups freshly grated
coconut

About 1 quart

Homemade coconut ice cream with a fresh slice of pound cake (the vanilla, nut, spice, or cream variety) tastes so good that I frequently feel compelled to bake a pound cake just because I have some coconut ice cream in the freezer. Scoops of this ice cream are sublime with most any of the pound cakes, as I've mentioned, as well as with slices of Coconut Layer Cake (page 166), Black Walnut and Chocolate Pan Cake (page 158), Chocolate Pan Cake with Chocolate Fudge Frosting (page 196), Fresh Peach Cake (page 242), and warm Vanilla Cakes (page 260).

———❖❖❖———

Place the cream of coconut, light cream, and milk in a medium-size saucepan, set over moderate heat, and scald the mixture. Once scalded, remove from the heat and let cool for 10 minutes.

Beat the egg yolks, sugar, and salt in a medium-size saucepan with a handheld mixer until light and creamy, about 3 minutes. Add the scalded and cooled liquid in a slow, steady stream, stirring. Place the pot over low heat and cook, stirring all the while, until a light custard is formed, about 10 to 12 minutes, or until the custard coats the back of a wooden spoon. Remove from the heat and pour into a bowl. Cool slightly, then stir in the heavy cream, the vanilla and coconut extracts, and the grated coconut.

Thoroughly chill the ice cream base, covered, in the refrigerator; the base should be chilled for at least 6 hours or, preferably, overnight.

Churn the ice cream mixture in a machine, following directions supplied by the manufacturer. Turn the ice cream into a sturdy storage container, cover, and freeze for at least 1 to 2 hours so that it has a chance to mellow.

THE COUNTRY CAKE TEA PARTY

Wendy Wheeler

When I was a child, I played "having tea" in my grandmother's library with a miniature tea service made out of sterling silver and china. I'd serve my imaginary guests imaginary tea with an equally imaginary array of sweets. My grandmother would play with me for hours, then we'd bake a real cake and enjoy a real teatime. (I drank lemonade.)

Years later, I learned the pleasures of tea anew. Now I often invite over a congenial group of people for tea and sweets—a plate of little cakes, a loaf cake sliced up, a fresh fruit cake, a pound cake—and a pot of freshly made tea (or a pitcher of iced tea). I put out my adult-size china tea set, which I purchased years ago in London, with its matching cups and saucers, serving plates, and cake platters. I tuck sprigs of flowers into crisp linen napkins and fill the platters and cake-stands with cakes. I mound one or two kinds of fresh berries in one bowl and whipped cream in another. Everyone has a divine time eating cake, sipping tea, and exchanging bits of gossip.

For your own tea party, bake cakes of different textures and tastes; choose a fruit-based cake, a chocolate cake, a nutty cake, and a spice-charged cake. Offer hot tea with a small pitcher of cream, a bowl of sugar, and a plate of lemon slices. Set out the cakes attractively, using lacy doilies underneath them for a special effect, and let your guests settle down before you fill the teapot and pour the tea. In summer you might prefer to serve a pitcher of plain or minted iced tea or an iced herbal tea. (I like to offer my own very special "house blend" iced tea, which

I make with two or three different kinds of tea bags and then sweeten it with a fresh fruit syrup.)

A tea party is a fine time for introducing new neighbors to the community, visiting with old friends, getting together with colleagues, or just plain relaxing. It is a welcome interlude that warms the heart and brightens the day.

Bake Sale Cakes

———— ❖❖❖ ————

Buttermilk Chocolate Layer Cake   164
Coconut Layer Cake   166
Cocoa-Nut Swirl Coffee Cake   172
Coconut-Cinnamon Pan Cake   174
Banana-Coconut Coffee Cake   182
Date Coffee Cake   186
Blueberry–Walnut–Brown Sugar Buckle   194
Chocolate Pan Cake with Chocolate Fudge Frosting   196
Pecan Carrot Cake with Raisins   198
Fudgy Chocolate–Walnut Cake   200
Best Vanilla Pound Cake   218
Bourbon Pound Cake   224
Spice Pound Cake   226
Rich Nut Pound Cake   228
Cream Pound Cake   230
Chocolate Pound Cake   232
Blueberry Cakes   256
Cream Cheese–Chocolate Chip Cakes   258
Vanilla Cakes   260

Country Cakes That Use "Goods on Hand" (Basic Dairy and Pantry Staples)

———— ❖❖❖ ————

Marbled German Chocolate Cake   156
Black Walnut and Chocolate Pan Cake   158
Buttermilk Chocolate Layer Cake   164
Coconut Layer Cake   166
Cocoa-Nut Swirl Coffee Cake   172
Coconut-Cinnamon Pan Cake   174
Caramel Upside-Down Sticky Cake   188
Chocolate Pan Cake with Chocolate Fudge Frosting   196
Fudgy Chocolate–Walnut Cake   200
Best Vanilla Pound Cake   218
Grandma Lilly's Hot Milk Cake   220
Cream Pound Cake   230
Chocolate Pound Cake   232
Ginger Cakes   254
Cream Cheese–Chocolate Chip Cakes   258
Vanilla Cakes   260

Country Cakes That Use Fresh Fruits and Vegetables

—————— ❖❖❖ ——————

Orange Cake   160
Apple-Raisin Coffee Cake   176
Maple-Pumpkin Coffee Cake   178
Walnut–Sweet Potato Coffee Cake   180
Banana-Coconut Coffee Cake   182
Raspberry Coffee Cake   184
Blueberry–Walnut–Brown Sugar Buckle   194
Pecan Carrot Cake with Raisins   198
Peach Upside-Down Cake   206
Spiced Nectarine Upside-Down Cake   208
Apple-Ginger Upside-Down Cake   210
Plum Cake   238
Spicy Apple Cake   240
Fresh Peach Cake   242
Nectarine Cake   244
Blueberry Gingerbread   246
Chunky Apple Cakes with Pecans   252
Blueberry Cakes   256
Pear Cakes with Walnuts and Currants   262

Keeping Cakes

✦✦✦

Apple-Raisin Coffee Cake   176
Date Coffee Cake   186
Best Vanilla Pound Cake   218
Lemon–Poppy Seed Pound Cake   222
Bourbon Pound Cake   224
Spice Pound Cake   226
Rich Nut Pound Cake   228
Cream Pound Cake   230

THE JOY OF COUNTRY COOKIES

A heap of Sugar Cookie Hearts piled high in a basket lined with a gingham cloth, Cinnamon-Cashew "Dunking" Cookies tucked into an old enameled cookie box, a batch of crunchy Ginger Crisps or Heavenly Hash Brownies layered on a Depression-glass plate, several dozen Oatmeal-Raisin Saucers nestled in an earthenware batter bowl—these are country cookies, sweet morsels that are homey and good to eat.

Like pie and cake baking, cookie making is an established specialty of the American kitchen. While the soup pot simmered away on a corner of the stovetop, old-time cooks would stir together a mound of cookie dough; in between chores, they'd pinch off gobs, arrange them on sheet pans in neat rows, and bake the cookies in shifts. Later, lucky family members and friends would raid the cookie jar and munch away.

The old-fashioned cookies in this section taste of pure and familiar ingredients. They are made up of such things as oatmeal, nuts, dried and fresh fruit, aromatic spices, buttermilk, molasses, coconut, and chocolate. These goodies are perfect for filling up big glass apothecary jars or shiny metal cookie tins.

There are fat, cakelike cookies that, once upon a time, you would have found at the corner bakery or cooling on racks in your grandmother's kitchen. And there are handcrafted cookies that are just waiting to become part of your holiday tradition. These are the cookies that I love to bake—the meltingly rich rolled cookies made with butter and plenty of vanilla, soft molasses drops or fudgy chocolate morsels—and they seem to recapture all the textures and flavors we remember from childhood.

GOOD AND FRESH:
NOTES FROM A
COOKIE KITCHEN

When I was growing up, my mother always mixed up a batch of cookie dough in an enormous crockery bowl with a wooden spoon—even though an electric mixer stood ready and waiting to do the job on a countertop nearby. Step by step, she'd blend together the ingredients, then drop spoonfuls of dough onto lightly buttered and floured sheets; she'd shove the pans into the oven (sometimes Mother was a "hurry up" kind of baker) and remove them when golden, firm to the touch, and just right.

It must be true—a plate of warm cookies, made from many wholesome things, creates memories that linger on and on.

THE COUNTRY CUPBOARD

There's nothing quite like the sight and scent of fresh cookies moving from spatula to cooling rack and the process for making them is simple and rewarding. Home-made cookies have a distinctively rich flavor and "crumb"; they are made from ingredients we use in everyday baking.

In my kitchen, I keep a "cookie larder"—a few shelves in the cupboard that hold all the baking essentials. (The cookie larder has many of the same ingredients used for making pies and cakes.) One shelf holds both all-purpose and cake flour, stored in large wide-mouth jars, and sugar (granulated, superfine, soft brown, confectioners', and the flavored sugars I love to make). On another shelf, I arrange extracts (vanilla, chocolate, almond, lemon, coconut, maple), cornstarch, narrow tubes of plump vanilla beans, leaveners (baking powder, baking soda), dried fruit (raisins, figs, dates, apricots, peaches, pears, currants), oatmeal (plus homemade granola), cans of shortening, and a range of chocolate (bittersweet bars, unsweetened squares, chocolate chips).

In the refrigerator I stockpile fresh butter and eggs, buttermilk and whole milk, sour cream, and containers of both light and heavy cream. The cookies in this book are made with extra-large eggs and fresh, not previously frozen, unsalted butter. Dairy ingredients should be brought to room temperature before adding them to cookie batters and doughs so that they blend in easily with the other ingredients.

Cookie Dough Enhancements

Using flavored granulated or confectioners' sugar is a favorite way of mine to strengthen the taste of many cookie doughs. Air-dried lemon peel or several split vanilla beans can be added to a jar of sugar, stored for a while to mellow, then used when mixing up a bowlful of dough.

Each sugar is easy to make and lovely to have on hand.

For Vanilla-Scented Granulated Sugar or Vanilla-Scented Confectioners' Sugar, see page 219.

For Lemon-Scented Confectioners' Sugar, remove 16 strips of peel from 2 large lemons using a swivel-bladed peeler. Place the strips on a sheet of waxed paper and let them air-dry for about 12 to 24 hours, or until they are leathery. Turn the strips from time to time. Place 2 pounds of confectioners' sugar in a large clean jar. Bury the dried lemon strips in the sugar. Cover the jar with the lid. Store the sugar in a cool, dark place for at least 1 week before using. Use the sugar without the peels.

Most of the cookies in this book are made in a freestanding electric mixer according to the following method: Butter or shortening (or a combination of both) is creamed until soft and malleable for 2 to 3 minutes. Sugar is added to the butter and the two are mixed together at moderate speed until fluffy. Eggs or egg yolks (or some of each) are beaten in, followed by flavorings, any liquid, fruit puree or melted chocolate (if used), and a flour mixture (which generally contains leavening and some spices). Assorted ingredients, such as chocolate or butterscotch chips, diced fruit, chopped nuts, or marshmallow cream, may be folded into the dough at the last moment.

Other cookies are made by combining melted butter (or melted butter and chocolate) in a bowl with sugar, eggs, flavoring, and flour, using a wooden spoon or spatula. And a few of the bar cookies are made in two layers—the bottom layer consisting of a creamed cookie dough covered by a top layer of fruit, nuts, sugar, eggs, and flavorings stirred together in a bowl.

A soft drop-cookie dough is formed into teaspoon- or tablespoon-size mounds (as specified in each recipe) and arranged on buttered and floured cookie sheets or on sheets lined with cooking parchment paper. Batterlike doughs for brownies and some bar cookies are spooned directly into baking pans; these bars or squares emerge from the oven baked as a solid "cake." The "cake" is then cut into small pieces when it reaches room temperature. (I refer to each pan of uncut brownies, bars, squares, and so on as a "cake" because it describes what you will be working with.)

Yet another kind of cookie dough, which is firm enough to press into a decorative pan, is baked into huge nibbling cookies. This is the kind of dough used in the recipe for Giant Double Chocolate Rounds on page 364. The rounds are baked in fluted tart pans and are handy to serve at picnics or casual suppers.

To make a batch of cookies, all you really need is a great big bowl, a long wooden spoon, and some heavy cookie sheets, nothing more than what good cooks have been using for years.

An electric mixer, though, does make fast work out of creaming and blending ingredients and is indispensable for making large quantities of cookie dough, a real time-saver if you are baking for a function, a holiday sweet table, or a cookie swap. But any of the doughs in this book may be made by hand with excellent results.

Country cookies are usually baked on heavy aluminum cookie sheets; bar cookies, brownies, or squares are baked in standard baking pans. My cookie sheets measure about 14 x 18 inches; the long sides are flat and the short sides have slight rims. Cookies baked on these sheets emerge from the oven evenly baked and with a delicate crumb.

If you are outfitting your cookie kitchen with these sheets, buy three or four of them. While one batch of cookies is baking, you can assemble the next; when the just-baked cookies are removed from the sheets onto racks, cool those sheets before placing more mounds of dough on them. Rotating the sheets in this fashion and cooling them in between baking also works well when you use sheets of parchment paper: Lay out the sheets on the countertop and space the mounds or cutout shapes of dough on them as directed in each recipe. Just before baking (or as soon as the sheets have cooled), carefully slide the parchment onto the sheets.

Usually, I line the sheets with cooking parchment paper, which is available in twenty-square-foot rolls at cookware and hardware stores and at some supermarkets. Buttering and flouring the sheets is a time-honored ritual for some, but I think cookies baked on ungreased parchment are far easier to slip off with a spatula. (The paper can be wiped clean with a damp cloth and used over again for your next cookie-baking session.)

Rolled cookie dough, which is generally sensitive to heat, should be cut out into shapes when the dough is well chilled; if you are working with thoroughly chilled rolled dough (such as the dough for my Sugar Cookie Hearts on page 352), stamp out cookies from one sheet of dough at a time. And unless your kitchen is very, very hot, drop cookie dough can stand at room temperature while you are working with it.

The cookies, ready to be sent into the oven, must be baked with care. I prefer to bake one tray of cookies at a time on the middle-level rack of the oven. If you are in a hurry, you can bake the cookies on the upper and lower third-level racks, but be sure to switch the sheets from top to bottom and front to back halfway through the baking time.

Brownies and other bar cookies are baked in 8-, 9-, or 10-inch square baking pans, a 13 x 9 x 2-inch rectangular baking pan, or a 15 x 10 x 1-inch jelly roll pan. For these sizes, I prefer to use heavy aluminum; my favorite pans have straight sides, which lets you cut the cookies into neat bars or squares. Cookies baked in aluminum turn out even textured, with a good crumb.

The batter for my Cinnamon-Cashew "Dunking" Cookies (page 370), Chocolate Chip Rusks (page 374), and Layered Ginger Rusks (page 394) gets baked in empty aluminum ice cube trays. In the trays, the batter bakes into a small loaf that cuts into perfect rectangular slices; these trays work better than anything else. Thankfully, metal ice cube trays are still available at hardware stores. The trays come in two finishes, smooth and textured. I prefer the smooth-surfaced trays because the batter is less likely to stick to the surface when baked.

I love to shop at flea markets, tag sales, and antique shows. At them, I add such things to my collection of cooking equipment as old pie tins, baking molds for corn bread and other batter breads, cookie plaques, and cookie cutters. Over the years, I have found such lovely—and sometimes odd-shaped—cookie cutters as ornate angels, gingerbread ladies, fussy Victorian hearts, a man in the moon, and even cutters in the shape of a muffin or loaf of bread. These are fun to collect and are a fine addition to your own heritage of baking equipment.

Keeping a full cookie jar is a tradition I heartily recommend—it seems that everyone loves to come home to a plate of fresh cookies. And I hope that the recipes in this section encourage and preserve the art of cookie baking.

ON COOKIE
BASKETS

Wendy Wheeler

*M*y favorite cookie basket is made out of clear Depression glass; it has a fluted rim and tall handle. Small cabbage roses are impressed around the base. When the basket is filled with Sugar Cookie Hearts or Fruit Clusters, it seems the essence of country—comforting, casual, and charming.

Cookies look appealing layered in all kinds of baskets, whether they are made out of spindly twigs or wooden slats, porcelain or colored glass. Depending upon the depth of the basket, you can line it with several lacy paper doilies or a bright checkered tea towel just before adding the cookies. If the basket has a handle, it can be fussied up with a raffia bow tied to one side; or you can tie a small stack of cinnamon sticks with satin ribbon and attach that to the side of the basket.

Little packages of cookies look pretty arranged in a basket. Tie up handfuls of cookies in squares of cellophane to resemble small pouches. Set the pouches in a basket that has been lined with curly Spanish moss. (For this, choose among the Vanilla Melt-a-Ways on page 300, Lemon Butter Balls on page 326, Sugar Cookie Hearts on page 352, Double Vanilla "Dog Bones" on page 322, Maple Bars on page 320, or Milk Chocolate–Almond Bars on page 368.)

Lots of miniature baskets, lined with moss and filled with single packages of cookies, are wonderful for handing out to dinner party guests or to children during the holiday season. And a huge basket filled with a still life of assorted cookies is a handsome addition to the Thanksgiving groaning board; be sure to include turkey-shaped sugar cookies made from the dough used in the recipe for Sugar Cookie Hearts (page 352).

HEART TO HEART

Heart-shaped baking implements—from cookie molds, to cutters, to individual cookie tins—are especially pleasing to use in the making of country cookies.

Over the years, I've amassed a whole range of these culinary implements and I use them frequently in baking and as tabletop accessories. Old-time bakeware, such as small cutters and tiny molds, can be used to decorate teatime trays or they can be tied to the sides of cookie baskets. Cookies look beautiful arranged in old heart-shaped wooden bowls or baskets lined with a linen cloth. Heart-shaped trays made of porcelain, if you can find them, are ideal for serving tender rolled cookies or bar cookies; the trays have deeply scalloped edges and come in a variety of colors.

Heart-shaped cookie cutters come in many sizes, from the tiny one-inchers to the large five-inchers. There are several cookie doughs in this book that, once rolled out, are especially suited to stamping out with a heart-shaped cutter (these doughs must hold their shape while baking): the vanilla-rich dough in the recipe for Double Vanilla ''Dog Bones'' (page 322), the buttery chocolate dough on page 364 in the recipe for Giant Double Chocolate Rounds (omit the chocolate chips and bake the smaller cookies at 325 degrees for 20 minutes, or until firm), and, of course, the sugar cookie dough in the recipe for Sugar Cookie Hearts on page 352.

Soft, moldable doughs, such as the kind used for Vanilla Melt-a-Ways on page 300, Black Walnut Butter Drops on page 362, or Lemon Butter Balls on page 326 can be pressed into tin cookie plaques. The plaques look like madeleine molds, only each depression is in the shape of a heart. To fill these plaques, film the inside of each form with nonstick cookware spray, then gently press about a tablespoon of dough into each form (more or less according to size); gently smooth over the top with a flexible palette knife. After the cookies have been baked, invert them into cooling racks and dust with granulated or confectioners' sugar (if you are using the Vanilla Melt-a-Way dough, omit the final rolling in sugar; sprinkle the cookies with the sugar while they are warm).

COOKIE JAR TREATS

COOKIE JAR TREATS

———————— ❖❖❖ ————————

Vanilla Melt-a-Ways 300
Sour Cream–Spice Cookies 302
Orange-Raisin Drops 304
Chocolate Gems 306
Applesauce Pillows 308
Mint Chocolate Crisps 310
Pear-Oatmeal Drops 312
Pumpkin-Fig Mounds 314

*I*t's the little things that count: pints of homemade cranberry-pear butter lining the shelves of the kitchen pantry, a bottle of fresh raspberry syrup tucked into the refrigerator, a huge jar of cookies sitting on the kitchen counter. These are the small pleasures of life and they are so nice to have around.

The cookie jar of my childhood was made out of pressed glass and its sweet contents were protected by a ground glass lid that kept the contents fresh and appealing. More than likely, you'd find my mother's famous Layered Ginger Rusks in the jar or Oatmeal-Raisin Saucers. I could never resist any of those cookies and I ate them a handful at a time. Between baking days, when the inside of the cookie jar was reduced to crumbs, Mother would fill the jar with caramels. Caramels were never a satisfactory substitute for cookies and this was a sad state of affairs.

To me, the sight of a full cookie jar evokes feelings of comfort and contentment. So I always keep my mother's big glass jar stuffed with cookies, varying the flavor and texture from week to week—to continue the nostalgic tradition and to have something good and sweet on hand.

In this chapter, you'll find soft applesauce cookies filled with raisins, oatmeal cookies flecked with bits of chopped pears and pecans, and chewy chocolate cookies dotted with pools of chopped bittersweet chocolate. Once baked, these cookies are very hard to resist and they just beg for a pitcher of ice-cold milk or a pot of hot coffee for serving alongside a basket of them.

Other cookies in this book that would fill up the cookie jar handsomely are my Double Vanilla "Dog Bones" (page 322), Ginger Crisps (page 346), Apple Butter Cookies (page 348), Pumpkin-Spice Cookies (page 357), Sugar Cookie Hearts (page 352), Black Walnut Butter Drops (page 362), Cinnamon-Cashew "Dunking" Cookies (page 370), Chocolate Chip Rusks (page 374), Fruit Clusters (page 388), Butterscotch-Granola Disks (page 390), or Banana-Oatmeal Pillows (page 382).

❖❖❖❖❖❖❖❖❖❖❖❖❖❖❖❖❖

Vanilla Melt-a-Ways

3¼ cups *unsifted* all-purpose flour

1 cup plus 3 tablespoons *unsifted* cake flour

1 teaspoon baking soda

¼ teaspoon baking powder

1 teaspoon cream of tartar

1 teaspoon salt

¾ teaspoon freshly grated nutmeg

These featherlight cookies, dotted with the seed scrapings from a plump vanilla bean, are tender and crisp—the combination of oil and butter makes them so. The cookie dough, which is uncommonly easy to work with, can be shaped into plump mounds, crescents, or logs. Rolled in vanilla-scented sugar and baked until just golden, these sweet morsels are delicious served with a bowl of poached fruit or ice cream, or simply on their own, washed down with big cups of Hot Spiced Cider (page 401).

———❖❖❖———

Lightly butter and flour 4 cookie sheets or line the sheets with lengths of cooking parchment paper; set aside. Preheat the oven to 375 degrees.

½ pound (2 sticks) unsalted butter, softened at room temperature

1 cup vegetable oil

1 cup *unsifted* Vanilla-Scented Granulated Sugar (page 219)

1 cup *unsifted* Vanilla-Scented Confectioners' Sugar (page 219)

Seed scrapings from the inside of 1 vanilla bean

1 extra-large egg plus 2 extra-large egg yolks, at room temperature

2 teaspoons pure vanilla extract

2 teaspoons milk, at room temperature

FOR ROLLING THE COOKIES:

About 1½ cups Vanilla-Scented Granulated Sugar (page 219)

About 60 cookies

Sift the all-purpose flour, cake flour, baking soda, baking powder, cream of tartar, salt, and nutmeg onto a sheet of waxed paper.

Cream the butter in the large bowl of an electric mixer on moderate speed for 2 minutes. Add the oil and beat for 2 minutes. Blend in the granulated sugar and beat for 2 minutes. Add the confectioners' sugar and beat for 2 minutes. Blend in the vanilla bean scrapings, egg, egg yolks, vanilla extract, and milk; beat 2 minutes, scraping down the sides of the mixing bowl frequently. On low speed (or by hand), blend in the sifted dry ingredients in 3 additions, beating just until the particles of flour have been absorbed.

Form balls, crescents, or logs from level tablespoons of dough and carefully roll them in the granulated sugar. Place the cookies 1½ inches apart on the prepared cookie sheets. If you have formed the dough into balls, flatten each ball with the tines of a fork, making a crisscross pattern.

Bake the cookies, one sheet at a time, on the middle-level rack of the oven for 10 to 12 minutes, or until pale golden and firm to the touch.

Transfer the cookies to cooling racks, using a wide spatula. Cool for 20 minutes. Store the cookies in an airtight tin.

Sour Cream–Spice Cookies

2 cups *sifted* all-purpose flour

1 cup plus 2 tablespoons *sifted* cake flour

¾ teaspoon baking powder

¾ teaspoon baking soda

¾ teaspoon salt

2 teaspoons ground cinnamon

1 teaspoon freshly grated nutmeg

1 teaspoon ground ginger

½ teaspoon ground allspice

¼ teaspoon ground cloves

12 tablespoons (1½ sticks) unsalted butter, softened at room temperature

¼ cup shortening

1 cup Vanilla-Scented Granulated Sugar (page 219)

These are dreamy cookies, rich in sour cream and eggs, and touched by five different spices. The cinnamon, nutmeg, ginger, allspice, and cloves form a gentle backdrop to the dairy ingredients. I love them plain but sometimes fancy them up with drizzles of confectioners' sugar glaze (see Baking Note).

A batch of Sour Cream–Spice Cookies is a perfect companion for a big earthenware bowl filled with Hot Spiced Cider (page 401).

Lightly butter and flour 4 cookie sheets or line the sheets with lengths of cooking parchment paper; set aside. Preheat the oven to 375 degrees.

Resift the all-purpose flour and cake flour with the baking powder, baking soda, salt, cinnamon, nutmeg, ginger, allspice, and cloves onto a sheet of waxed paper.

Cream the butter and shortening in the large bowl of an electric mixer on moderate speed for 2 minutes. Add the granulated sugar in 2 additions, beating for 1 minute after each portion is added. Add the light brown sugar and beat for 1 minute. Blend in the egg and egg yolks; beat 1 minute. On low speed (or by hand), blend in half of the sifted mixture. Blend in all of the sour cream, then the remaining sifted mixture.

Drop the dough by level tablespoons onto the prepared cookie sheets, placing the mounds 2 inches apart.

⅓ cup firmly packed light brown sugar

1 extra-large egg plus 2 extra-large egg yolks, at room temperature

1 cup sour cream blended with 2 teaspoons pure vanilla extract

---

About 42 cookies

Bake the cookies, one sheet at a time, on the middle-level rack of the oven for 11 to 12 minutes, or until light brown and firm to the touch.

Transfer the cookies to cooling racks, using a wide spatula. Cool for 20 minutes. Store the cookies in an airtight tin.

Baking Note: To make the confectioners' sugar glaze for this cookie, combine 3 tablespoons light cream, ¼ teaspoon pure vanilla extract, and about ¾ cup confectioners' sugar. The glaze should be smooth and fluid enough to pour from a spoon (if not, stir in a teaspoon of sugar at a time if it is too thin or several drops of milk if it is too thick). Drizzle the glaze over each cookie from a small spoon and let it firm up completely before storing the cookies between sheets of waxed paper.

Orange-Raisin Drops

2½ cups *unsifted* all-purpose flour

½ cup *unsifted* cake flour

¾ teaspoon baking soda

¼ teaspoon baking powder

¾ teaspoon salt

½ teaspoon ground cinnamon

½ teaspoon freshly grated nutmeg

¼ teaspoon ground allspice

¼ teaspoon ground ginger

8 tablespoons (1 stick) unsalted butter, softened at room temperature

½ cup shortening

1 cup maple sugar

½ cup granulated sugar

3 tablespoons freshly grated orange rind

2 teaspoons pure orange extract

The tangy flavor of freshly grated orange rind and orange juice winds through this cookie dough, partnering nicely with the golden raisins, maple sugar, and spices. Soft, old-fashioned Orange-Raisin Drops are particularly good teamed up with tall glasses of milk or mugs of hot chocolate, and they are a welcome addition to the school (or office) brown bag lunch.

My paternal grandmother, Lilly Yockelson, and I used to bake these cookies together on many an afternoon. Grandma loved golden raisins and used them here, along with a cupful of chopped dates. I like the cookies without the dates, and I have made the dough a bit more delicate by replacing a small amount of the all-purpose flour with cake flour.

Lightly butter and flour 4 cookie sheets or line the sheets with lengths of cooking parchment paper; set aside. Preheat the oven to 375 degrees.

Sift the all-purpose flour, cake flour, baking soda, baking powder, salt, cinnamon, nutmeg, allspice, and ginger onto a sheet of waxed paper. Cream the butter and shortening in the large bowl of an electric mixer on moderate speed for 2 minutes. Add the maple sugar and beat for 2 minutes. Add the granulated sugar and beat for 1 minute longer. Beat in the orange peel and orange extract. Blend in the eggs, one at a time, beating well after each addition. Beat in the egg yolks. Blend in the orange juice. On low speed (or by hand), blend

2 extra-large eggs plus 2
    extra-large egg yolks, at
    room temperature
¼ cup freshly squeezed
    orange juice
1¾ cups golden raisins

About 48 cookies

in the sifted dry ingredients in 2 additions, beating just until
the particles of flour have been absorbed. By hand, stir in the
raisins.

Drop the dough by rounded tablespoons onto the prepared
cookie sheets, placing the mounds 2 inches apart.

Bake the cookies, one sheet at a time, on the middle-level
rack of the oven for 12 to 14 minutes, or until light brown and
just firm to the touch.

Transfer the cookies to cooling racks, using a wide spatula.
Cool for 20 minutes. Store the cookies in an airtight tin.

Chocolate Gems

2 cups *sifted* cake flour

1 cup *sifted* all-purpose flour

¾ teaspoon baking powder

¾ teaspoon baking soda

1 teaspoon salt

½ teaspoon ground cinnamon

12 tablespoons (1½ sticks) unsalted butter, softened at room temperature

1 cup Vanilla-Scented Granulated Sugar (page 219)

Seed scrapings from the inside of 1 vanilla bean

1 extra-large egg plus 1 extra-large egg yolk, at room temperature

5 ounces (5 squares) unsweetened chocolate, melted and cooled

1 teaspoon pure vanilla extract

Indeed, these cookies are gems: crisp-chewy, buttery, with soft chocolate overtones. The chopped bittersweet chocolate that meanders through the dough forms tiny chocolate "puddles" throughout the baked cookie, giving this sweet a candylike quality.

Cookies made from heaping tablespoons of this dough look homey when piled into a beautiful woven basket and served forth with a pitcher of cold milk. Smaller, teaspoon-size mounds of dough bake into daintier, two-bite-size cookies, and these are lovely piled onto a softly colored pressed glass plate for nibbling with cups of espresso.

Lightly butter and flour 4 cookie sheets or line the sheets with lengths of cooking parchment paper; set aside. Preheat the oven to 350 degrees.

Resift the cake flour and all-purpose flour with the baking powder, baking soda, salt, and cinnamon onto a sheet of waxed paper.

Cream the butter in the large bowl of an electric mixer on moderate speed for 2 minutes. Add the granulated sugar in 2 additions, beating for 1 minute after each portion is added. Beat in the vanilla bean scrapings and egg. Beat in the egg yolk and blend well. On low speed, add the melted chocolate and vanilla and chocolate extracts and beat slowly until the chocolate is evenly blended in. On low speed (or by hand), blend in half of the sifted mixture. Blend in all of the cream,

1 teaspoon chocolate
   extract
½ cup light cream
1 cup chopped
   bittersweet chocolate

About 50 cookies

then the remaining sifted mixture. Stir in the chopped bitter-sweet chocolate.

Drop the dough by rounded tablespoons onto the prepared cookie sheets, placing the mounds 1½ inches apart.

Bake the cookies, one sheet at a time, on the middle-level rack of the oven for 10 to 12 minutes, or until just firm to the touch.

Transfer the cookies to cooling racks, using a wide spatula. Cool for 20 minutes. Store the cookies in an airtight tin.

Applesauce Pillows

2¾ cups *unsifted* all-purpose flour

¾ cup *unsifted* cake flour

1 teaspoon baking soda

¾ teaspoon baking powder

¾ teaspoon salt

2 teaspoons ground cinnamon

1 teaspoon freshly grated nutmeg

½ teaspoon ground ginger

¼ teaspoon ground allspice

¼ teaspoon ground cloves

½ pound (2 sticks) unsalted butter, softened at room temperature

1 cup granulated sugar

¾ cup firmly packed light brown sugar

Making cookies with applesauce, spices, and molasses has come to be one of my fall baking rituals—along with baking apple breads, apple muffins, and apple cakes and putting up jars of apple butter made with fresh cider.

These cushions of apple goodness are moist, soft, and chewy with raisins. Serve the pillows with a pitcher of hot or cold cider, brewed lemon tea, or hot coffee.

Lightly butter and flour 4 cookie sheets or line the sheets with lengths of cooking parchment paper; set aside. Preheat the oven to 375 degrees.

Sift the all-purpose flour, cake flour, baking soda, baking powder, salt, cinnamon, nutmeg, ginger, allspice, and cloves onto a sheet of waxed paper.

Cream the butter in the large bowl of an electric mixer on moderate speed for 2 minutes. Add the granulated sugar in 2 additions, beating for 1 minute after each portion is added. Add the light brown sugar and beat for 2 minutes. Beat in the egg and continue beating for 1 minute; add the egg yolk and beat for a minute longer. On low speed, blend in the molasses, applesauce, and shredded apple. With the mixer still on low speed (or by hand), blend in the sifted mixture in 2 additions, beating just until the particles of flour have been absorbed. By hand, stir in the raisins and walnuts.

Drop the dough by rounded tablespoons onto the prepared cookie sheets, placing the mounds 2½ inches apart.

1 extra-large egg plus 1
  extra-large egg yolk, at
  room temperature
¼ cup light molasses
¾ cup applesauce
½ cup shredded apple
  (about half a
  medium-size apple)
¾ cup dark seedless
  raisins
¾ cup chopped walnuts

About 48 cookies

Bake the cookies, one sheet at a time, on the middle-level rack of the oven for 11 to 13 minutes, or until just firm to the touch.

Transfer the cookies to cooling racks, using a wide spatula. Cool for 20 minutes. Store the cookies in an airtight tin.

Mint Chocolate Crisps

1½ cups plus 3 tablespoons *sifted* all-purpose flour

¾ teaspoon baking soda

¾ teaspoon salt

12 tablespoons (1½ sticks) unsalted butter, softened at room temperature

1½ cups granulated sugar

1 extra-large egg plus 1 extra-large egg yolk, at room temperature

1 teaspoon pure vanilla extract

1 teaspoon peppermint extract

½ teaspoon chocolate extract

2 teaspoons light corn syrup

3 ounces (3 squares) unsweetened chocolate, melted and cooled

Enriched with melted unsweetened chocolate, thoroughly loaded with mint-flavored chocolate chips and good butter, this dough makes cookies that are crisp and crunchy. While the cookies are baking, the whole house is filled with an intriguing scent—a combination of mint and chocolate—and before you know it, everyone begins to snatch still-warm cookies from the cooling rack.

Serve the crisps piled into a basket (of woven wood, ceramic, or glass) lined with a gingham cloth along with big tumblers of iced coffee or thick vanilla milk shakes.

Lightly butter and flour 4 cookie sheets or line the sheets with lengths of cooking parchment paper; set aside. Preheat the oven to 400 degrees.

Resift the flour with the baking soda and salt onto a sheet of waxed paper.

Cream the butter in the large bowl of an electric mixer on moderate speed for 2 minutes. Add the granulated sugar in 2 additions, beating for 1 minute after each portion is added. Beat in the egg and egg yolk. Blend in the vanilla, peppermint, and chocolate extracts. Slowly blend in the corn syrup and melted chocolate. On low speed (or by hand), add the sifted mixture in 2 additions, beating just until the particles of flour have been absorbed. By hand, fold in the chocolate chips.

1½ cups mint-flavored
chocolate chips

About 48 cookies

Drop the dough by level tablespoons onto the prepared cookie sheets, placing the mounds 1½ inches apart.

Bake the cookies, one sheet at a time, on the middle-level rack of the oven for 10 to 12 minutes, or until set and just firm to the touch.

Transfer the cookies to cooling racks using a wide spatula. Cool for 20 minutes. Store the cookies in an airtight tin.

Pear-Oatmeal Drops

1½ cups *unsifted* all-purpose flour

¾ cup plus 2 tablespoons *unsifted* cake flour

1¼ teaspoons baking powder

¾ teaspoon baking soda

¾ teaspoon salt

2½ teaspoons ground cinnamon

1 teaspoon freshly grated nutmeg

¾ teaspoon ground ginger

½ teaspoon ground allspice

¼ teaspoon ground cloves

8 tablespoons (1 stick) unsalted butter, softened at room temperature

½ cup shortening

1 cup firmly packed light brown sugar

½ cup superfine sugar

These soft mounds are a specialty of my autumn baking kitchen, the season when I love to work with all the harvest fruits and vegetables—pumpkins, cranberries, apples, chestnuts, and the entire jewel-like range of dried fruit. Chopped dried pears taste wonderful in this oatmeal cookie, but you can substitute dried peaches or apricots with excellent results.

Pear-Oatmeal Drops look pretty layered in a woodenware or wireware basket that has been lined with a checkered or striped tea towel. With the cookies, sip a cup of English Breakfast tea or Hot Spiced Cider (page 401).

———— ❖❖❖ ————

Lightly butter and flour 4 cookie sheets or line the sheets with lengths of cooking parchment paper; set aside. Preheat the oven to 400 degrees.

Sift the all-purpose flour, cake flour, baking powder, baking soda, salt, cinnamon, nutmeg, ginger, allspice, and cloves onto a sheet of waxed paper.

Cream the butter and shortening in the large bowl of an electric mixer on moderate speed for 2 minutes. Add the light brown sugar and beat for 2 minutes. Add the superfine sugar and beat for 1 minute longer. Beat in the eggs, one at a time, blending well after each addition. Beat in the egg yolks. Blend in the sour cream–vanilla mixture. On low speed (or by hand), add the sifted mixture in 2 additions, beating just until

2 extra-large eggs plus 2
extra-large egg yolks, at
room temperature

¾ cup sour cream
blended with 2½
teaspoons pure vanilla
extract

2¾ cups quick-cooking
oatmeal

1¾ cups chopped moist
dried pears

1 cup chopped pecans

About 48 cookies

the particles of flour have been absorbed. By hand, stir in the oatmeal, pears, and pecans.

Drop the dough by rounded tablespoons onto the prepared cookie sheets, placing the mounds 2 inches apart.

Bake the cookies, one sheet at a time, on the middle-level rack of the oven for 12 minutes, or until set, just firm to the touch, and light golden.

Transfer the cookies to cooling racks, using a wide spatula. Cool for 20 minutes. Store the cookies in an airtight tin.

Pumpkin-Fig Mounds

2½ cups *unsifted* all-purpose flour

½ cup *unsifted* cake flour

1¼ teaspoons baking powder

¾ teaspoon baking soda

¾ teaspoon salt

2 teaspoons ground cinnamon

1 teaspoon ground ginger

1 teaspoon freshly grated nutmeg

¼ teaspoon ground cloves

¼ teaspoon ground allspice

½ pound (2 sticks) unsalted butter, softened at room temperature

½ cup shortening

1 cup granulated sugar

½ cup firmly packed light brown sugar

Several years ago, I baked these cookies a few days before the big Thanksgiving feast. I packed them up, two dozen at a time, in shiny tins embossed with autumn leaves. I gave a tin to each guest invited for Thanksgiving dinner—a bread-and-butter gift that was a token of friendship. This was my way of celebrating the harvest. Pumpkin-Fig Mounds taste good accompanied by big cups of mulled wine, Hot Spiced Cider (page 401), or freshly brewed coffee.

Lightly butter and flour 4 cookie sheets or line the sheets with lengths of cooking parchment paper; set aside. Preheat the oven to 375 degrees.

Sift the all-purpose flour, cake flour, baking powder, baking soda, salt, cinnamon, ginger, nutmeg, cloves, and allspice onto a sheet of waxed paper.

Cream the butter and shortening in the large bowl of an electric mixer on moderate speed for 2 minutes. Add the granulated sugar and beat for 2 minutes. Add the brown sugar and beat for a minute longer. Beat in the egg and egg yolk. Blend in the vanilla, molasses, and pumpkin puree (the mixture may look curdled at this point and that's okay). On low speed (or by hand), add the sifted mixture in 2 additions, beating just until the particles of flour have been absorbed. By hand, stir in the figs and walnuts.

Drop the dough by rounded tablespoons onto the prepared cookie sheets, placing the mounds 2½ inches apart.

1 extra-large egg plus 1
extra-large egg yolk, at
room temperature

2 teaspoons pure vanilla
extract

1 tablespoon light
molasses

1½ cups unsweetened
pumpkin puree

1½ cups stemmed and
chopped dried figs

½ cup chopped walnuts

About 42 cookies

Bake the cookies, one sheet at a time, on the middle-level rack of the oven for 12 to 14 minutes, or until set and just firm to the touch.

Transfer the cookies to cooling racks, using a wide spatula. Cool for 20 minutes. Store the cookies in an airtight tin.

BAKE SALE
GEMS

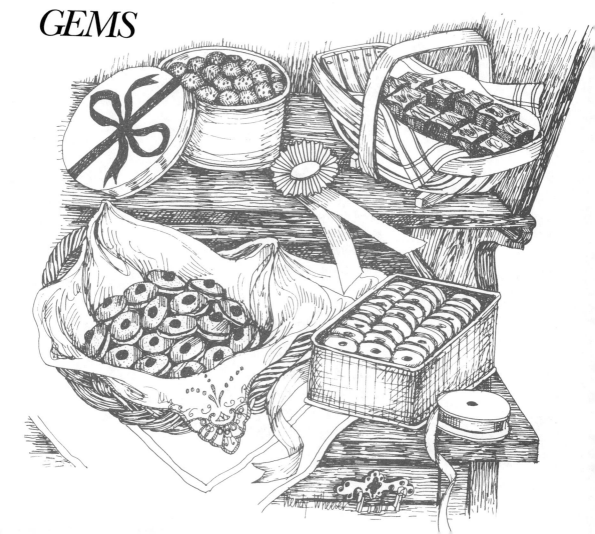

BAKE SALE GEMS

—◈◈◈—

Maple Bars   320

Double Vanilla "Dog Bones"   322

Chocolate Nut Crunch Squares   324

Lemon Butter Balls   326

Three Nut Bars   328

Coconut Dreams   330

BAKE SALE BROWNIES

Grandma Lilly's Brownies   332

Heavenly Hash Brownies   334

Double Chocolate–Walnut Fudgies   336

Coconut-Chocolate "Swirlies"   338

Chocolate Toffee Squares   340

*O*ftentimes, the best of home baking is represented at school bake sales and other charity functions when good cooks contribute cookies, pies, and cakes made from scratch. Cookies, it seems, are often snapped up by the dozen, parceled out in clear cellophane bags, sacks, or pouches. (And cakes, depending on their size and shape, are sold sliced or whole.)

Those people who love to bake and share their handmade sweets generally use some heirloom recipe that has become a specialty of their kitchen. Over the years, I have baked miniature pound cakes and fruit cakes, plus all sorts of sweet and savory breads. And I have baked dozens and dozens of Grandma Lilly's Brownies (page 332), Chocolate Toffee Squares (page 340), stacks of Lemon Butter Balls (page 326), and huge sheet pans full of Maple Bars (page 320)—all for events that raised funds for increasing benefits and wages for schoolteachers or for enlarging staffs at day-care centers.

Any of the cookies in this chapter can be made in quantity and held for safekeeping in tightly sealed tins or rigid storage containers. The Double Vanilla "Dog Bones" or Lemon Butter Balls can be tied up in bundles of six or twelve and secured with a curly ribbon. The brownies and bar cookies can be packed individually in plastic wrap, or in neat bundles of four or six and enclosed in heavy cellophane. Individual brownies look appealing stacked in baskets or galvanized steel pails lined with lacy paper doilies.

In addition to the recipes in this chapter, the Ginger Crisps (page 346),

Butterscotch-Granola Disks (page 390), Bittersweet Chocolate–Caramel Bars (page 354), Milk Chocolate–Almond Bars (page 368), Pecan Pie Squares (page 393), or Peanut Delights (page 380) would make a fine contribution to a bake sale. Any of these cookies are a welcome hostess gift: Place the cellophane-wrapped goodies in a good-looking stenciled tin or wooden box lined with fresh lemon or galax leaves.

❖❖❖❖❖❖❖❖❖❖❖❖❖❖❖❖❖

Maple Bars

½ cup *unsifted* all-purpose flour

½ cup *unsifted* cake flour

¼ teaspoon baking powder

¼ teaspoon salt

¼ teaspoon freshly grated nutmeg

8 tablespoons (1 stick) unsalted butter, melted and cooled

¾ cup firmly packed light brown sugar

2 extra-large egg yolks, at room temperature

1½ teaspoons pure vanilla extract

Chewy and dense, these bars are a favorite of many people I know who love things like butterscotch brownies, translucent nut pies (especially walnut and pecan), and toffee bars.

Maple Bars can be made in great quantity (this recipe doubles or triples easily) and baked five to six days before you plan to serve them or sell them at a bake sale. Arrange in bars in shallow tins or heavy plastic containers in two layers, separating the top and bottom layer with a sheet of waxed paper.

These bars are heavenly with a cup of hot cider, a glass of ice-cold Real Lemonade (page 400), or a mug of freshly brewed coffee.

———❖❖❖———

Lightly butter and flour a 9-inch square baking pan. Line the bottom of the pan with a square of waxed paper; set aside. Preheat the oven to 350 degrees.

½ teaspoon maple extract
¼ cup pure maple syrup
1 cup chopped walnuts

18 bars

Sift the all-purpose flour, cake flour, baking powder, salt, and nutmeg onto a sheet of waxed paper.

Whisk the melted butter, brown sugar, and egg yolks in a large mixing bowl. Blend in the vanilla and maple extracts. Stir in the maple syrup. Toss the walnuts with 2 teaspoons of the sifted flour mixture in a separate bowl. Stir in the walnuts and the sifted mixture, blending just until the particles of flour have been absorbed.

Spoon the batter into the prepared pan.

Bake on the middle-level rack of the oven for 30 to 35 minutes, or until light golden on top and just firm to the touch. (The entire cake will begin to pull away from the sides of the baking pan when done.)

Cool in the pan on a rack until it reaches room temperature, about 2 hours. Invert onto a second cooling rack, peel away the waxed paper, and invert again onto a cutting board.

Cut into 18 bars and store them in an airtight tin.

Double Vanilla "Dog Bones"

3½ cups *unsifted* all-purpose flour

½ cup *unsifted* cake flour

2 teaspoons cornstarch

½ teaspoon baking powder

¾ teaspoon salt

1 pound (4 sticks) unsalted butter, softened at room temperature

1 cup plus 2 tablespoons *unsifted* Vanilla-Scented Confectioners' Sugar (page 219)

2½ teaspoons pure vanilla extract

1 tablespoon milk, at room temperature

Seed scrapings from the inside of 1 vanilla bean

One holiday season several years ago, I baked many, many cookies for gifts and to have around the house. Tired of working with cutters in the shape of angels, bells, and holly sprigs, I pulled out some whimsical cutters—a pear, a teddy bear, a hand, a foot, and a dog bone. I rolled out many batches of the buttery, vanilla-flavored dough given below. I stamped out the sheets of dough with the 3-inch dog bone cutter (it turned out to be the perfect size for these cookies). Friends received their tin of "bones" and every year look forward to these cookies, now a tradition I can't seem to escape.

The "dog bones" are terrific keeping cookies, perfect for making ahead, storing in tins, and carrying to bake sales.

Any of the refreshments on pages 400 to 402 can be offered with a plate of these cookies.

Lightly butter and flour 3 or 4 cookie sheets or line the sheets with lengths of cooking parchment paper; set aside.

Sift the all-purpose flour, cake flour, cornstarch, baking powder, and salt onto a sheet of waxed paper.

Cream the butter in the large bowl of an electric mixer on moderate speed for 3 minutes. Add the confectioners' sugar in 2 batches, beating for 1 minute after each portion is added; scrape down the sides of the mixing bowl several times after adding the sugar. Blend in the vanilla extract, milk, and vanilla bean scrapings. On low speed (or by hand), blend in the sifted mixture in 3 additions, beating just until the particles of flour have been absorbed.

About ⅓ cup
  Vanilla-Scented
  Granulated Sugar
  (page 219)

About 42 cookies

Divide the dough into 2 portions and form each into a rough cake. Roll each cake between sheets of waxed paper to a thickness of a scant ½ inch. Refrigerate the sheets of dough on a cookie sheet until they are very firm, about 6 hours. (The sheets of dough can be kept in the refrigerator for up to 3 days before baking; once the dough has firmed up, double-wrap the sheets in plastic wrap.)

Working with one sheet at a time, remove the sheet from the refrigerator and peel off the top layer of waxed paper. Stamp out the entire sheet of dough with the dog bone cutter. Remove each cookie from the bottom sheet of waxed paper with a small, thin palette knife. Place the cookies 1½ inches apart on the prepared cookie sheets. (Reroll the scraps between sheets of waxed paper, chill, and cut out more cookies.)

Preheat the oven to 350 degrees.

Bake the cookies, one sheet at a time, on the middle-level rack of the oven for 15 minutes, or until pale golden and firm to the touch.

Transfer the cookies to cooling racks using a wide spatula. Sprinkle a little vanilla sugar over the tops of the cookies while they are still warm. Cool for 20 minutes. Store the cookies in an airtight tin.

Chocolate Nut Crunch Squares

FOR THE WALNUT COOKIE LAYER:

1½ cups *unsifted* all-purpose flour

¼ cup *unsifted* cake flour

2 teaspoons cornstarch

¼ teaspoon salt

8 tablespoons (1 stick) unsalted butter, softened at room temperature

½ cup firmly packed light brown sugar

¼ teaspoon pure vanilla extract

1 teaspoon milk, at room temperature

¼ cup finely chopped walnuts

These homestyle squares are made up of a crumbly short-breadlike base that's punctuated with chopped walnuts, and a topping of eggs, walnuts, brown sugar, and chocolate.

Chocolate Nut Crunch Squares look attractive—and tempting—piled in a shallow basket or in an open cookie tin lined with a pastel-colored tea towel. And remember to take a batch of them on a summer picnic and serve with a windfall of fresh raspberries.

Lightly butter and flour a 13 x 9 x 2-inch baking pan; set aside. Preheat the oven to 350 degrees.

For the walnut cookie layer, sift the all-purpose flour, cake flour, cornstarch, and salt onto a sheet of waxed paper.

Cream the butter in the large bowl of an electric mixer on moderate speed for 2 minutes. Add the brown sugar and beat for 1 minute. Add the vanilla and milk and beat for 1 minute longer. On low speed (or by hand), blend in the sifted mixture in 2 additions, beating just until the particles of flour have been absorbed. Stir in the chopped walnuts.

Press the cookie dough evenly on the bottom of the prepared pan. Bake the cookie layer on the middle-level rack of the oven for 15 to 20 minutes, or until an even golden color and firm to the touch. Remove from the oven and set aside on a cooling rack.

For the chocolate and nut topping, combine the brown sugar, granulated sugar, corn syrup, salt, vanilla, egg, and egg yolks

½ cup firmly packed light
brown sugar

¼ cup granulated sugar

¼ cup light corn syrup

¼ teaspoon salt

1 teaspoon pure vanilla
extract

1 extra-large egg plus 2
extra-large egg yolks, at
room temperature

1½ cups chopped walnuts

1 cup chopped
bittersweet chocolate

36 squares

in a large mixing bowl. Beat well. Stir in the chopped walnuts
and chocolate.

Spoon the topping evenly over the cookie base. Bake on the
middle-level rack of the oven for 20 to 25 minutes, or until the
topping is set and firm to the touch.

Cool in the pan on a rack until it reaches room temperature,
about 2 hours. Cut into 36 squares and store in an airtight tin.

Lemon Butter Balls

1¾ cups *unsifted*
    all-purpose flour

¼ cup *unsifted* cake flour

¼ teaspoon baking soda

Pinch of salt

½ pound (2 sticks)
    unsalted butter,
    softened at room
    temperature

½ cup *unsifted*
    Lemon-Scented
    Confectioners' Sugar
    (page 287)

2 teaspoons pure lemon
    extract

1 tablespoon freshly
    grated lemon peel

¼ cup ground walnuts

FOR ROLLING THE COOKIES:

About 1½ cups *unsifted*
    Lemon-Scented
    Confectioners' Sugar
    (page 287)

About 42 cookies

Lemon Butter Balls are softly flavored with finely grated lemon peel, lemon extract, and Lemon-Scented Confectioners' Sugar. The dough, which is a joy to work with, can be shaped into crescents and logs in addition to balls. For quantity baking, you can make up several batches of the dough and refrigerate each in a tightly sealed container for up to five days. On baking day, remove each package of dough about 15 minutes before you're going to form the balls.

These meltingly rich cookies are just the thing to serve with tall glasses of my Real Lemonade (page 400), Summer Fruit Medley (page 402), or minted iced tea.

———❖❖❖———

Lightly butter and flour 4 cookie sheets or line the sheets with lengths of cooking parchment paper; set aside. Preheat the oven to 325 degrees.

Sift the all-purpose flour, cake flour, baking soda, and salt onto a sheet of waxed paper.

Cream the butter in the large bowl of an electric mixer on moderate speed for 2 minutes. Add the confectioners' sugar and beat for 1 minute. Blend in the lemon extract, lemon peel, and walnuts. On low speed (or by hand), blend in the sifted mixture in 2 additions, beating just until the particles of flour have been absorbed.

Roll rounded teaspoonfuls of dough into balls. Place the balls 2 inches apart on the prepared cookie sheets.

Bake the cookies, one sheet at a time, on the middle-level rack of the oven for 10 to 12 minutes, or until set and firm to the touch.

Transfer the cookies to cooling racks, using a wide spatula. While the cookies are still warm, roll them in the Lemon-Scented Confectioners' Sugar and return them to the rack. Cool for 20 minutes. Store the cookies in an airtight tin.

Three Nut Bars

FOR THE BROWN SUGAR
COOKIE DOUGH:

1¼ cups *sifted* all-purpose
flour

1 tablespoon cornstarch

¼ teaspoon salt

8 tablespoons (1 stick)
unsalted butter,
softened at room
temperature

½ cup firmly packed light
brown sugar

½ teaspoon pure vanilla
extract

½ teaspoon pure almond
extract

In addition to baking panfuls of these rich bars for bake sales, I love to have a few dozen of them stockpiled during the winter holidays. In the late fall, when the fresh crop of nuts abounds in the market (in big burlap sacks), buy several pounds of walnuts, pecans, and almonds. Freshly cracked nuts keep well in the freezer stored in self-sealing plastic bags and they lend a distinctive taste to this bar cookie.

Rich and satisfying, Three Nut Bars are lovely served with a pot of hot lemon tea, goblets of mulled wine, or cold glasses of my Real Lemonade (page 400).

Lightly butter and flour a 10-inch square baking pan; set aside. Preheat the oven to 350 degrees.

For the brown sugar cookie dough, resift the flour with the cornstarch and salt onto a sheet of waxed paper.

Cream the butter in the large bowl of an electric mixer on moderate speed for 2 minutes. Add the brown sugar and beat for 1 minute. Blend in the vanilla and almond extracts. On low speed (or by hand), blend in the sifted mixture in 2 additions, beating just until the particles of flour have been absorbed.

Spread the cookie dough evenly on the bottom of the prepared pan. Bake the cookie layer on the middle-level rack for 15 minutes, or until golden and firm to the touch. Remove from the oven and set aside on a cooling rack.

¾ cup firmly packed light
  brown sugar

¼ cup granulated sugar

3 tablespoons *sifted*
  all-purpose flour

½ teaspoon baking
  powder

¼ teaspoon salt

1 extra-large egg plus 2
  extra-large egg yolks, at
  room temperature

1 teaspoon pure vanilla
  extract

1 teaspoon pure almond
  extract

2 tablespoons unsalted
  butter, melted and
  cooled

½ cup chopped walnuts

½ cup chopped pecans

½ cup chopped almonds

24 bars

For the nut topping, combine the brown sugar, granulated sugar, flour, baking powder, and salt in a large mixing bowl. Beat in the egg, egg yolks, and vanilla and almond extracts. Blend in the melted butter. Stir in the walnuts, pecans, and almonds.

Spoon the topping evenly over the cookie base. Bake on the middle-level rack of the oven for 20 to 25 minutes, or until the topping is set and firm to the touch.

Cool the cake of nut bars on a rack until it reaches room temperature, about 2 hours. Cut into 24 bars and store in an airtight tin.

Coconut Dreams

1 cup *sifted* cake flour

1/4 teaspoon baking powder

1/2 teaspoon salt

1/2 teaspoon freshly grated nutmeg

1/2 pound (2 sticks) unsalted butter, melted and cooled

1 cup firmly packed light brown sugar

1/3 cup granulated sugar

3 extra-large eggs plus 2 extra-large egg yolks, at room temperature

2 teaspoons pure vanilla extract

2 teaspoons coconut extract

1/4 cup light cream, at room temperature

2 2/3 cups flaked coconut

18 squares

Coconut Dreams are chewy and moist—they will remind you of macaroons and blondies. The squares are sweetened by a combination of light brown sugar and granulated sugar, giving them a soft caramel flavor that plays nicely against the coconut. Two good variations of this bar cookie are: macadamia nuts and white chocolate and walnuts and miniature chocolate chips. For the macadamia nut version, decrease the coconut by 2/3 cup and with it fold in 1 cup grated white chocolate and 1 cup chopped macadamia nuts. For the walnut version, decrease the coconut by 2/3 cup and with it fold in 1 cup chopped walnuts and 1 cup miniature semisweet chocolate chips. A tin of Coconut Dreams is a perfect mate to a pitcher of Real Lemonade (page 400).

Lightly butter and flour two 8-inch square baking pans. Line the bottom of each pan with a square of waxed paper. Set aside. Preheat the oven to 325 degrees.

Resift the cake flour with the baking powder, salt, and nutmeg onto a sheet of waxed paper.

Pour the melted butter into a large mixing bowl. Blend in the light brown sugar, granulated sugar, eggs, and egg yolks, mixing well. Stir in the vanilla and coconut extracts. Blend in the light cream and coconut.

Spoon the batter into the prepared pans, dividing it evenly between them.

Bake the dreams on the middle-level rack of the oven for 40

minutes, or until the top of each is golden and just firm to the touch (the cakes will begin to pull away from the sides of the baking pan when done).

Cool each cake in the pan on a rack until it reaches room temperature, about 2 hours. Invert each cake onto a second cooling rack, peel away the waxed paper, and invert again onto a cutting board.

Cut each cake into 9 squares and store them in an airtight tin.

BAKE SALE BROWNIES

Moist and fudgy, brownies offered up by the dozen are a favorite bake sale item. They look appealing layered in slatted wooden baskets lined with a cloth or several doilies. All of the recipes that follow have been designed to double successfully if you need an extra big batch. And when I make lots of brownies in advance, I store each cake (the whole block of baked brownie) uncut in a tightly sealed container; several hours or the day before the brownies are needed, I cut each cake into squares or bars.

❖❖❖❖❖❖❖❖❖❖❖❖❖❖❖❖

Grandma Lilly's Brownies

½ pound (2 sticks) unsalted butter, cut into chunks

4 ounces (4 squares) unsweetened chocolate, chopped

My Grandma Lilly was well known for her brownies (among other tasty things). These chocolate squares are at once cakelike and chewy, and she underbaked them slightly to make them extra fudgy. For years, I'd been terrified of changing the original recipe but knew that reducing the amount of baking powder by half would result in a better brownie, one that was a little more dense. Finally, I altered Grandma's recipe and I think she would approve.

These brownies are usually the first item to sell out at bake sales (they always did when she brought them to such

1½ cups *sifted* cake flour

1 teaspoon baking powder (Grandma used 2 teaspoons)

½ teaspoon salt

½ cup chopped black walnuts

4 extra-large eggs, at room temperature

2 cups Vanilla-Scented Granulated Sugar (page 219)

2 teaspoons pure vanilla extract

---

24 brownies

events when I was in school), so be sure to bake a lot of them.

In my family, it was always traditional to sift confectioners' sugar over the tops of the brownies just before serving.

———❖❖❖———

Lightly butter and flour a 13 x 9 x 2-inch baking pan; set aside. Preheat the oven to 350 degrees.

Melt the butter and chocolate in a heavy saucepan over very low heat; stir well and set aside to cool.

Resift the cake flour with the baking powder and salt onto a sheet of waxed paper. Put the walnuts in a bowl and toss with 1 teaspoon of the sifted mixture.

Pour the melted chocolate-butter mixture into a large mixing bowl. Beat in the eggs, one at a time. Blend in the sugar and vanilla. Stir in the sifted mixture, mixing just until the particles of flour have been absorbed. Fold in the floured walnuts.

Pour and scrape the batter into the prepared pan.

Bake the brownies on the middle-level rack of the oven for 25 minutes (for a *very* fudgy brownie, bake for 20 minutes).

Cool the brownie cake in the pan on a rack until it reaches room temperature, about 2 hours. Cut the cake into 24 squares and store them in an airtight tin.

Heavenly Hash Brownies

12 tablespoons (1½ sticks) unsalted butter, cut into chunks

4 ounces (4 squares) unsweetened chocolate, chopped

½ cup *unsifted* all-purpose flour

¼ cup *unsifted* cake flour

¼ teaspoon baking powder

½ teaspoon salt

½ cup miniature semisweet chocolate chips

½ cup chopped walnuts

2 extra-large eggs plus 2 extra-large egg yolks, at room temperature

1¼ cups Vanilla-Scented Granulated Sugar (page 219)

2 teaspoons pure vanilla extract

These brownies taste like a creamy (and chewy) chocolate and nut candy bar. The buttery batter traps swirls of marshmallow cream, miniature chocolate chips, and chopped walnuts. For an indulgent dessert, serve the squares warm, topped with a scoop of vanilla ice cream and a spoonful of hot fudge sauce. And to make the ultimate brownie ice cream, cut several brownies into cubes and mash them lightly with the broad side of a knife (or cleaver); fold these chocolate gobs through softened vanilla ice cream and refreeze for an hour or so. This is delicious.

I serve lots of Heavenly Hash Brownies from an old wide-mouth apothecary jar with a pot of freshly brewed coffee.

I have baked these brownies for years and years. The brownie batter can hold almost any kind of embellishment you can think of (coconut, macadamia nuts, pecans, chopped caramel, or praline) and still bakes up tender and moist inside.

Lightly butter and flour a 9-inch square baking pan. Line the bottom of the pan with a square of waxed paper. Set aside. Preheat the oven to 350 degrees.

Melt the butter and chocolate in a heavy saucepan over very low heat; stir well. Set aside to cool.

Sift the all-purpose flour, cake flour, baking powder, and salt onto a sheet of waxed paper.

1 teaspoon chocolate
extract

½ cup marshmallow
cream

---

9 large brownies

Combine the chocolate chips and walnuts in a small bowl and toss with 2 teaspoons of the sifted flour mixture.

Beat the eggs and egg yolks in a large mixing bowl. Whisk in the granulated sugar and vanilla and chocolate extracts. Blend in the cooled butter-chocolate mixture. Stir in the sifted mixture, blending just until the particles of flour have been absorbed. Fold in the chocolate chips and walnuts. Spoon the marshmallow cream on top of the chocolate batter and swirl it in with a few quick strokes (leave the cream in rather large patches to prevent it from dissolving into the batter).

Carefully pour and scrape the batter into the prepared pan.

Bake the brownies on the middle-level rack of the oven for 40 to 45 minutes, or until the brownie cake begins to pull away from the sides of the baking pan.

Cool the cake in the pan on a rack until it reaches room temperature, about 2 hours. Invert the cake onto a second cooling rack, peel away the waxed paper, and invert again onto a cutting board.

Cut the brownie cake into 9 squares and store them in an airtight tin.

Double Chocolate–Walnut Fudgies

½ pound (2 sticks) unsalted butter, cut into chunks

6 ounces (6 squares) unsweetened chocolate, chopped

½ cup *unsifted* cake flour

½ cup *unsifted* all-purpose flour

1 teaspoon salt

1 cup chopped walnuts

⅔ cup miniature semisweet chocolate chips

3 extra-large eggs plus 2 extra-large egg yolks, at room temperature

2 cups Vanilla-Scented Granulated Sugar (page 219)

2½ teaspoons pure vanilla extract

1 teaspoon chocolate extract

Fudgies are moist, candylike squares packed with a double dose of chocolate—melted unsweetened chocolate colors the batter while semisweet chocolate chips add little pockets of chocolate richness. These are easy to pack and carry in the lunch bag or box if wrapped securely in waxed paper or popped into self-sealing plastic pouches. At home, sprinkle the walnut-flecked tops of the fudgies with a light sifting of confectioners' sugar and serve with a pot of steaming hot coffee or pitcher of milk.

Lightly butter and flour two 8-inch square baking pans. Line the bottom of each pan with a square of waxed paper; set aside. Preheat the oven to 350 degrees.

Melt the butter and chocolate in a heavy saucepan over very low heat; stir well. Set aside to cool.

Sift the cake flour, all-purpose flour, and salt onto a sheet of waxed paper.

Combine the walnuts and chocolate chips in a small bowl and toss with 1 tablespoon of the sifted flour mixture.

Beat the eggs and egg yolks in a large mixing bowl. Blend in the granulated sugar and mix well. Blend in the vanilla and chocolate extracts. Stir in the melted chocolate-butter mixture. Stir in the sifted mixture, blending just until the particles of flour have been absorbed. Fold in the chocolate chips and walnuts.

Spoon the batter into the prepared pans, dividing it evenly

⅔ cup chopped walnuts

---

18 brownies

between them. Sprinkle the top of each pan of batter with ⅓ cup chopped walnuts.

Bake the fudgies on the middle-level rack of the oven for 40 minutes, until the top is set and shiny and each cake pulls away slightly from the sides of the baking pan.

Cool each cake in the pan on a rack until it reaches room temperature, about 2 hours. Invert each cake onto a second cooling rack, peel away the waxed paper, and invert again onto a cutting board.

Cut each cake into 9 squares and store them in an airtight tin.

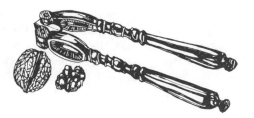

Coconut-Chocolate "Swirlies"

½ pound (2 sticks)
  unsalted butter,
  softened at room
  temperature

4 ounces (4 squares)
  unsweetened
  chocolate, chopped

1¼ cups *sifted* cake flour

1 tablespoon *unsifted*
  unsweetened cocoa
  powder

½ teaspoon salt

3 extra-large eggs plus 2
  extra-large egg yolks, at
  room temperature

2 cups Vanilla-Scented
  Granulated Sugar
  (page 219)

2 teaspoons pure vanilla
  extract

1 teaspoon chocolate
  extract

"Swirlies" are like brownies, but better: Drifts of marshmallow cream and flaked coconut wind through the chocolate batter in an intriguing pattern. I have been baking this brownielike confection for many, many years; I've taken them to country fairs and bazaars, teas, picnics, and charity events. They are a toothsome lunch box or picnic dessert.

Serve a big plate of "swirlies" with tall glasses of strong iced coffee, a pot of hot coffee, or a pitcher of cold milk.

———❖❖❖———

Lightly butter and flour two 8-inch square baking pans. Line the bottom of each pan with a square of waxed paper; set aside. Preheat the oven to 350 degrees.

Melt the butter and chocolate in a heavy saucepan over very low heat; stir well. Set aside to cool.

Resift the cake flour with the cocoa and salt onto a sheet of waxed paper. Beat the eggs and egg yolks in a large mixing bowl. Blend in the granulated sugar and mix well. Beat in the vanilla and chocolate extracts. Blend in the cooled chocolate-butter mixture. Stir in the sifted mixture, blending just until the particles of flour have been absorbed. Spoon the marshmallow cream on top of the chocolate batter, sprinkle over the flaked coconut, and swirl both in with a few quick strokes of a wooden spoon (leave the cream in patches to prevent it from dissolving into the batter).

Pour and scrape the batter into the prepared pans, dividing it evenly between them.

¾ cup marshmallow
   cream
½ cup flaked coconut

---

18 brownies

Bake the "swirlies" on the middle-level rack of the oven for 35 to 40 minutes, until the top is set and each cake pulls away slightly from the sides of the baking pan.

Cool each cake of "swirlies" in the pan on a rack until it reaches room temperature, about 2 hours. Invert each cake onto a second cooling rack, peel away the waxed paper, and invert again onto a cutting board.

Cut each cake into 9 squares and store them in an airtight tin.

Chocolate Toffee Squares

1¼ cups *unsifted* all-purpose flour

¼ cup *unsifted* cake flour

¾ teaspoon baking powder

½ teaspoon salt

1 cup *unsifted* unsweetened cocoa powder

¾ pound (3 sticks) unsalted butter, melted and cooled

1 square (1 ounce) unsweetened chocolate, melted

5 extra-large eggs plus 1 extra-large egg yolk, at room temperature

2 tablespoons milk, at room temperature

2 tablespoons light corn syrup

2 teaspoons pure vanilla extract

1 teaspoon chocolate extract

These thick squares are rich in chocolate; chopped chocolate-covered toffee bars get stirred through a buttery cocoa batter and more chopped toffee is sprinkled on top right before baking. My mother baked these brownies frequently; this is my version of her recipe. (I've added chocolate extract for a full chocolate bouquet and use Vanilla-Scented Granulated Sugar.) The squares are quite moist and tender; they keep very well at room temperature when packed in a tightly sealed tin. If you are making the squares to sell at a bake sale, wrap each in clear cellophane and arrange them in shallow baskets. At home, I present these fudgy wonders in an antique cake tin or cookie box lined with heart-shaped doilies.

Chocolate Toffee Squares are delicious served with cups of hot coffee, tall glasses of iced coffee, or cold milk.

❖❖❖

Lightly butter and flour a 13 x 9 x 2-inch baking pan. Line the bottom with a square of waxed paper. Set aside. Preheat the oven to 350 degrees.

Sift the all-purpose flour, cake flour, baking powder, salt, and cocoa onto a sheet of waxed paper.

Whisk the melted butter, chocolate, eggs, egg yolk, and milk in a large mixing bowl. Blend in the corn syrup and vanilla and chocolate extracts. Beat in the granulated sugar.

Put the chopped toffee candy in a bowl and toss with 2 teaspoons of the sifted dry ingredients. Stir the sifted mixture into the egg and sugar mixture, mixing just until the particles

2⅔ cups Vanilla-Scented
  Granulated Sugar
  (page 219)
6 packages (1.20 ounces
  each) chocolate-
  covered toffee bars
  (such as Heath Bars),
  chopped (about
  1¼ cups)

FOR SPRINKLING:

4 packages (1.20 ounces
  each) chocolate-
  covered toffee bars,
  chopped (about
  ¾ cup)

About 32 brownies

of flour have been absorbed. Fold in the floured chopped toffee.

Spoon the batter into the prepared pan. Sprinkle the chopped toffee candy on top of the batter.

Bake the squares on the middle-level rack of the oven for 40 minutes, or until the cake begins to pull away from the sides of the baking pan.

Cool the cake in the pan on a rack until it reaches room temperature, about 2 hours. Invert the cake onto a second cooling rack, peel away the waxed paper, and invert again onto a cutting board.

Cut the cake into 32 squares and store them in an airtight tin.

Baking Note: My mother also made marvelous brownies using almond butter crunch, chopped up and folded through the dense batter. To vary this recipe, you can substitute the same amount of almond butter crunch candy for the toffee; then substitute 1 teaspoon pure almond extract for the chocolate extract called for in the recipe.

LUNCH BOX COOKIES

LUNCH BOX COOKIES

———————— ❖❖❖ ————————

Ginger Crisps   346
Apple Butter Cookies   348
Pecan Butter Crunch Squares   350
Sugar Cookie Hearts   352
Bittersweet Chocolate–Caramel Bars   354
Oatmeal-Raisin Saucers   356
Pumpkin-Spice Cookies   357

ookies that get packed up in lunch boxes should satisfy that craving for something sweet, whether they are crisp and buttery (like my Sugar Cookie Hearts on page 352) or substantial and hearty (like my Pecan Butter Crunch Squares on page 350 or the Oatmeal-Raisin Saucers on page 356).

The cookies in this chapter are good for munching on during the afternoon, with or without a piece of fresh fruit. The Bittersweet Chocolate–Caramel Bars rely on the combination of butter and chocolate to keep them moist and tasty, so they can be made over the weekend and enjoyed for days to follow (if they last that long). The Ginger Crisps, Apple Butter Cookies, and Pumpkin-Spice Cookies contain lots of spices and the usual "goods on hand" that cookie bakers keep stocked in the pantry.

These cookies are perfect for stashing in the lunch box or briefcase because they are a full-flavored, easy-to-carry sweet—and much more delicious than a packaged candy bar! Any of the fruit and spice cookies would be a nourishing dessert for school-bound children; the cookies taste good after a sandwich or thermos of soup.

Also, remember that the Pecan Butter Crunch Squares are a welcome addition to boxed picnic lunches, along with some fresh seasonal fruit such as plums, peaches, and nectarines. Wrap the squares in clear cellophane wrap before packing them.

Besides the cookies in this chapter, there are many others in this book that are handy to have ready-made and in the cupboard for tucking into lunch boxes. Among them: Mint Chocolate Crisps (page 310), Heavenly Hash Brownies (page 334), Chocolate Toffee Squares (page 340), Maple Bars (page 320), Chocolate Nut Crunch Squares (page 324), Peanut Delights (page 380), Butterscotch-Granola Disks (page 390), Fruit Clusters (page 388), Banana-Oatmeal Pillows (page 382), Sour Cream–Molasses–Spice Rounds (page 386), and Grandma Lilly's Brownies (page 332).

❖❖❖❖❖❖❖❖❖❖❖❖❖❖❖❖❖

Ginger Crisps

2¾ cups *sifted* all-purpose flour

¼ cup plus 1 tablespoon *sifted* cake flour

1 tablespoon baking soda

¾ teaspoon salt

2½ teaspoons ground ginger

2 teaspoons ground cinnamon

½ teaspoon ground allspice

¼ teaspoon ground cloves

¼ teaspoon freshly grated nutmeg

One of my favorite ginger cookies, these wafers really snap when you bite into them. Ground ginger is the keynote of the spices, of course, but its flavor is supported by aromatic ground cinnamon, allspice, cloves, and nutmeg.

Keep Ginger Crisps in the cookie jar for friends and family to snack on. And when a dessert of baked or poached fruit—particularly apples and pears—calls for something crisp and spicy as an accompaniment, remember these cookies.

Ginger Crisps are delicious paired with glasses of Real Lemonade (page 400), mulled wine, or Hot Spiced Cider (page 401).

———❖❖❖———

Lightly butter and flour 4 cookie sheets or line the sheets with lengths of cooking parchment paper; set aside. Preheat the oven to 375 degrees.

1 cup plus 2 tablespoons
  shortening

1⅓ cups superfine sugar

2 tablespoons firmly
  packed light brown
  sugar

5 tablespoons light
  molasses

1 extra-large egg plus 1
  extra-large egg yolk, at
  room temperature

1 teaspoon milk

1½ teaspoons pure
  vanilla extract

FOR ROLLING THE COOKIES:

1 cup granulated sugar
  blended with 1
  teaspoon ground
  ginger

About 50 cookies

Resift the all-purpose and cake flours with the baking soda, salt, ginger, cinnamon, allspice, cloves, and nutmeg onto a sheet of waxed paper.

Cream the shortening in the large bowl of an electric mixer on moderate speed for 2 minutes. Add the superfine sugar in 2 additions, beating for 1 minute after each portion is added. Beat in the light brown sugar. Add the molasses and beat for 1 minute. Add the egg and egg yolk; beat for 1 minute. Blend in the milk and vanilla extract. On low speed (or by hand), add the sifted mixture in 2 additions, beating just until the particles of flour have been absorbed.

Roll level tablespoons of dough into balls. Roll each ball in the ginger-spiced sugar. Place the balls 2½ inches apart on the prepared cookie sheets. (The dough is soft, so in very hot or humid weather, refrigerate it for 1 hour, or until just firm enough to roll.)

Bake the cookies, one sheet at a time, on the middle-level rack of the oven for 12 to 14 minutes, or until set and firm to the touch (the dough will rise up during baking, then flatten and firm up).

Transfer the cookies to cooling racks, using a wide spatula. Cool for 20 minutes. Store the cookies in an airtight tin.

Apple Butter Cookies

3 cups *sifted* all-purpose flour

1 cup plus 2 tablespoons *sifted* cake flour

1 teaspoon baking soda

1 teaspoon baking powder

1 teaspoon salt

2½ teaspoons ground cinnamon

1¼ teaspoons freshly grated nutmeg

¾ teaspoon ground ginger

½ teaspoon ground allspice

¼ teaspoon ground cloves

12 tablespoons (1½ sticks) unsalted butter, softened at room temperature

¼ cup shortening

1 cup firmly packed light brown sugar

Every fall, I put up jars of silky apple butter to use as a spread for muffins, toast, and sweet yeast breads and to add to holiday fruit cakes and pie fillings. Apple butter (as well as peach, pear, or cranberry butter) lends an incomparable satiny quality to many baked goods. Cookies made with apple butter bake up golden, with a fine crumb and delectable flavor.

These Apple Butter Cookies are spicy and soft, and they are a fine accompaniment for a helping of poached fruit. A heap of cookies, presented in an old wicker basket, is just the right thing to serve with cups of hot buttered rum or freshly brewed coffee.

Lightly butter and flour 4 cookie sheets or line the sheets with lengths of cooking parchment paper; set aside. Preheat the oven to 375 degrees.

Resift the all-purpose and cake flour with the baking soda, baking powder, salt, cinnamon, nutmeg, ginger, allspice, and cloves onto a sheet of waxed paper.

Cream the butter and shortening in the large bowl of an electric mixer on moderate speed for 2 minutes. Add the light brown sugar and beat for 1 minute. Add the superfine sugar and beat for a minute longer. Add the egg and beat for 1 minute; add the egg yolks and beat for a minute longer. Blend in the apple butter, sour cream, and shredded apples. On low speed (or by hand), blend in the sifted mixture in 3 additions,

⅓ cup superfine sugar

1 extra-large egg plus 2 extra-large egg yolks, at room temperature

½ cup apple butter

2 tablespoons sour cream

1½ cups firmly packed shredded tart cooking apples (about 2 medium-size)

½ cup chopped pecans

½ cup dried currants

About 48 cookies

beating just until the particles of flour have been absorbed. By hand, stir in the pecans and currants.

Drop the dough by rounded tablespoons onto the prepared cookie sheets, placing the mounds 2½ inches apart.

Bake the cookies, a sheet at a time, on the middle-level rack of the oven for 12 to 13 minutes, or until firm to the touch.

Transfer the cookies to cooling racks, using a wide spatula. Cool for 20 minutes. Store the cookies in an airtight tin.

Baking Note: This recipe has been in my file for many cookie-baking years. My grandmother made them with applesauce (instead of the apple butter) and golden raisins (instead of the currants). I add a little sour cream to smooth out the cookie dough and sift lots of spices with the flour.

Pecan Butter Crunch Squares

1¼ cups *unsifted* all-purpose flour

¼ cup *unsifted* cake flour

½ teaspoon baking soda

½ teaspoon baking powder

½ teaspoon salt

¾ teaspoon freshly grated nutmeg

¼ teaspoon ground allspice

8 tablespoons (1 stick) unsalted butter, melted and cooled

2 tablespoons shortening, melted and cooled

1½ cups firmly packed brown sugar

½ cup granulated sugar

1 extra-large egg plus 2 extra-large egg yolks, at room temperature

1 teaspoon pure vanilla extract

Soft and chewy, these pecan butter squares are easily mixed in a large bowl. The topping is a sweet and crunchy finish to the cookies: The crumble of brown sugar, butter, and chopped pecans caramelizes lightly during baking, adding another texture.

In the summertime, arrange Pecan Butter Crunch Squares in a willow basket and serve with fresh seasonal berries (such as a mixture of blackberries, raspberries, and blueberries); in fall and winter, accompany the squares with a bowl of homemade applesauce or poached pears.

Lightly butter and flour a 9-inch square baking pan. Line the bottom of the pan with a square of waxed paper; set aside. Preheat the oven to 350 degrees.

Sift the all-purpose flour, cake flour, baking soda, baking powder, salt, nutmeg, and allspice onto a large sheet of waxed paper.

Combine the butter and shortening in a large mixing bowl. Stir in the brown sugar and granulated sugar. Beat in the egg and egg yolks. Blend in the vanilla and maple extracts. Add the sifted mixture, sprinkle over the pecans, and blend everything together until the particles of flour have been absorbed.

Spoon the batter into the prepared pan, spreading it into the corners and smoothing over the top.

For the pecan-sugar topping, combine the pecans, light

½ teaspoon maple extract
1½ cups chopped pecans

FOR THE PECAN-SUGAR
TOPPING:

½ cup chopped pecans
1 tablespoon firmly
    packed light brown
    sugar
1 tablespoon unsalted
    butter, melted and
    cooled

12 squares

brown sugar, and butter in a small mixing bowl. Crumble everything together with your fingertips and sprinkle evenly over the pan of batter.

Bake the crunches on the middle-level rack of the oven for 25 minutes, or until the top is set and the cake pulls away slightly from the sides of the baking pan.

Cool the cake in the pan on a rack until it reaches room temperature, about 2 hours. Carefully invert the cake onto a second cooling rack, peel away the waxed paper, and invert again onto a cutting board.

Cut the cake into 12 squares and store them in an airtight tin.

Sugar Cookie Hearts

4½ cups *unsifted*
    all-purpose flour

¾ teaspoon baking
    powder

⅛ teaspoon baking soda

1 teaspoon salt

½ teaspoon freshly grated
    nutmeg

¾ pound (3 sticks)
    unsalted butter,
    softened at room
    temperature

2¼ cups Vanilla-Scented
    Granulated Sugar
    (page 219)

2 extra-large eggs plus 2
    extra-large egg yolks, at
    room temperature

2½ teaspoons pure
    vanilla extract

Seed scrapings from the
    inside of ½ a vanilla
    bean

2 tablespoons plus 1
    teaspoon milk, at room
    temperature

I am partial to baking cookies, muffins, rolls, and miniature pastries in the shape of hearts. I always cut out sheets of this thin cookie dough with an antique heart-shaped cutter: It has finely scalloped edges and makes beautiful cookies.

Sugar Cookie Hearts are wonderful to have on hand for adding to lunch bags and the holiday cookie basket would not be complete without them.

In the summer, serve the cookies with Real Lemonade (page 400).

———❖❖❖———

Sift the all-purpose flour, baking powder, baking soda, salt, and nutmeg onto a sheet of waxed paper.

Cream the butter in the large bowl of an electric mixer on moderate speed for 3 minutes. Add the sugar in 3 additions, beating for 1 minute after each portion is added; scrape down the sides of the mixing bowl frequently. Beat in the eggs, one at a time, blending well after each addition. Beat in the egg yolks. Blend in the vanilla extract, vanilla bean scrapings, and milk. On low speed (or by hand), blend in the sifted mixture in 3 additions, beating just until the particles of flour have been absorbed.

Divide the dough into 3 portions and form each into a rough cake. Roll each cake between sheets of waxed paper to a thickness of ¼ inch. Freeze the sheets of dough stacked on cookie sheets until they are very firm, about 3 to 4 hours. (The sheets of dough can be kept in the freezer for up to 1 week before cutting and baking; once the dough has firmed

FOR SPRINKLING:

About ⅔ cup
   Vanilla-Scented
   Granulated Sugar
   (page 219)

About 72 cookies

up, double-wrap the sheets in plastic wrap and aluminum foil.)

Lightly butter and flour 4 cookie sheets or line the sheets with lengths of cooking parchment paper; set aside. Preheat the oven to 375 degrees.

Stamp out each sheet of dough with a 3-inch heart-shaped cutter. Place the cookies 1 to 1½ inches apart on the prepared cookie sheets. (Reroll the scraps between sheets of waxed paper, chill, and cut out more cookies.) Sprinkle the cookies lightly with the Vanilla-Scented Granulated Sugar.

Bake the cookies, one sheet at a time, on the middle-level rack of the oven for 10 to 12 minutes, or until light golden and firm to the touch.

Transfer the cookies to cooling racks, using a wide spatula. Cool for 20 minutes. Store the cookies in an airtight tin.

Baking Note: Prior to freezing, this cookie dough is quite sticky. Once the sheets of dough are frozen firm, the dough is easy to stamp out with a cutter and holds its shape nicely during baking. Although you might be tempted, adding additional flour to the dough will spoil the texture and make the cookies a lot less delicate-crisp than they should be. Freezing the dough takes care of the handling and the baked cookies will be light and tender as a result.

Bittersweet Chocolate–Caramel Bars

1¾ cups *unsifted*
  all-purpose flour

¼ cup *unsifted* cake flour

¼ teaspoon salt

½ pound (2 sticks)
  unsalted butter,
  softened at room
  temperature

¾ cup firmly packed light
  brown sugar

¼ cup granulated sugar

2 extra-large egg yolks, at
  room temperature

1 teaspoon pure vanilla
  extract

1 cup vanilla caramels

4 tablespoons milk

1¼ cups chopped
  bittersweet chocolate

¾ cup chopped lightly
  toasted walnuts

---

48 bars

All the good larder ingredients—chocolate, butter, brown sugar, eggs, and walnuts—are combined to make a bar cookie that's sweet and crunchy-chewy. A butter cookie dough made with brown sugar and egg yolks forms the base for a topping of chopped bittersweet chocolate, walnuts, and caramel. These are rich.

Offer a plate of Bittersweet Chocolate–Caramel Bars with bowls of plain vanilla ice cream, mousse, or a summer compote of fresh berries.

Lightly butter and flour a 15 x 10 x 1-inch jelly roll pan; set aside. Preheat the oven to 350 degrees.

Blend together the all-purpose flour, cake flour, and salt in a mixing bowl.

Cream the butter in the large bowl of an electric mixer on moderate speed for 2 minutes. Add the light brown sugar and beat for 1 minute. Add the granulated sugar and beat for a minute longer. Beat in the egg yolks. Blend in the vanilla. On low speed (or by hand), blend in the flour mixture in 2 additions, mixing just until the particles of flour have been absorbed.

Press the cookie dough evenly on the bottom of the prepared pan. Bake the cookie layer on the middle-level rack of the oven for 15 to 20 minutes, or until golden and firm to the touch. Leave the oven on.

In the meantime, melt the caramels with the milk in a saucepan, stirring occasionally; keep warm.

As soon as the cookie dough has been removed from the oven, scatter the chopped chocolate evenly over the top. Return to the oven for 1 to 2 minutes longer, or until the chocolate has softened. Gently spread the chocolate in large patches over the top of the cookie dough, leaving small spaces of the dough showing. Drizzle the melted caramel over with a teaspoon, then sprinkle with chopped walnuts.

Cool the cake in the pan on a rack until it reaches room temperature, about 2 hours. Cut into 48 bars with a sharp knife and store them in an airtight tin.

Baking Note: In very hot or humid weather, or if your kitchen is warm, it may be necessary to chill the pan of bars before cutting to firm up the chocolate and caramel. Place the pan in the refrigerator for 1 hour or in the freezer for about 15 to 20 minutes.

Oatmeal-Raisin Saucers

2½ cups *unsifted*
  all-purpose flour

½ cup *unsifted* cake flour

2 teaspoons baking soda

1 teaspoon baking
  powder

1 teaspoon salt

1½ teaspoons ground
  cinnamon

1 teaspoon freshly grated
  nutmeg

1 cup shortening, melted
  and cooled

8 tablespoons (1 stick)
  unsalted butter, melted
  and cooled

2 cups firmly packed light
  brown sugar

1 cup granulated sugar

2 extra-large eggs plus 2
  extra-large egg yolks, at
  room temperature

2 teaspoons pure vanilla
  extract

These saucers are thin and chewy, with a soft butterscotch flavor. The ground cinnamon and nutmeg gently spice the oatmeal-coconut-raisin dough. Still warm from the oven and fragrant, the cookies are easy to devour along with a glass of cold milk or a cup of tea.

Lightly butter and flour 4 cookie sheets or line the sheets with lengths of cooking parchment paper; set aside. Preheat the oven to 350 degrees.

Sift the all-purpose flour, cake flour, baking soda, baking powder, salt, cinnamon, and nutmeg onto a sheet of waxed paper.

Whisk the shortening and butter together in a large mixing bowl. Stir in the brown sugar and granulated sugar. Beat in the eggs, one at a time; beat in the egg yolks. Blend in the vanilla. Blend in the sifted mixture in 2 additions, stirring just until the particles of flour have been absorbed. Stir in the oatmeal, coconut, and raisins.

Drop the dough by heaping tablespoons onto the prepared cookie sheets, placing the mounds 3 inches apart.

Bake the cookies, a sheet at a time, on the middle-level rack of the oven for 12 to 15 minutes, or until just set (the cookies will be slightly soft on top).

2½ cups quick-cooking
 oatmeal

1¾ cups flaked coconut

1 cup dark seedless
 raisins

About 60 cookies

Transfer the cookies to cooling racks, using a wide spatula. Cool for 20 minutes. Store the cookies in an airtight tin.

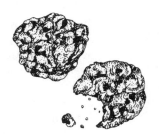

❖·❖·❖·❖·❖·❖·❖·❖·❖·❖·❖·❖·❖

Pumpkin-Spice Cookies

2 cups *unsifted* all-purpose
 flour

½ cup *unsifted* cake flour

1 teaspoon baking soda

1 teaspoon baking
 powder

¾ teaspoon salt

2 teaspoons ground
 cinnamon

¾ teaspoon freshly grated
 nutmeg

Pumpkin puree and a mingling of five pungent spices create a few dozen moist and ruddy-colored cookies. These are soft mounds, packed with chewy dates and chopped cashews. For body and substance, I like to add a few spoonfuls of bran to the dough. Pumpkin-Spice Cookies go well with Hot Spiced Cider (page 401), rum toddies, or cold milk.

———❖❖❖———

Lightly butter and flour 3 cookie sheets or line the sheets with lengths of cooking parchment paper; set aside. Preheat the oven to 375 degrees.

Sift the all-purpose flour, cake flour, baking soda, baking

(continued)

½ teaspoon ground
   ginger

¼ teaspoon ground
   allspice

¼ teaspoon ground
   cloves

8 tablespoons (1 stick)
   unsalted butter,
   softened at room
   temperature

8 tablespoons shortening

1 cup firmly packed light
   brown sugar

1 extra-large egg plus 1
   extra-large egg yolk, at
   room temperature

1 tablespoon molasses

2 teaspoons pure vanilla
   extract

1 cup unsweetened
   pumpkin puree

¾ cup chopped pitted
   dates

¾ cup chopped unsalted
   cashews

3 tablespoons bran

About 36 cookies

powder, salt, cinnamon, nutmeg, ginger, allspice, and cloves onto a sheet of waxed paper.

Cream the butter and shortening in the large bowl of an electric mixer on moderate speed for 2 minutes. Add the sugar and beat for 1 minute. Beat in the egg and egg yolk. Blend in the molasses and vanilla. Add the pumpkin puree and blend well. On low speed (or by hand), blend in the sifted mixture in 2 additions, beating just until the particles of flour have been absorbed. By hand, stir in the dates, cashews, and bran.

Drop the dough by rounded tablespoons onto the prepared cookie sheets, placing the mounds 2½ inches apart.

Bake the cookies, one sheet at a time, on the middle-level rack of the oven for 12 to 14 minutes, or until firm to the touch.

Transfer the cookies to cooling racks, using a wide spatula. Cool 20 minutes. Store the cookies in an airtight tin.

COFFEE AND TEA
SWEETS

Wendy Wheeler

COFFEE AND TEA SWEETS

———————◆◆◆———————

Black Walnut Butter Drops   362
Giant Double Chocolate Rounds   364
Apricot-Date Bars   366
Milk Chocolate–Almond Bars   368
Cinnamon-Cashew "Dunking" Cookies   370
Peach Squares   372
Chocolate Chip Rusks   374

I love to set out a coffee or tea service with sweets on a well-worn pine table in my library. (The library is a cozy place—where a jumble of books and lots of porcelain collected over the years fills all the nooks.) I decorate the table with all the expected accompaniments and a few unexpected things, too: a pitcher of cream and bowl of sugar, a plate of lemon slices (if tea is served), embroidered napkins, pastel china plates, a dish of homemade potpourri to scent the room, or a posy of dried flowers.

For the coffee or tea hour, it's a nice gesture to offer at least two different kinds of cookies and present them in an appealing way. Arrange them in baskets, in napkin-lined tins, or in fancy copper molds. Make a simple fresh fruit compote, if you like, and serve that with a bowl of softly whipped cream for spooning over.

The cookies in this chapter are crisp and buttery, soft and chewy, or firm and not too sweet—in my house, they are the traditional accompaniments to coffee or tea. The Giant Double Chocolate Rounds are 9-inch circles of dough laced with miniature chocolate chips and baked in shallow tart pans. This is a break-apart cookie, meant for guests to nibble on a little at a time. The Cinnamon-Cashew "Dunking" Cookies and the Chocolate Chip Rusks are crisp and softly flavored—ideal for dipping into cups of steamy hot cappuccino or strong coffee.

Many cookies that are ideal for filling the cookie jar or bringing to a bake sale (from the Cookie Jar Treats and Bake Sale Gems chapters) are equally good to serve with coffee or tea. They are: the Vanilla Melt-a-Ways (page 300), Chocolate Gems (page 306), Mint Chocolate Crisps (page 310), Chocolate Toffee Squares (page 340), Maple Bars (page 320), Double Vanilla "Dog Bones" (page 322), Lemon Butter Balls (page 326), Three Nut Bars (page 328), and Coconut Dreams (page 330).

❖❖❖❖❖❖❖❖❖❖❖❖❖❖❖❖❖

Black Walnut Butter Drops

1¾ cups *unsifted* all-purpose flour

¼ cup *unsifted* cake flour

¼ teaspoon baking powder

½ teaspoon salt

½ teaspoon freshly grated nutmeg

½ pound (2 sticks) unsalted butter, softened at room temperature

1 cup Vanilla-Scented Granulated Sugar (page 219)

Simple and sweet, these butter drops have a cakelike texture —which makes them delicate little mouthfuls. Bits of black walnuts wind through each cookie for flavor and crunch. Apart from serving with hot coffee or iced tea to regenerate the spirit in the morning or afternoon, the cookies are a welcome accompaniment to mousse, ice cream, or fruit salad.

——————❖❖❖——————

Lightly butter and flour 4 cookie sheets or line the sheets with lengths of cooking parchment paper; set aside. Preheat the oven to 300 degrees.

Sift the all-purpose flour, cake flour, baking powder, salt, and nutmeg onto a sheet of waxed paper.

Cream the butter in the large bowl of an electric mixer on moderate speed for 2 minutes. Add the sugar in 2 additions,

2 teaspoons pure vanilla
    extract
1 extra-large egg, at room
    temperature
¾ cup chopped black
    walnuts (English
    walnuts may be
    substituted)

About 48 cookies

beating for 1 minute after each portion is added. Beat in the vanilla and egg. On low speed (or by hand), add the sifted mixture in 2 additions, beating just until the particles of flour have been absorbed. By hand, stir in the walnuts.

Drop the dough by rounded teaspoons onto the prepared cookie sheets, placing the mounds 1 inch apart.

Bake the cookies, one sheet at a time, on the middle-level rack of the oven for 20 to 25 minutes, or until very pale golden and firm to the touch.

Transfer the cookies to cooling racks, using a wide spatula. Store the cookies in an airtight tin.

Baking Note: This recipe was my mother's. She added golden raisins (¼ cup) to the dough along with the walnuts and used 2 cups of all-purpose flour.

Giant Double Chocolate Rounds

2¾ cups *unsifted* all-purpose flour

¼ cup *unsifted* cake flour

1 teaspoon cornstarch

¾ cup *unsifted* unsweetened cocoa powder

¼ teaspoon baking soda

⅛ teaspoon baking powder

½ teaspoon salt

¾ pound (3 sticks) unsalted butter, softened at room temperature

1½ cups Vanilla-Scented Confectioners' Sugar (page 219)

2 teaspoons pure vanilla extract

½ teaspoon chocolate extract

2 teaspoons light cream, at room temperature

This recipe makes two huge buttery chocolate cookies, flecked with miniature chocolate chips. The dough is pressed into fluted metal tart pans with removable bottoms and baked; what you pull from the oven are firm, yet meltingly rich disks, perfect for nibbling on with coffee or tea.

The rounds look pretty sitting on a flat, doily-lined plate, with sprigs of fresh lavender, holly, or apple blossom encircling the cookie. Giant Double Chocolate Rounds are wonderful to take on a picnic or to offer at an *al fresco* supper, accompanied by a bowl of fresh cherries.

With nonstick cookware spray, spray the inside of two 9-inch tart pans with removable bottoms. Line the bottom of the pans with a circle of waxed paper or parchment paper; set aside. Preheat the oven to 325 degrees.

Sift the all-purpose flour, cake flour, cornstarch, cocoa, baking soda, baking powder, and salt onto a sheet of waxed paper.

Cream the butter in the large bowl of an electric mixer on moderate speed for 2 minutes. Add the Vanilla-Scented Confectioners' Sugar and beat for 2 minutes, scraping down the sides of the mixing bowl frequently. Blend in the vanilla and chocolate extracts and light cream. On low speed (or by hand), blend in the sifted mixture in 3 additions, beating just until the particles of flour have been absorbed. By hand, stir in the chocolate chips.

¾ cup miniature
semisweet chocolate
chips

FOR SPRINKLING:

About 1½ tablespoons
Vanilla-Scented
Granulated Sugar
(page 219)

---

*Two 9-inch round break-apart
cookies*

Divide the dough into 2 disks. Place the disks between sheets of waxed paper and roll out into a 9-inch circle. For each cookie, peel off the top sheet of waxed paper, then invert the dough into the prepared tart pan. Press each round of dough evenly into the pan.

Bake the rounds on the middle-level rack of the oven for about 35 minutes, or until just firm to the touch.

Cool the cookies in the pans on 2 racks for 10 minutes. After 10 minutes, carefully set 1 tart pan on top of a small heatproof bowl (about 3 to 3½ inches in diameter), letting the outside frame drop to the countertop, then transfer the cookie (still on the metal bottom) back to the cooling rack. Repeat with the second tart pan. After about 20 minutes, carefully slide off each large cookie from the bottom of the tart pan onto the cooling rack, using a long, thin flexible palette knife. Invert each cookie and peel away the waxed or parchment paper; invert again to right side up.

Sprinkle the top of each cookie with ¾ tablespoon of the Vanilla-Scented Granulated Sugar. Cool the cookies for 1 hour, then store them in an airtight tin.

Apricot-Date Bars

FOR THE BROWN SUGAR COOKIE LAYER:

1¼ cups *unsifted* all-purpose flour

¼ teaspoon salt

8 tablespoons (1 stick) unsalted butter, softened at room temperature

½ cup firmly packed light brown sugar

1 teaspoon pure vanilla extract

¼ teaspoon maple extract

This is a two-layer bar cookie—a soft apricot and date spread bound with whole eggs and egg yolks covers a plain brown sugar cookie base. A plate of Apricot-Date Bars and one of Cinnamon-Cashew "Dunking" Cookies (page 370) would make a lovely midafternoon treat served with a pot of hot Earl Grey tea.

———❖❖❖———

Lightly butter and flour a 13 x 9 x 2-inch baking pan; set aside. Preheat the oven to 350 degrees.

For the brown sugar cookie layer, sift the flour and salt onto a sheet of waxed paper.

Cream the butter in the large bowl of an electric mixer on moderate speed for 2 minutes. Beat in the brown sugar. Blend in the vanilla and maple extracts. On low speed (or by hand), blend in the sifted mixture in 2 additions, beating just until the particles of flour have been absorbed.

Press the cookie dough evenly on the bottom of the prepared pan. Bake the cookie layer on the middle-level rack of the oven for 15 to 20 minutes, or until firm to the touch. Remove from the oven and set aside on a cooling rack.

For the apricot-date spread, sift the cake flour, baking soda, salt, cinnamon, and nutmeg into a large mixing bowl. Stir in the light brown sugar and granulated sugar. Beat in the egg and egg yolks. Stir in the preserves, dates, and pecans. Spoon the topping evenly over the cookie base.

3 tablespoons *unsifted* cake flour

½ teaspoon baking soda

⅛ teaspoon salt

½ teaspoon ground cinnamon

¼ teaspoon freshly ground nutmeg

½ cup firmly packed light brown sugar

¼ cup granulated sugar

1 extra-large egg plus 2 extra-large egg yolks, at room temperature

¾ cup apricot preserves

1¼ cups chopped pitted dates

½ cup chopped pecans

36 bars

Bake on the middle-level rack of the oven for 25 minutes, or until the topping is set and firm to the touch.

Cool the baked cake in the pan on a rack until it reaches room temperature, about 2 hours. Cut the cake into 36 bars and store in an airtight tin.

Milk Chocolate–Almond Bars

½ pound (2 sticks) unsalted butter, cut into chunks

2 cups (about 12 ounces) chopped milk chocolate

1½ cups *unsifted* all-purpose flour

½ cup *unsifted* cake flour

½ teaspoon baking powder

¾ teaspoon salt

¾ cup chopped almonds

3 extra-large eggs plus 2 extra-large egg yolks, at room temperature

1¾ cups Vanilla-Scented Granulated Sugar (page 219)

2 teaspoons pure vanilla extract

1 teaspoon pure almond extract

½ teaspoon chocolate extract

36 bars

The mellow taste of milk chocolate and almonds, plus enough butter to enrich, makes this bar cookie distinctive. The batter is reinforced by vanilla-scented sugar and vanilla extract to complement the chocolate flavor.

As a summertime treat, serve the bars with glasses of iced tea or frosty goblets of iced coffee (add a cinnamon stick to each glass, if you like).

Lightly butter and flour two 9-inch square baking pans. Line the bottom of each pan with a square of waxed paper; set aside. Preheat the oven to 350 degrees.

Melt the butter and 1¼ cups milk chocolate in a heavy saucepan over very low heat; stir well, then set aside to cool.

Sift the all-purpose flour, cake flour, baking powder, and salt onto a sheet of waxed paper. Put the remaining ¾ cup chopped milk chocolate and almonds in a bowl and toss with 1 tablespoon of the sifted mixture.

Beat the eggs and egg yolks in a large mixing bowl. Beat in the sugar and vanilla, almond, and chocolate extracts. Pour in the cooled chocolate-butter mixture and mix well. Stir in the sifted mixture in 2 additions, mixing just until the particles of flour have been absorbed. Fold in the floured chocolate and almonds.

Spoon the batter into the prepared pans, dividing it evenly between them.

Bake the bars on the middle-level rack of the oven for 30 to 35 minutes, or until set and each cake begins to pull away from the sides of the baking pan.

Cool the cakes in the pans on racks until they reach room temperature, about 2 hours. Invert each cake onto a second cooling rack, peel away the waxed paper, and invert again onto a cutting board.

Cut each cake into 18 bars and store them in an airtight tin.

Cinnamon-
Cashew
"Dunking"
Cookies

2¼ cups *sifted* all-purpose
flour

1 teaspoon baking
powder

½ teaspoon salt

1 cup finely chopped
unsalted cashews

3 extra-large eggs, at
room temperature

1 cup granulated sugar

1 cup vegetable oil

2 teaspoons pure vanilla
extract

FOR SPRINKLING:

½ cup granulated sugar
blended with 2
teaspoons ground
cinnamon

About 36 cookies

These rectangular cookies are crisp and tender. The batter (made of oil, eggs, sugar, flour, leavening, and cashews) is baked in old-fashioned ice cube trays—without the metal dividers. The trays hold just the right amount of batter, which bakes up into a soft, rounded loaf. The loaf is cut into ½-inch-thick slices and the slices are doused with a haze of cinnamon sugar. Then you bake the slices in a low oven until they are quite crisp.

This recipe is from my mother's file. She used almonds instead of cashews and the results are just as good. The idea for putting cashews in the batter comes from my friend and good cook, Mimi Davidson. This is one of my most requested cookie recipes and it is so popular that I decided to work up some variations; they appear in this book as Chocolate Chip Rusks on page 374 and Layered Ginger Rusks on page 394. Cinnamon-Cashew "Dunking" Cookies keep magnificently in a cookie tin for several weeks—but only if you hide them.

Lightly butter and flour two 11 x 4 x 1½-inch metal ice cube trays (with the divider inserts removed); set aside. Preheat the oven to 350 degrees.

Resift the flour with the baking powder and salt onto a sheet of waxed paper. Put the cashews in a bowl and toss with 2 teaspoons of the sifted mixture.

Beat the eggs and sugar in the large bowl of an electric mixer on moderate speed for 2 minutes. Add the oil in a slow, steady stream, beating well. Increase the speed to moderately high and beat for 1 minute. Blend in the vanilla. On low speed (or by hand), add the sifted mixture in 2 additions, beating just until the particles of flour have been absorbed. By hand, stir in the cashews.

Spoon the batter into the prepared pans, dividing it evenly between them.

Bake on the middle-level rack of the oven for 30 minutes, or until well risen, firm to the touch, and a wooden pick inserted into the center of each cake withdraws clean and dry.

Cool each cake in the pan on a rack for 3 to 5 minutes. Reduce the oven temperature to 250 degrees.

Invert each cake onto a second cooling rack and invert again to cool right side up. Let the cakes cool for 15 minutes.

Cut each cake into 18 slices with a sharp serrated knife. Arrange the slices on a large jelly roll pan (or large shallow baking pan). Sprinkle the slices evenly with half of the cinnamon sugar, turn the slices over, and sprinkle with the remaining cinnamon sugar.

Bake the slices on the middle-level rack of the oven for about 20 to 30 minutes to dry and crisp them. Turn the slices every 10 minutes with a pair of tongs. The slices should be quite firm—the tops should feel like toast instead of soft cake.

Transfer the cookies to cooling racks, using a wide spatula. Cool for 20 minutes. Store the cookies in an airtight tin.

Peach Squares

1¼ cups *unsifted*
  all-purpose flour

¼ cup *unsifted* cake flour

¼ teaspoon baking soda

¼ teaspoon baking
  powder

½ teaspoon salt

1 teaspoon ground
  cinnamon

¾ teaspoon freshly grated
  nutmeg

½ teaspoon ground
  ginger

½ teaspoon ground
  allspice

¼ teaspoon ground
  cloves

8 tablespoons (1 stick)
  unsalted butter,
  softened at room
  temperature

½ cup firmly packed light
  brown sugar

¼ cup granulated sugar

1 extra-large egg plus 2
  extra-large egg yolks, at
  room temperature

These squares are chewy, spicy, and chockablock full of dried peaches and pecans. I love them with a midafternoon cup of brewed decaffeinated coffee or mug of warm cider.

At my house, Peach Squares are served on a pale pink Depression-glass cookie plate, lined with heart-shaped paper doilies.

———◆◆◆———

Lightly butter and flour a 13 x 9 x 2-inch baking pan; set aside. Preheat the oven to 350 degrees.

Sift the all-purpose flour, cake flour, baking soda, baking powder, salt, cinnamon, nutmeg, ginger, allspice, and cloves onto a sheet of waxed paper.

Cream the butter in the large bowl of an electric mixer on moderate speed for 2 minutes. Add the brown sugar and beat for 2 minutes; add the granulated sugar and beat for 1 minute longer. Beat in the egg and the egg yolks, one at a time, blending well after each addition. Blend in the preserves-vanilla mixture. On low speed (or by hand), beat in the sifted mixture in 2 additions, beating just until the particles of flour have been absorbed. By hand, stir in the dried peaches, raisins, and pecans.

Spoon the batter into the prepared pan, spreading it into an even layer with a spatula or flexible palette knife.

Bake the squares on the middle-level rack of the oven for 25 minutes, or until set and firm to the touch. (The cake will

½ cup peach preserves blended with 1 teaspoon pure vanilla extract

1 cup chopped dried peaches

¾ cup golden raisins

¾ cup chopped pecans

---

24 squares

begin to pull away from the sides of the baking pan when done.)

Cool the cake in the pan on a rack until it reaches room temperature, about 2 hours. Cut the cake into 24 squares and store them in an airtight tin.

Chocolate Chip Rusks

2¼ cups *sifted* all-purpose flour

1 teaspoon baking powder

½ teaspoon salt

¾ cup miniature semisweet chocolate chips

3 extra-large eggs, at room temperature

1 cup Vanilla-Scented Granulated Sugar (page 219)

1 cup vegetable oil

1½ teaspoons pure vanilla extract

½ teaspoon chocolate extract

FOR SPRINKLING:

⅓ cup Vanilla-Scented Granulated Sugar (page 219)

About 36 rusks

Chocolate Chip Rusks are the perfect cappuccino, hot chocolate, or coffee cookie—they are sweet enough, tender textured but firm, with enough chocolate to satisfy. Packed in a checkered tin, they make a divine hostess gift.

Lightly butter and flour two 11 x 4 x 1½-inch metal ice cube trays (with the divider inserts removed); set aside. Preheat the oven to 350 degrees.

Resift the flour with the baking powder and salt onto a sheet of waxed paper. Put the chocolate chips in a bowl and toss with 2 teaspoons of the sifted mixture.

Beat the eggs and sugar in the large bowl of an electric mixer for 2 minutes. Add the oil in a slow, steady stream, beating well. Increase the speed to moderately high and beat for 1 minute. Blend in the vanilla and chocolate extracts. On low speed (or by hand), add the sifted mixture in 2 additions, beating just until the particles of flour have been absorbed. By hand, stir in the chocolate chips.

Spoon the batter into the prepared pans, dividing it evenly between them.

Bake on the middle-level rack of the oven for 30 minutes, or until well risen, firm to the touch, and a wooden pick inserted into the center of each cake withdraws clean and dry.

Cool each cake in the pan on a rack for 2 to 3 minutes. Reduce the oven temperature to 250 degrees.

Invert each cake onto a second cooling rack and invert again to cool right side up. Let the cakes cool for 15 minutes.

Cut each cake into 18 slices with a sharp serrated knife. Arrange the slices on a large jelly roll pan (or large shallow baking pan). Sprinkle the slices evenly with half of the sugar, turn the slices over, and sprinkle with the remaining sugar.

Bake the slices on the middle-level rack of the oven for about 20 to 30 minutes to dry and crisp them. Turn the slices over every 10 minutes with a pair of tongs. The slices should be quite firm—the tops should feel like toast instead of soft cake.

Transfer the cookies to cooling racks, using a wide spatula. Cool for 20 minutes. Store the cookies in an airtight tin.

"SNACKING" COOKIES

"SNACKING" COOKIES

————————— ❖❖❖ —————————

Peanut Delights 380

Banana-Oatmeal Pillows 382

Brown Sugar–Fruit and Nut Mounds 384

Sour Cream–Molasses–Spice Rounds 386

Fruit Clusters 388

Butterscotch-Granola Disks 390

Pecan Pie Squares 393

Layered Ginger Rusks 394

Full of character and flavor, "snacking" cookies are those sweets made from nuts, oatmeal, dried fruit, or preserves. Whether they are layered in tins or stacked in big jars, these cookies are good keepers. I have found it wise to have a few dozen of them on hand for those who sneak into the kitchen at midnight for cookies and milk.

Brown Sugar–Fruit and Nut Mounds, Butterscotch-Granola Disks, and Fruit Clusters are big and thick, bursting with a whole market list of ingredients: oatmeal, coconut, peanuts, cashews, sunflower seeds, bran, apricots, currants, raisins, figs, and dates. These hearty cookies were made for pairing with goblets of cold milk or Hot Spiced Cider (page 401).

The Pecan Pie Squares and Layered Ginger Rusks are just sweet enough to accompany a pot of English Breakfast or Darjeeling tea for a four o'clock tea-and-cookie break.

There are other recipes in this book for big-batch cookies that store well and are pleasing to have around for offering to children after school or taking to the office and stashing in your desk drawer. My favorites are: Applesauce Pillows (page 308) and Apple Butter Cookies (page 348), Pear-Oatmeal Drops (page 312) and Oatmeal-Raisin Saucers (page 356), Pumpkin-Fig Mounds (page 314), Pumpkin-Spice Cookies (page 357), and Ginger Crisps (page 346).

Peanut Delights

2¾ cups *unsifted*
　all-purpose flour

¼ cup *unsifted* cake flour

¾ teaspoon baking soda

¾ teaspoon baking
　powder

¾ teaspoon salt

1½ teaspoons ground
　cinnamon

½ teaspoon ground
　ginger

½ teaspoon ground
　allspice

½ teaspoon freshly grated
　nutmeg

12 tablespoons (1½
　sticks) unsalted butter,
　softened at room
　temperature

¾ cup shortening

¾ cup firmly packed light
　brown sugar

¾ cup superfine sugar

2 extra-large eggs plus 2
　extra-large egg yolks, at
　room temperature

This big-batch recipe makes enough cookies to fill up a few cookie jars. These delights are full of the savor of smooth peanut butter and roasted peanuts. Spices and brown sugar complement the peanut flavor.

This is my mother's recipe for peanut butter cookies, one that I have changed slightly. I add a little light cream and molasses to the drop cookie dough and replace part of the all-purpose flour with cake flour. Peanut Delights are always welcome at bake sales. If you are faced with baking many more dozens than this recipe turns out, know that great quantities of this dough can be made up and stored in the refrigerator for 2 to 3 days before baking. (And if your schedule is really frantic, turn these drop cookies into the slice-and-bake variety: Chill the dough thoroughly, then form into logs, 3 inches in diameter. Freeze the logs, then slice and bake as needed.)

———✦✦✦———

Lightly butter and flour 4 cookie sheets or line the sheets with lengths of cooking parchment paper; set aside. Preheat the oven to 375 degrees.

Sift the all-purpose flour, cake flour, baking soda, baking powder, salt, cinnamon, ginger, allspice, and nutmeg onto a sheet of waxed paper.

Cream the butter and shortening in the large bowl of an electric mixer on moderate speed for 3 minutes. Add the brown sugar and beat for 1 minute; add the superfine sugar

1 teaspoon pure vanilla
extract

3 tablespoons light
molasses

3 tablespoons light
cream, at room
temperature

1⅓ cups smooth peanut
butter

1¼ cups chopped lightly
salted peanuts

About 48 cookies

and beat for 2 minutes. Add the eggs and egg yolks one at a time, blending well after each addition; scrape down the sides of the mixing bowl frequently with a rubber spatula. Beat in the vanilla, molasses, and cream. Beat in the peanut butter. On low speed (or by hand), blend in the sifted mixture in 2 additions, beating just until the particles of flour have been absorbed.

Drop the dough by level tablespoons onto the prepared cookie sheets, placing the mounds 1½ inches apart.

Bake the cookies, one sheet at a time, on the middle-level rack of the oven for 12 to 14 minutes, or until set and firm to the touch.

Transfer the cookies to cooling racks, using a wide spatula. Cool for 20 minutes. Store the cookies in an airtight tin.

Banana-Oatmeal Pillows

2½ cups *sifted* all-purpose flour

1 cup *sifted* cake flour

1½ teaspoons baking soda

1 teaspoon baking powder

¾ teaspoon salt

2½ teaspoons ground cinnamon

1 teaspoon freshly grated nutmeg

½ teaspoon ground ginger

¼ teaspoon ground allspice

¼ teaspoon ground cloves

¾ cup shortening

4 tablespoons unsalted butter, softened at room temperature

1¼ cups firmly packed light brown sugar

¾ cup superfine sugar

2 extra-large eggs plus 2 extra-large egg yolks, at room temperature

This recipe is from my grandmother's cookie file: The pillows are soft, cakelike, and full of the taste of ripe bananas and oatmeal. Over the years, I have modified the recipe to include lots more spices, flaked coconut, walnuts, and a little molasses (some of the same ingredients that can be found in my favorite banana quick bread).

Banana-Oatmeal Pillows should be served with thick vanilla milk shakes or large cups of piping-hot coffee.

Lightly butter and flour 4 cookie sheets or line the sheets with lengths of cooking parchment paper; set aside. Preheat the oven to 375 degrees.

Resift the all-purpose flour and cake flour with the baking soda, baking powder, salt, cinnamon, nutmeg, ginger, allspice, and cloves onto a sheet of waxed paper.

Cream the shortening and butter in the large bowl of an electric mixer on moderate speed for 2 minutes. Add the brown sugar in 2 additions, beating for 1 minute after each portion is added. Add the superfine sugar and beat for 2 minutes. Add the eggs, one at a time, blending well after each addition. Beat in the egg yolks. Blend in the vanilla and almond extracts; blend in the molasses and bananas. On low speed (or by hand), blend in the sifted mixture in 2 additions, beating just until the particles of flour have been absorbed. By hand, stir in the oatmeal, coconut, and walnuts.

Drop the dough by rounded tablespoons onto the prepared cookie sheets, placing the mounds 1½ inches apart.

2 teaspoons pure vanilla
   extract

1 teaspoon pure almond
   extract

1 tablespoon light
   molasses

1½ cups mashed ripe
   bananas (about 3
   bananas)

2¾ cups quick-cooking
   oatmeal

¾ cup flaked coconut

¾ cup chopped walnuts

About 60 cookies

Bake the cookies one sheet at a time, on the middle-level rack of the oven for 13 to 14 minutes, or until set and just firm to the touch.

Transfer the cookies to cooling racks, using a wide spatula. Cool for 20 minutes. Store the cookies in an airtight tin.

Brown Sugar–Fruit and Nut Mounds

1¾ cups *unsifted* all-purpose flour

¼ cup *unsifted* cake flour

1 teaspoon baking soda

1 teaspoon baking powder

1 teaspoon salt

1 teaspoon ground cinnamon

1 teaspoon freshly grated nutmeg

½ teaspoon ground allspice

½ pound (2 sticks) unsalted butter, softened at room temperature

1½ cups firmly packed brown sugar

½ cup superfine sugar

1 extra-large egg plus 2 extra-large egg yolks, at room temperature

2 teaspoons pure vanilla extract

Filled with dried fruit and oatmeal, these mounds are thick and hearty. Every year, around about the middle of December, my mother and I made these cookies in anticipation of the holidays. Weeks earlier, she'd order all the nuts, dried fruit, and seeds from a supplier in California and store them in the pantry; with everything on hand, you knew that fruit cookies, fruitcakes, and fruit-and-nut loaves were soon to be baked. Nowadays, the ingredients for these cookies are available at grocery stores, health food stores, and most small markets.

Brown Sugar–Fruit and Nut Mounds can be made with almost any combination of dried fruit and nuts you can imagine. I am passing on our family recipe to you and this list of substitutions: a mixture of filberts, Brazil nuts, and almonds can replace the sunflower seeds, peanuts, and cashews; currants or golden raisins can replace the dark seedless raisins; apricots or prunes can replace the peaches; and honey can replace the molasses.

———— ❖❖❖ ————

Lightly butter and flour 4 cookie sheets or line the sheets with lengths of cooking parchment paper; set aside. Preheat the oven to 350 degrees.

Sift the all-purpose flour, cake flour, baking soda, baking powder, salt, cinnamon, nutmeg, and allspice onto a sheet of waxed paper.

Cream the butter in the large bowl of an electric mixer for 2 minutes. Add the brown sugar and beat for 2 minutes; add

1 tablespoon light
  molasses

1 tablespoon light corn
  syrup

2¼ cups quick-cooking
  oatmeal

1 cup dark seedless
  raisins

1 cup flaked coconut

½ cup chopped lightly
  salted cashews

½ cup chopped lightly
  salted peanuts

¼ cup roasted unsalted
  sunflower seeds

1 cup chopped pitted
  dates

About 48 cookies

the superfine sugar and beat for 1 minute. Beat in the egg and egg yolks, blending well. Beat in the vanilla, molasses, and corn syrup. On low speed (or by hand), blend in the sifted mixture in 2 additions, beating just until the particles of flour have been absorbed. By hand, stir in the oatmeal, raisins, coconut, cashews, peanuts, sunflower seeds, and dates.

Drop the dough by level tablespoons onto the prepared cookie sheets, placing the mounds 1½ inches apart.

Bake the cookies, one sheet at a time, on the middle-level rack of the oven for 10 to 12 minutes, or until just set and firm to the touch.

Transfer the cookies to cooling racks, using a wide spatula. Cool for 20 minutes. Store the cookies in an airtight tin.

Sour Cream–Molasses–Spice Rounds

2½ cups *unsifted* all-purpose flour

½ cup *unsifted* cake flour

1 teaspoon baking soda

½ teaspoon baking powder

1 teaspoon salt

2 teaspoons ground cinnamon

1½ teaspoons freshly grated nutmeg

½ teaspoon ground ginger

¼ teaspoon ground allspice

8 tablespoons (1 stick) unsalted butter, softened at room temperature

2 tablespoons shortening

½ cup firmly packed light brown sugar

¼ cup superfine sugar

⅓ cup molasses

¼ cup honey

These rounds are soft and golden brown, as good molasses cookies should be. The cinnamon and nutmeg, which I think of as sweet spices, balance out the assertive flavor of the molasses.

Cups of Hot Spiced Cider (page 401) or icy glasses of Real Lemonade (page 400) and a basket of Sour Cream–Molasses–Spice Rounds would make a delightful afternoon snack.

———❖❖❖———

Lightly butter and flour 4 cookie sheets or line the sheets with lengths of cooking parchment paper; set aside. Preheat the oven to 375 degrees.

Sift the all-purpose flour, cake flour, baking soda, baking powder, salt, cinnamon, nutmeg, ginger, and allspice onto a sheet of waxed paper.

Cream the butter and shortening in the large bowl of an electric mixer on moderate speed for 2 minutes. Add the brown sugar and beat for 1 minute; add the superfine sugar and beat for 1 minute. Blend in the molasses and honey (the mixture may look curdled, but it's okay). Beat in the egg and egg yolk. Blend in the vanilla extract. On low speed (or by hand), blend in the sifted mixture in 2 additions alternately with the sour cream in 1 addition, beginning and ending with the sifted mixture. By hand, stir in the raisins.

Drop the dough by level tablespoons onto the prepared cookie sheets, placing the rounds 1½ to 2 inches apart. Lightly sprinkle the cookies with the spiced sugar.

1 extra-large egg plus 1 extra-large egg yolk, at room temperature

1 teaspoon pure vanilla extract

¾ cup sour cream, at room temperature

¾ cup dark seedless raisins

FOR SPRINKLING:

½ cup granulated sugar blended with ¼ teaspoon ground cinnamon and ¼ teaspoon ground ginger

About 48 cookies

Bake the cookies, one sheet at a time, on the middle-level rack of the oven for 10 to 12 minutes, or until set and just firm to the touch.

Transfer the cookies to cooling racks, using a wide spatula. Cool for 20 minutes. Store the cookies in an airtight tin.

Fruit Clusters

¾ cup buttermilk, at
 room temperature

1 teaspoon baking soda

3 cups *sifted* all-purpose
 flour

¾ cup *sifted* cake flour

1 teaspoon baking
 powder

1 teaspoon salt

2½ teaspoons ground
 cinnamon

1½ teaspoons freshly
 grated nutmeg

1 teaspoon ground ginger

½ teaspoon ground
 allspice

½ pound (2 sticks)
 unsalted butter,
 softened at room
 temperature

1¼ cups firmly packed
 light brown sugar

¾ cup superfine sugar

3 extra-large eggs plus 1
 extra-large egg yolk, at
 room temperature

Fruit clusters are soft, chewy, and crammed full of apricots, dates, currants, and figs; they will remind you of a good light fruitcake. The little kick of rum added to the cookie dough along with the vanilla extract intensifies the flavor of the fruit and nuts.

I serve a mound of Fruit Clusters from a pretty porcelain basket with cups of eggnog, mulled wine, Hot Spiced Cider (page 401), or coffee.

———❖❖❖———

Lightly butter and flour 4 cookie sheets or line the sheets with lengths of cooking parchment paper; set aside. Preheat the oven to 350 degrees.

Pour the buttermilk into a bowl, stir in the baking soda, and set aside.

Resift the all-purpose flour and cake flour with the baking powder, salt, cinnamon, nutmeg, ginger, and allspice onto a sheet of waxed paper.

Cream the butter in the large bowl of an electric mixer on moderate speed for 3 minutes. Add the brown sugar and beat for 2 minutes; add the superfine sugar and beat for 1 minute. Beat in the eggs, one at a time, blending well after each addition. Beat in the egg yolk. Blend in the vanilla and rum. On low speed (or by hand), blend in the sifted mixture in 3 additions alternately with the buttermilk in 2 additions, beginning and ending with the sifted mixture. By hand, stir in the apricots, dates, figs, currants, raisins, walnuts, and pecans.

1 tablespoon pure vanilla
  extract

3 tablespoons light rum

1½ cups chopped glazed
  apricots

¾ cup chopped pitted
  dates

¾ cup chopped stemmed
  dried figs

½ cup currants

½ cup dark seedless
  raisins

1 cup chopped walnuts

½ cup chopped pecans

About 60 cookies

Drop the dough by level tablespoons onto the prepared cookie sheets, placing the mounds 2 inches apart.

Bake the cookies, one sheet at a time, on the middle-level rack of the oven for 15 minutes, or until golden, set, and just firm to the touch.

Transfer the cookies to cooling racks, using a wide spatula. Cool for 20 minutes. Store the cookies in an airtight tin.

Butterscotch-Granola Disks

1¾ cups *unsifted* all-purpose flour

¼ cup *unsifted* cake flour

2 teaspoons baking powder

1½ teaspoons baking soda

¾ teaspoon salt

1 teaspoon ground cinnamon

¾ teaspoon freshly grated nutmeg

¼ teaspoon ground allspice

8 tablespoons (1 stick) unsalted butter, softened at room temperature

½ cup shortening

1¼ cups firmly packed light brown sugar

¼ cup superfine sugar

2 extra-large eggs, at room temperature

2 tablespoons light molasses

Making your very own "house blend" of granola is a quick and satisfying project. While no two mixtures ever come out the same, it's fun to mix and match the oats, bran, wheat germ, spices, nuts, fruit, seeds, and sweeteners. Homemade granola makes a very good batch of cookies, but store-bought granola works well too. If you are using commercially produced granola and it lacks coconut or raisins, add about ⅓ cup raisins to this cookie dough, along with ¼ cup flaked coconut. Following this recipe is my own quirky recipe for granola, which I keep in a large wide-mouth apothecary jar on the kitchen counter.

Accompany a heaping plateful of Butterscotch-Granola Disks with a large pitcher of ice-cold milk.

Lightly butter and flour 4 cookie sheets or line the sheets with lengths of cooking parchment paper; set aside. Preheat the oven to 375 degrees.

Sift the all-purpose flour, cake flour, baking powder, baking soda, salt, cinnamon, nutmeg, and allspice onto a sheet of waxed paper.

Cream the butter and shortening in the large bowl of an electric mixer on moderate speed for 2 minutes. Add the brown sugar and beat for 2 minutes; add the superfine sugar and beat for a minute longer. Beat in the eggs, one at a time, blending well after each addition. Blend in the molasses and vanilla and maple extracts. On low speed (or by hand), blend in the sifted mixture in 2 additions, beating just until the

2 teaspoons pure vanilla extract

1 teaspoon maple extract

1½ cups granola (homemade or store-bought)

1 cup butterscotch chips

About 48 cookies

particles of flour have been absorbed. By hand, stir in the granola and butterscotch chips.

Drop the dough by level tablespoons onto the prepared cookie sheets, placing the mounds 1½ inches apart.

Bake the cookies, one sheet at a time, on the middle-level rack of the oven for 12 to 14 minutes, or until set and just firm to the touch.

Transfer the cookies to cooling racks, using a wide spatula. Cool for 20 minutes. Store the cookies in an airtight tin.

Homemade Granola

7 cups oats,
  quick-cooking or
  old-fashioned

1 cup bran

1 cup wheat germ

2 cups flaked coconut

1 cup unsalted sunflower
  seeds

1 cup chopped walnuts

1 cup chopped pecans

1 teaspoon ground
  cinnamon

¾ teaspoon freshly grated
  nutmeg

1 cup pure maple syrup,
  or to taste

1 tablespoon plus 1
  teaspoon pure vanilla
  extract

2 teaspoons maple extract

1½ cups dark seedless
  raisins

About 16½ cups

Full of what's good for you.

Lightly oil two 15 x 10 x 1-inch jelly roll pans; set aside. Preheat the oven to 275 degrees.

Combine the oatmeal, bran, wheat germ, coconut, sunflower seeds, walnuts, pecans, cinnamon, and nutmeg in a large (8 to 10 quart) mixing bowl. Whisk together the maple syrup and vanilla and maple extracts; pour over the oat mixture and toss well.

Spread the granola evenly on the jelly roll pans, dividing the mixture between them. Bake the granola on the upper-level and lower-third-level racks of the oven for about 45 minutes, or until lightly toasted, stirring the mixture from time to time.

Cool the granola in the pans on a rack until room temperature, about 1½ hours. Crumble the granola into a large storage container, add the raisins, and toss. Cover tightly and store at room temperature.

Pecan Pie Squares

1 cup *unsifted* all-purpose flour

⅓ cup *unsifted* cake flour

½ teaspoon baking soda

½ teaspoon baking powder

½ teaspoon salt

½ teaspoon ground cinnamon

½ teaspoon freshly grated nutmeg

¼ teaspoon ground allspice

1½ cups chopped pecans

12 tablespoons (1½ sticks) unsalted butter, melted and cooled

1½ cups firmly packed light brown sugar

3 tablespoons dark corn syrup

3 extra-large eggs, at room temperature

2 teaspoons pure vanilla extract

24 squares

These golden-colored squares are thick with chopped pecans, sweetened with brown sugar and corn syrup, and enriched with butter. Serve them with a pot of hot tea (or pitcher of iced lemon tea), cups of spiced wine, or a good bourbon-spiked eggnog.

Lightly butter and flour a 13 x 9 x 2-inch baking pan; set aside. Preheat the oven to 350 degrees.

Sift the all-purpose flour, cake flour, baking soda, baking powder, salt, cinnamon, nutmeg, and allspice onto a sheet of waxed paper. Put the pecans in a bowl and toss with 1 tablespoon of the sifted mixture.

Whisk the melted butter, brown sugar, corn syrup, and eggs in a large mixing bowl, beating well. Blend in the vanilla. Stir in the sifted mixture in 2 additions, beating just until the particles of flour have been absorbed. Stir in the pecans.

Spoon the batter into the prepared pan, smoothing over the top with a spatula.

Bake on the middle-level rack of the oven for 30 to 35 minutes, or until set and firm to the touch (the cake will begin to pull away from the sides of the baking pan when done).

Cool the cake in the pan on a rack until it reaches room temperature, about 2 hours. Cut into 24 squares and store them in an airtight tin.

Layered Ginger Rusks

2¼ cups *sifted* all-purpose flour

1 teaspoon baking powder

½ teaspoon salt

¼ teaspoon ground ginger

¾ cup finely chopped roasted almonds

3 extra-large eggs, at room temperature

1 cup granulated sugar

1 cup vegetable oil

2 tablespoons freshly squeezed orange juice

1 tablespoon freshly grated orange peel

½ cup ginger preserves, at room temperature

FOR SPRINKLING:

⅓ cup granulated sugar

About 36 rusks

Patterned after the luscious Cinnamon-Cashew "Dunking" Cookies on page 370, these rusks are flavored with ginger preserves, orange juice, and grated orange rind.

For a splendid teatime treat, serve a basket of Layered Ginger Rusks with cups of hot orange or English Breakfast tea, or a pitcher of minted iced tea. For dessert, offer the rusks with poached pears, a toss of summer berries, or homemade caramel ice cream.

Lightly butter and flour two 11 x 4 x 1½-inch metal ice cube trays (with the divider inserts removed); set aside. Preheat the oven to 350 degrees.

Resift the flour with the baking powder, salt, and ginger onto a sheet of waxed paper.

Put the almonds in a bowl and toss with 2 teaspoons of the sifted flour mixture.

Beat the eggs and sugar in the large bowl of an electric mixer on moderate speed for 2 minutes. Add the oil in a slow, steady stream, beating well. Increase the speed to moderately high and beat for 1 minute. Beat in the orange juice and orange peel. On low speed (or by hand), add the sifted flour mixture in 2 additions, beating just until the particles of flour have been absorbed. By hand, stir in the almonds.

Divide the batter in half. Spoon *half* of 1 portion of batter into the prepared pans, dividing it evenly between them. Spoon ¼ cup preserves over the top of each pan of batter, leaving a ¾-inch border. Spoon the remaining portion of batter on top of the ginger layer, dividing it evenly between the 2 pans.

Bake on the middle-level rack of the oven for 30 minutes, or until well risen, firm to the touch, and a wooden pick inserted into the center of each comes out clean and dry.

Cool the rusks in the pans on a rack for 3 to 5 minutes. Reduce the oven temperature to 250 degrees.

Invert each onto a second cooling rack and invert again to cool right side up. Let the cakes cool for 20 minutes.

Cut each cake into 18 slices with a sharp serrated knife. Arrange the slices on a large jelly roll pan (or large shallow baking pan). Sprinkle the slices evenly with half of the sugar, turn the slices over, and sprinkle with the remaining sugar.

Bake the slices on the middle-level rack of the oven for 20 to 30 minutes to dry and crisp them. Turn the slices every 10 minutes with a pair of tongs. The slices should be quite firm —the tops should feel like toast instead of soft cake.

Transfer the cookies to cooling racks, using a wide spatula. Cool for 20 minutes. Store the cookies in an airtight tin.

REFRESHMENTS
FOR A COUNTRY DAY

Wendy Wheeler

REFRESHMENTS FOR A COUNTRY DAY

———————— ❖❖❖ ————————

Real Lemonade   400
Hot Spiced Cider   401
Summer Fruit Medley   402

eal Lemonade, Hot Spiced Cider, and Summer Fruit Medley are all splendid beverages to serve alongside a plate of just-baked cookies. The lemonade and the mixed fruit drink, a pair of fresh and lively thirst quenchers, taste mighty good with many of the cookies in this book, especially the Vanilla Melt-a-Ways (page 300), Sugar Cookie Hearts (page 352), Double Vanilla "Dog Bones" (page 322), Ginger Crisps (page 346), Lemon Butter Balls (page 326), or Black Walnut Butter Drops (page 362). A pitcher of warm cider is a heavenly match for a basket of Applesauce Pillows (page 308), Pumpkin-Fig Mounds (page 314), Maple Bars (page 320), Apple Butter Cookies (page 348), Apricot-Date Bars (page 366), or Oatmeal-Raisin Saucers (page 356). On a snowy weekend afternoon, offer mugs of cider and a tin of fresh cookies to neighbors; on a hot and balmy summer day, present tall glasses of lemonade with a dish of buttery cookies to friends and family after an outing to the pool or farmers' market.

Real Lemonade

FOR THE LEMON SYRUP:

2 cups water

2²/₃ cups granulated sugar

3 cups freshly squeezed
   lemon juice (about 16
   lemons)

TO FINISH:

About 4¹/₂ cups ice-cold
   water (more or less, to
   taste)

Thin slices of lemon,
   optional

Sprigs of fresh mint,
   optional

*About 8 cups, enough for 12
tall glasses*

With a sweet-tart taste, fresh lemonade is perfect for washing down a few cookies—or a slice of cake or wedge of pie. The base of this cooling drink is made up of a sugar syrup into which you pour freshly squeezed lemon juice. For serving, simply add several cupfuls of ice-cold water to dilute the syrup; the lemon-enhanced syrup can be made several days in advance and kept in the refrigerator in a tightly sealed container. This recipe also turns out a sprightly batch of limeade if you substitute the same amount of lime juice for the lemon juice.

———❖❖❖———

Place the water and sugar in a medium-size stainless steel saucepan; cover and set over low heat. Cook slowly until every last granule of sugar has dissolved. Uncover the saucepan, raise the heat to moderately high, and bring the liquid to a boil. Boil 5 minutes. Cool. Stir the lemon juice into the sugar syrup. (The syrup can be prepared up to this point, stored in a tightly sealed container, and refrigerated for 5 to 7 days.)

To serve the lemonade, add most of the water (about 3¹/₂ cups) to the lemon syrup. Add the rest of the water, a little at a time, tasting as you go: The lemonade should be nicely balanced. If the drink is too heavy on the syrup, just add a little more water.

Pour the lemonade into tall glasses that have been filled with ice. Tuck a mint sprig into the glass to one side and enjoy.

❖·❖·❖·❖·❖·❖·❖·❖·❖·❖·❖·❖·❖·❖·❖

Hot Spiced Cider

6 cups fresh apple cider

¼ cup pure maple syrup
(more or less, to taste)

2 cinnamon sticks

6 whole cloves

6 whole allspice berries

6 strips orange peel

6 strips lemon peel

---

*About 6 cups, enough for 6
large mugs*

This is a comforting concoction that's far from fussy: It is unfiltered cider, sweetened with maple syrup, charged with spices, and warmed to bring out all the pleasing aromas and flavors.

Pour the apple cider and maple syrup into a large stainless steel saucepan. Place the cinnamon sticks, cloves, allspice berries, orange peel, and lemon peel in the center of a washed square of cheesecloth; fold up the sides of the cheesecloth to enclose the spices in a bundle, then tie it up with a length of kitchen string. Drop the spice bundle into the cider mixture. Place the saucepan over moderate heat for 5 to 10 minutes, or until the cider is very hot but not boiling.

Remove the cider from the heat. Discard the spice bundle. Ladle the cider into big cups or mugs, adding a fresh cinnamon stick to each serving, if you like.

Summer Fruit
Medley

2 cups chilled freshly
   squeezed grapefruit
   juice
1½ cups chilled guava
   juice
1 cup chilled peach
   nectar
1 cup chilled pear nectar
1 cup chilled freshly
   squeezed orange juice
⅓ cup fresh fruit syrup
   (homemade or
   store-bought)
2 tablespoons freshly
   squeezed lime juice
⅔ cup chilled club soda

*About 7½ cups, enough for 6
tall glasses*

A blend of fruit juices, lightly sweetened with fresh fruit syrup and served in pretty glass tumblers, is a good drink to have on hand during summer's sun-drenched days. A few splashes of light rum can be stirred into each drink, if the spirit moves you.

———❖❖❖———

Combine the grapefruit juice, guava juice, peach nectar, pear nectar, orange juice, fruit syrup, and lime juice in a large pitcher. Stir in the club soda.

Pour the fruit medley into large ice-filled glasses and serve.

Note: Fruit syrups are wonderful to have on hand for adding to summer drinks, fruit salads, and ice cream. The method for making a whole range of the syrups is outlined on pages 37 and 38.

THE COUNTRY COOKIE EXCHANGE

Wheeler

*D*uring the winter holidays when everyone loves to bake and have plenty of cookies squirreled away in tins, it's fun to organize an informal gathering to swap cookies and recipes. Participating in such an exchange is a good way to sample lots of baked things and take home masses of cookies besides.

As the host or hostess, invite twelve of the best cooks you know to take part in the exchange. Ask each person to send you his or her three favorite cookie recipes, then select one recipe from each submission, making sure that many flavors and textures are represented. Assign each cook one of his or her own recipes and tell everyone to prepare twelve dozen cookies (or more, if you like). Along with the load of cookies, remind every baker to bring copies of the recipe and big containers for holding all the cookies they'll be taking home.

On the day of the swap, clear a large table. Set out packages of plastic bags, boxes of waxed paper, twist ties, and cellophane wrap.

Arrange a big pot of coffee or tea or eggnog on a sideboard to accompany the cookies you'll be sampling.

Ask each baker to set out his or her batch of cookies on the table and parcel them out into bags or boxes. The table, holding a mountain of cookies, will remind you of Santa's workshop. And the aroma of spices, butter, chocolate, nuts, and fruit is a festive reminder of the days to come.

Country Cookies That Use "Goods on Hand" (Basic Dairy and Pantry Staples)

❖❖❖

Vanilla Melt-a-Ways   300
Sour Cream–Spice Cookies   302
Chocolate Gems   306
Applesauce Pillows   308
Mint Chocolate Crisps   310
Pear-Oatmeal Drops   312
Maple Bars   320
Double Vanilla "Dog Bones"   322
Chocolate Nut Crunch Squares   324
Three Nut Bars   328
Coconut Dreams   330
Grandma Lilly's Brownies   332
Heavenly Hash Brownies   334
Double Chocolate–Walnut Fudgies   336
Coconut-Chocolate "Swirlies"   338
Chocolate Toffee Squares   340
Ginger Crisps   346
Pecan Butter Crunch Squares   350

Sugar Cookie Hearts   352
Bittersweet Chocolate–Caramel Bars   354
Oatmeal-Raisin Saucers   356
Black Walnut Butter Drops   362
Giant Double Chocolate Rounds   364
Milk Chocolate–Almond Bars   368
Cinnamon-Cashew "Dunking" Cookies   370
Chocolate Chip Rusks   374
Peanut Delights   380
Brown Sugar–Fruit and Nut Mounds   384
Sour Cream–Molasses–Spice Rounds   386
Fruit Clusters   388
Butterscotch-Granola Disks   390
Pecan Pie Squares   393

Country Cookies That Use Fresh or Dried Fruit

Orange-Raisin Drops   304

Applesauce Pillows   308

Pear-Oatmeal Drops   312

Pumpkin-Fig Mounds   314

Lemon Butter Balls   326

Apple Butter Cookies   348

Oatmeal-Raisin Saucers   356

Pumpkin-Spice Cookies   357

Apricot-Date Bars   366

Peach Squares   372

Banana-Oatmeal Pillows   382

Brown Sugar–Fruit and Nut
    Mounds   384

Fruit Clusters   388

Keeping Cookies

———◆◆◆———

Vanilla Melt-a-Ways   300
Applesauce Pillows   308
Pear-Oatmeal Drops   312
Pumpkin-Fig Mounds   314
Double Vanilla "Dog Bones"   322
Lemon Butter Balls   326
Chocolate Toffee Squares   340
Ginger Crisps   346
Oatmeal-Raisin Saucers   356
Giant Double Chocolate Rounds   364
Cinnamon-Cashew "Dunking" Cookies   370
Chocolate Chip Rusks   374
Brown Sugar–Fruit and Nut Mounds   384
Fruit Clusters   388
Layered Ginger Rusks   394

Index

❖❖❖

Acorn squash, golden
  pie, brandied, 84–85
  puree, 85
Almond(s)
  –milk chocolate bars, 368–69
  pie, lemon-, 122
  three nut bars with, 328–29
Apple(s)
  butter cookies, 348–49
  cake, spicy, 240–41
  cakes, chunky, with pecans, 252–53
  cider, in hot spiced cider, 401
  cider syrup, 65
  -ginger mincemeat pie, 63
  -pear pie, with apple cider syrup, 66–67
  pie, double-crust, 62
  -raisin coffee cake, 176–77
  -raspberry pie, 53
  streusel pie, 104–5
  upside-down cake, ginger-, 210–11
Apricot pie
  fresh, 55–56
  yam-, 81

Bake sale cakes, 276
Bake sale gems, 317–31
  chocolate nut crunch squares, 324–25
  coconut dreams, 330–31
  double vanilla "dog bones," 322–23
  lemon butter balls, 326–27
  maple bars, 320–21
  three nut bars, 328–29
Bakeware and tools, 146–48
Banana(s)
  -coconut coffee cake, 182–83

cream pie, 100–101
  -oatmeal pillows, 382–83
Bar cookies, baking, 290
Baskets, cookie, 294–95
Black walnut(s)
  butter drops, 362–63
  and chocolate pan cake, 158–59
  in Grandma Lilly's brownies, 332–33
Blackberry pie, deep-dish, 52
Blueberry(-ies)
  cakes, 256–57
  gingerbread, 246–47
  -peach pie, double-crust, 42–43
  pie, deep-dish, 44
  –walnut–brown sugar buckle, 194–95
Bourbon
  pecan pie, 75
  pound cake, 224–25
Brandied golden acorn squash pie, 84–85
Brown sugar
  –fruit and nut mounds, 384–85
  pie, 87
Brownies, 319, 332–41
  chocolate
    -coconut "swirlies," 338–39
    toffee squares, 340–41
    –walnut fudgies, double, 336–37
  Grandma Lilly's, 332–33
  heavenly hash, 334–35
  pans for baking, 290
Butter
  balls, lemon, 326–27
  cookies, apple, 348–49
  crunch squares, pecan, 350–51
  drops, black walnut, 362–63

Buttermilk
  cake, 162–63
  chocolate layer cake, 164–65
  pie, 106–7
Butternut squash
  pie, orange-, 82–83
  puree, 83
Butterscotch-granola disks, 390–91

Cake(s)
  apple-ginger upside-down, 210–11
  apple-raisin coffee, 176–77
  bake sale, 276
  banana-coconut coffee, 182–183
  best vanilla pound, 218–19
  black walnut and chocolate pan, 158–59
  blueberry, 256–57
  blueberry gingerbread, 246–47
  blueberry–walnut–brown sugar buckle, 194–95
  bourbon pound, 224–25
  buttermilk, 162–63
  buttermilk chocolate layer, 164–65
  caramel upside-down sticky, 188–89
  chocolate pan, with chocolate fudge frosting, 196–97
  chocolate pound, 232–33
  chunky apple, with pecans, 252–53
  cocoa-nut swirl coffee, 172–73
  coconut layer, 166–68
  coconut-cinnamon pan, 174–75
  cream cheese–chocolate chip, 258–59

Cake(s) (*cont.*)
  cream pound, 230–31
  date coffee, 186–87
  easy to keep, 279
  with fresh fruits and vegetables, 278
  fresh peach, 242–43
  fudgy chocolate–walnut, 200–201
  ginger, 254–55
  Grandma Lilly's hot milk, 220–21
  ingredients, 149–50
  lemon–poppy seed pound, 222–23
  making batters for, 142–43
  maple-pumpkin coffee, 178–179
  marbled German chocolate, 156–57
  nectarine, 244–45
  orange, 160–61
  peach upside-down, 206–7
  pear, with walnuts and currants, 262
  pecan carrot, with raisins, 198–99
  plum, 238–39
  plates for, 151
  raspberry coffee, 184–85
  rich nut pound, 228–29
  spice pound, 226–27
  spiced nectarine upside-down, 208–9
  spicy apple, 240–41
  using "goods on hand," 277
  vanilla, 260–61
  walnut–sweet potato coffee, 180–81
"Candy" pie
  coconut, 116
    walnut-chocolate-chip, 86
Caramel
  –bittersweet chocolate bars, 354–55
  upside-down sticky cake, 188–89
Carrot-pecan cake with raisins, 198–99

Cashew(s)
  in brown sugar–fruit and nut mounds, 384–85
  -cinnamon "dunking" cookies, 370–71
  in pumpkin-spice cookies, 357–58
Cherry pie
  sour, 50
  yellow, glazed, 51
Chocolate
  –almond nut bars, milk, 368–69
  cake, marbled German, 156–57
  –caramel bars, bittersweet, 354–55
  chip rusks, 374–75
  -coconut "swirlies," 338–39
  cream cheese–, chip cakes, 258–59
  crisps, mint, 310–11
  frosting
    fudge, 197
    thin and rich, 164–65
  fudge pie, old-fashioned, 96–97
  gems, 306–7
  layer cake, buttermilk, 164–65
  nut crunch squares, 324–25
  pan cake, black walnut and, 158–59
  pan cake with chocolate fudge frosting, 196–97
  pie, shimmery, 117
  pound cake, 232–33
  rounds, giant double, 364–65
  silk pie, 102
  toffee squares, 340–41
  –walnut cake, fudgy, 200–201
  –walnut fudgies, double, 336–37
Chocolate chip rusks, 374–75
Chocolate-chip "candy" pie, coconut-walnut, 86
Cider, hot spiced, 401
Cinnamon
  -cashew "dunking" cookies, 370–71
  -coconut pan cake, 174–75
  ice cream, 268–69

-pear pie with walnut streusel, 69–70
-walnut topping, 181
Cocoa-nut swirl coffee cake, 172–73
Coconut
  about toasting, 183
  -banana coffee cake, 182–83
  in banana-oatmeal pillows, 382–83
  in brown sugar–fruit and nut mounds, 384–85
  -butter crumble topping, 175
  "candy" pie, 116
    walnut-chocolate-chip, 86
  -chocolate "swirlies," 338–39
  -cinnamon pan cake, 174–75
  cream pie, mile-high, 98–99
  custard pie, 93
  dreams, 330–31
  ice cream, 271–72
  layer cake, 166–68
  in oatmeal-raisin saucers, 356–57
Coffee cake(s), 169–89
  apple-raisin, 176–77
  banana-coconut, 182–83
  caramel upside-down sticky cake, 188–89
  cocoa-nut swirl, 172–73
  coconut-cinnamon pan cake, 174–75
  date, 186–87
  maple-pumpkin, 178–79
  raspberry, 184–85
  walnut–sweet potato, 180–81
Confectioners' sugar, about, 287
Cookies
  apple butter, 348–49
  applesauce pillows, 308–9
  apricot-date bars, 366–67
  banana-oatmeal pillows, 382–183
  bittersweet chocolate–caramel bars, 354–55
  black walnut butter drops, 362–63
  brown sugar–fruit and nut mounds, 384–85

butterscotch-granola disks,
        390–91
chocolate chip rusks, 374–75
chocolate gems, 306–7
chocolate nut crunch squares,
        324–25
chocolate toffee squares, 340–41
cinnamon-cashew "dunking,"
        370–71
coconut dreams, 330–31
coconut-chocolate "swirlies,"
        338–39
double chocolate–walnut
        fudgies, 336–37
double vanilla "dog bones,"
        322–23
easy to keep, 407
with fresh or dried fruit, 406
fruit clusters, 388–89
giant double chocolate rounds,
        364–65
ginger crisps, 346–47
Grandma Lilly's brownies, 332–
        33
heavenly hash brownies, 334–
        35
layered ginger rusks, 394–95
lemon butter balls, 326–27
maple bars, 320–21
milk chocolate–almond bars,
        368–69
mint chocolate crisps, 310–11
oatmeal-raisin saucers, 356–57
orange-raisin drops, 304–5
peach squares, 372–73
peanut delights, 380–81
pear-oatmeal drops, 312–13
pecan butter crunch squares,
        350–51
pecan pie squares, 393
pumpkin-fig mounds, 314–15
pumpkin-spice, 357–58
sour cream–molasses–spice
        rounds, 386–87
sour cream–spice, 302–3
sugar cookie hearts, 352–53
three nut bars, 328–29
using "goods on hand," 405
vanilla melt-a-ways, 300–301

Cookie jar treats, 297–315
    applesauce pillows, 308–9
    chocolate
        crisps, mint, 310–11
        gems, 306–7
    orange-raisin drops, 304–5
    pear-oatmeal drops, 312–13
    pumpkin-fig mounds, 314–15
    sour cream–spice cookies, 302–
        3
    vanilla melt-a-ways, 300–301
Cookie sheets, 289
Cranberry(-ies)
    preserve, 73
    -walnut mincemeat pie, 72–73
Cream, whipped, vanilla-scented,
        131
Cream cheese–chocolate chip
        cakes, 258–59
Cream pie
    banana, 100–101
    coconut, mile-high, 98–99
    lemon, mile-high, 118–19
    lime, 126
    maple, 94
Cream pound cake, 230–31
Currant(s)
    in apple butter cookies, 348–49
    in fruit clusters, 388–89
    pie, spiced pear-, 71–72
    and walnuts, pear cakes with,
        262
Custard
    pie
        coconut, 93
        pumpkin, 76–77
        vanilla, 92
    pouring vanilla, 129

Date(s)
    -apricot bars, 366–67
    in brown sugar–fruit and nut
        mounds, 384–85
    coffee cake, 186–87
    in fruit clusters, 388–89
    in pumpkin-spice cookies, 357–
        58
Double chocolate–walnut fudgies,
        336–37

Double vanilla "dog bones," 322–
        23
Dough, 287–91
Dried fruit and spice mincemeat,
        64–65

Edges for pie crusts, 27–29
Electric mixers, 289

Fig(s)
    in fruit clusters, 388–89
    -pumpkin mounds, 314–15
Filling(s)
    cinnamon-sugar, 189
    cocoa-nut, 172–73
Fresh fruit splash, 217
Frosting(s)
    billowy white, 167
    chocolate
        fudge, 197
        thin and rich, 164–65
    vanilla cream, 199
Fruit(s). See also specific fruits
    clusters, 388–89
    dried, and spice mincemeat,
        64–65
    medley, summer, 402
    nut mounds, brown sugar–,
        384–85
    syrups, to make, 37–38
Fudge pie, chocolate,
        old-fashioned, 96–97

Giant double chocolate rounds,
        364–65
Ginger(ed)
    -apple mincemeat pie, 63
    cakes, 254–55
    crisps, 346–47
    peach pie, deep-dish, 40–41
    rusks, layered, 394–95
    upside-down cake, apple-, 210–
        11
Gingerbread, blueberry, 246–47
Glaze(s)
    lemon, 162–63
    lemon-sugar, 223
    orange, 160–61
Golden pecan pie, 74

Grandma Lilly's brownies, 332–33
Granola
    -butterscotch disks, 390–91
    homemade, 392
Green tomato pie, late-season,
    56–57

Heart-shaped baking implements,
    295–96
Heavenly hash brownies, 334–35
Homemade granola, 392
Hot milk cake, Grandma Lilly's,
    220–21

Ice cream, 265
    cinnamon, 268–69
    coconut, 271–72
    lemon, 270
    vanilla
        double, 130–31
        pure, 266–67

Lattice cover for a double-crust
    pie, 33
Layered ginger rusks, 394–95
Lemon(s)
    -almond pie, 122
    butter balls, 326–27
    cream pie, mile-high, 118–19
    glaze, 162–63
    ice cream, 270
    meringue pie, 123
    –poppy seed pudding cake,
        222–23
    pudding pie, 121
    slice pie, 119–20
    -scented confectioners' sugar,
        287
    -sugar glaze, 223
Lemonade, real, 400
Lime cream pie, 126
Lunch box cookies, 343–58
    apple butter, 348–49
    bittersweet chocolate–caramel
        bars, 354–55
    ginger crisps, 346–47
    oatmeal-raisin saucers, 356–57
    pecan butter crunch squares,
        350–51

pumpkin-spice, 357–58
sugar cookie hearts, 352–53

Maple
    bars, 320–21
    cream pie, 94
    -pumpkin coffee cake, 178–79
    -walnut pie, 95
Marbled German chocolate cake,
    156–57
Marshmallow cream
    in coconut-chocolate "swirlies,"
        338–39
    in heavenly hash brownies,
        334–35
Meringue pie
    lemon, 123
    vanilla, 124–25
Mile-high coconut cream pie, 98–
    99
Mile-high lemon cream pie, 118–
    19
Milk chocolate–almond bars,
    368–69
Mint chocolate crisps, 310–11
Mincemeat
    dried fruit and spice, 64–65
    pie
        apple-ginger, 63
        cranberry-walnut, 72–73
        pear, 68–69
Molasses
    in applesauce pillows, 308–9
    –spice–sour cream rounds,
        386–87

Nectarine(s)
    cake, 244–45
    spice pie, double-crust, 48–49
    upside-down cake, spiced, 208–
        9
Nut(s). See also specific nuts
    bars, three, 328–29
    cocoa-swirl coffee cake, 172–73
    crunch squares, chocolate,
        324–25
    mounds, brown sugar–fruit,
        384–85
    pound cake, rich, 228–29

Oatmeal
    -banana pillows, 382–83
    in brown sugar–fruit and nut
        mounds, 384–85
    -pear drops, 312–13
    -raisin saucers, 356–57
Orange(s)
    –butternut squash pie, 82–83
    cake, 160–61
    glaze, 160–61
    peel, julienned, 161
    -raisin drops, 304–5
    -rhubarb pie, 115

Pastry cutouts
    to add to the top of a deep-dish
        or double-crust pie, 33–34
    to fashion a pie cover of, 32–33
Peach(es)
    -blueberry pie, double-crust,
        42–43
    cake, fresh, 242–43
    pie, gingered, deep-dish, 40–41
    square, 372–73
    streusel pie, 38–39
    upside-down cake, 206–7
Peanut(s)
    in brown sugar–fruit and nut
        mounds, 384–85
    delights, 380–81
Pear(s)
    -apple pie, with apple cider
        syrup, 66–67
    cakes with walnuts and
        currants, 262
    -cinnamon pie, with walnut
        streusel, 69–70
    -currant pie, spiced, 71–72
    mincemeat pie, 68
    -oatmeal drops, 312–13
    upside-down cake, 207
Pecan(s)
    in apple butter cookies, 348–49
    in apricot-date spread, 367
    butter crunch squares, 350–51
    -carrot cake with raisins, 198–99
    chunky apple cakes with, 252–
        53
    in fruit clusters, 388–89

in peach squares, 372–73
in pear-oatmeal drops, 312–13
pie
    bourbon, 75
    golden, 74
    squares, 393
in three nut bars, 328–29
Pie(s)
    apple-ginger mincemeat, 63
    apple-pear, with apple cider
        syrup, 66–67
    apple-raspberry, 53
    apple streusel, 104–5
    apricot-yam, 81
    banana cream, 100–101
    bourbon pecan, 75
    brandied golden acorn squash,
        84–85
    brown sugar, 87
    buttermilk, 106–7
    chocolate silk, 102
    cinnamon-pear, with walnut
        streusel, 69–70
    coconut "candy," 116
    coconut custard, 93
    coconut-walnut-chocolate-chip
        "candy," 86
    cranberry-walnut mincemeat,
        72–73
    deep-dish blackberry, 52
    deep-dish blueberry, 44
    deep-dish gingered peach, 40–
        41
    deep-dish strawberry-rhubarb,
        113
    deep-dish walnut-rum-plum,
        46–47
    double-crust apple, 62
    double-crust blueberry-peach,
        42–43
    double-crust nectarine spice,
        48–49
    fresh apricot, 55–56
    with fresh fruits and vegetables,
        135
    fresh sugar pumpkin, 80
    glazed strawberry, 112
    glazed yellow cherry, 51
    golden pecan, 74

ingredients, 15–16
late-season green tomato, 56–
    57
lemon-almond, 122
lemon meringue, 123
lemon pudding, 121
lemon slice, 119–20
lime cream, 126
maple cream, 94
maple-walnut, 95
mile-high coconut cream, 98–
    99
mile-high lemon cream, 118–19
old-fashioned chocolate fudge,
    96–97
orange–butternut squash, 82–
    83
orange-rhubarb, 115
pans, 18–19
peach streusel, 38–39
pear mincemeat, 68–69
plum-rhubarb, 114
pumpkin crunch, 78–79
pumpkin custard, 76–77
red raspberry, 54
shimmery chocolate, 117
sour cherry, 50
spiced pear-currant, 71–72
spiced red plum, 45–46
spicy sweet potato, 103
using "goods on hand," 136
vanilla custard, 92
vanilla meringue, 124–25
Pie crust, flaky, 20–34
    about, 20
    for double-crust pie, 30–34
        to add extra pastry cutouts,
            33–34
        cutout pastry top, 32–33
        to freeze pie crust dough, 31
        lattice cover for, 33
        to make the dough by hand,
            30
        to make the dough in a food
            processor, 30–31
        to line a rimmed pie pan for,
            31–32
        to roll out the pie dough, 31
        variations, 34

edges for, 27–29
for single-crust pie, 20–26
    about, 21
    to completely prebake a pie
        shell, 24
    to cover a deep-dish pie with
        a round of pie dough, 23–
        24
    to freeze a pie shell, 25
    to line a rimmed pie pan,
        22–23
    to make the dough by hand,
        21
    to make the dough in a food
        processor, 22
    to roll out the pie dough, 22
    variations, 25–26
    to waterproof the pie shell,
        24–25
Plum(s)
    cake, 238–39
    pie
        red, spiced, 45–46
        -rhubarb, 114
        walnut-rum-, deep-dish, 46–
            47
Poppy seed–lemon pound cake,
    222–23
Pound cake, 213–233
    best vanilla, 218–19
    bourbon, 224–25
    chocolate, 232–33
    cream, 230–31
    fresh fruit splash with, 217
    Grandma Lilly's hot milk cake,
        220–21
    lemon–poppy seed, 222–23
    rich nut, 228–29
    spice, 226–27
Prebaking pie shells, 24
Preserve, cranberry, 73
Pudding pie, lemon, 121
Pumpkin(s)
    -fig mounds, 314–15
    -maple coffee cake, 178–79
    pie
        crunch, 78–79
        custard, 76–77
        sugar pumpkin, fresh, 80

Pumpkin(s) (*cont.*)
  puree
    fresh, 77
    homemade, 179
    sugar pumpkin, fresh, 80
  -spice cookies, 357–58

Raisin(s)
  -apple coffee cake, 176–77
  in applesauce pillows, 308–9
  in brown sugar–fruit and nut
    mounds, 384–85
  in fruit clusters, 388–89
  in homemade granola, 392
  -oatmeal saucers, 356–57
  -orange drops, 304–5
  in peach squares, 372–73
  pecan carrot cake with, 198–99
  in sour cream–molasses–spice
    rounds, 386–87
Raspberry(-ies)
  coffee cake, 184–85
  pie
    apple-, 53
    red, 54
Red plum pie, spiced, 45–46
Rhubarb pie
  orange-, 115
  plum-, 114
  strawberry-, deep-dish, 113
Rolled cookie dough, 290
Rum
  -plum-walnut pie, deep-dish,
    46–47
  syrup, 47

Sheets, cookie, 289
Soft drop-cookie dough, 288
Sour cherry pie, 50
Sour cream
  –molasses–spice rounds, 386–
    87
  –spice cookies, 302–3
Spice
  pound cake, 226–27
  -pumpkin cookies, 357–58
  –sour cream
    cookies, 302–3
    –molasses rounds, 386–87

Spicy apple cake, 240–41
Squash
  butternut
    pie, orange-, 82–83
    puree, 83
  golden acorn
    pie, brandied, 84–85
    puree, 85
Strawberry pie
  glazed, 112
  rhubarb-, deep-dish, 113
Streusel topping
  apple pie with, 104–5
  peach pie with, 38–39
  walnut, cinnamon-pear pie
    with, 69–70
Sugar
  cookie hearts, 352–53
  flavored, 15–16
  –fruit and nut mounds, brown,
    384–85
  lemon-scented confectioners',
    287
  pie, brown, 87
  vanilla-scented confectioners',
    219
  vanilla-scented granulated,
    219, 287
Sugar pumpkin pie, fresh, 80
Summer fruit medley, 402
Sunflower seeds, in brown sugar–
    fruit and nut mounds,
    384–85
Sweet potato(es)
  pie, spicy, 103
  –walnut coffee cake, 180–81
Syrup
  apple cider, 65
    apple-pear pie with, 66–67
  to make, 37–38
  rum, 47

Three nut bars, 328–29
Toffee squares, chocolate, 340–41
Tools for baking, 146–48
Topping(s)
  cinnamon-walnut, 180–81
  coconut-butter crumble, 174–
    75

cream cheese–chocolate chip,
    258–59
  sugar and spice, 245
  walnut, 184–85
  walnut–brown sugar crumble,
    194–95

Upside-down cake, 203–11
  apple-ginger, 210–11
  caramel sticky, 188–89
  peach, 206–7
  pear, 207
  spiced nectarine, 208–9

Vanilla,
  cakes, 260–61
  cream frosting, 199
  custard pie, 92
  "dog bones," double, 322–23
  ice cream
    double, 130–31
    pure, 266–67
  melt-a-ways, 300–301
  meringue pie, 124–25
  pound cake, best, 218–19
  pouring custard, 129
  -scented confectioners' sugar, 219
  -scented granulated sugar, 219,
    287
    in black walnut butter drops,
      362–63
    in giant double chocolate
      rounds, 364–65
    in milk chocolate–almond
      bars, 368–69
    in sugar cookie hearts, 352–
      53
  -scented whipped cream, 131

Walnut(s)
  in applesauce pillows, 308–9
  in banana-oatmeal pillows, 382–
    83
  in bittersweet chocolate–
    caramel bars, 354–55
  black
    butter drops, 362–63
    and chocolate pan cake, 158–
      59

Grandma Lilly's brownies,
332–33
–blueberry–brown sugar
buckle, 194–95
cake, fudgy chocolate–, 200–
201
in chocolate nut crunch
squares, 324–25
in cocoa-nut swirl coffee cake,
172–73
-coconut-chocolate-chip
"candy" pie, 86
-cranberry mincemeat pie, 72–
73

and currants, pear cakes with,
262
–double chocolate fudgies,
336–37
in fruit clusters, 388–89
in heavenly hash brownies,
334–35
in maple bars, 320–21
-maple pie, 95
in pumpkin-fig mounds, 314–15
-rum-plum pie, deep-dish, 46–
47
streusel, cinnamon-pear pie
with, 69–70

–sweet potato coffee cake, 180–
81
in three nut bars, 328–29
topping, 184–85
–brown sugar crumble, 194–
95
-cinnamon, 180–81
Waterproofing pie shells, 24–25
White frosting, billowy, 167–68

Yam(s)
pie, apricot-, 81
puree, 81

About the Author

————❖❖❖————

LISA YOCKELSON, a graduate of the London Cordon Bleu, is the author of several baking books, including those in the American Baking Classics series: *Brownies and Blondies; Baking for Gift-Giving; Cobblers, Crisps, and Deep-Dish Pies;* and the forthcoming *Layer Cakes and Sheet Cakes*. As a food journalist with a concentration on baking, her recipes have also appeared in national magazines and in the food pages of the *Washington Post*.